Henriquet on
DRESSAGE

Henriquet on DRESSAGE

MICHEL HENRIQUET

CATHERINE DURAND

Translated by Hilda Nelson

J.A. ALLEN · LONDON

© Michel Henriquet and Catherine Durand
First published in France in 1991 by Maloine;
second French edition 2000
First published in Great Britain 2004

ISBN 0 85131 876 2

J. A. Allen
Clerkenwell House
Clerkenwell Green
London EC1R 0HT

J. A. Allen is an imprint of Robert Hale Limited

The right of Michel Henriquet and Catherine Durand to be identified
as authors of this work has been asserted by them in accordance
with the Copyright, Designs and Patents Act 1988

A catalogue record for this book is available from the British Library

Photographs by Frédéric Chéhu, except those on page xiv (J. Fadié),
page 8 (Werner Ernst), and 248 (P. Karl; Maloine)
Line illustrations by Yvan Benoist-Géronière

Translated by Hilda Nelson
Edited by Martin Diggle
Design and typesetting by Paul Saunders

Origination by Tenon & Polert Colour Scanning Limited, Hong Kong
Printed by Midas Printing International Limited, China

To Catherine for her indispensable collaboration

Contents

Translator's Note and Glossary

Within the text I have, in most cases, retained the use of French terms and expressions that pertain to movements and effects in schooling, rather than translating them into English. This is because some of these expressions are difficult to replace with an English equivalent that is both accurate and concise. This being the case, I have endeavoured, below, to convey the sense of these French terms in a manner that will be helpful to the reader. These terms are set here in italic.

There are also a few terms which I have translated into English, the meaning of which may be unfamiliar to newcomers to equitation. These are set below in bold text, with brief explanations.

Contraction: A term popularized in the 19th century by riders such as François Baucher to describe muscular tension in the horse that manifests itself in some form as a resistance.

Descente d'encolure: Literally, descent of the neck and shoulders; a degree of forward extension and lowering of neck and head, to allow and encourage relaxation and give the dorsal muscles their free play. The effect is promoted by the rider yielding with the hands, thus recompensing the horse for previous efforts in working completely "on the aids".

Descente de jambes: Reduction or cessation of the rider's forward-driving leg aids, especially to reward or acknowledge the horse's efforts.

Descente de main: Yielding the pressure of the hand and, consequently, the rein. Done in classical equitation to check the extent of the horse's self-carriage; therefore the horse should not change his speed, balance or outline – he is sometimes said to be "on parole". The *descente de main* is thus a different action, with a different effect from, *descente d'encolure*.

Dressage: In French, the term means, essentially, "training". However, to assist clarity, it has been used in this text only to indicate the competitive discipline; elsewhere, the term 'schooling' has been used to denote the actual training and gymnastic exercises of the horse.

Écouté: Said of a school trot or school walk, (q.v.) a trot or walk one can "hear" (*écouté* – "listen in"); gaits that are precise, shortened, cadenced. Movement of this nature was cherished by the former *écuyers* (q.v.).

Écuyer: While the term "equerry" has lost most of its original meaning in English, in France the term *écuyer* is very much alive, even though its meaning has changed somewhat. In the past, it implied someone who managed the stables of royalty and the nobility: now, it denotes someone who is an accomplished horseman or horsewoman, who teaches equitation to pupils of all levels and who may be active in competitive dressage. In this book, the author assumes that the person training the horse is an *écuyer* and thus this term, rather than "trainer" is used throughout.

L'effet d'ensemble: Combined or co-ordinated effect, specifically the effect of using the leg/spur simultaneously with the hand.

Manège: An enclosed area, either covered or open, used for schooling. Usually smaller than a competition arena.

Mise en main: Literally "putting in the hand"; to effect a yielding of the jaw; in association with flexion at the poll, contributes to putting the horse in the position of the *ramener* (q.v.).

Ramener, ramené: The flexing of the head at the poll (which must be associated with a yielding of the jaw), completed when the nose is in the vertical. NB Equestrian students should, in this case, be wary of literal translations of *ramener*, which include "to bring back"; "pull down", since they may have connotations of backward-pulling effects of the rein. While, in its equestrian context, *ramener* means simply the flexed outline of the head (however achieved), it is axiomatic that, under saddle, the horse is always ridden *forwards* into the hands.

Rassembler; rassemblé: Literally, "to gather together"; "gathered together" I have used the French term *rassembler* because the English term "collection", as generally understood, is not quite a full or accurate substitute, having a somewhat more limited meaning, in particular describing the bearing of a horse, especially the engagement of his hindquarters. While collection is, indeed, an essential component, *rassembler* refers to each and every part and action of the horse: the suppleness of his body – joints, muscles, etc. – and thus the pliancy of his *ressorts* (q.v.), his ease, harmony and generosity when moving; his cadence and rhythm and, above all, his lightness. *Rassembler* is thus the all-round perfection of a horse who is well schooled and moves with great impulsion matched with great lightness, which is the crowning glory of a trainer's efforts. Thus *rassembler* is, as described by Henry Wynmalen, "collection of the third and highest degree".

Ressorts: Literally, "springiness"; all of a horse's resources – pliancy of joints, muscles, tendons, etc. and his natural impulsion that combine to empower active movement.

School gaits: Gaits performed with the highest degree of collection.

Tride: An archaic term that was especially current in France during the 18th century and more or less disappeared with the 19th century. Essentially, a horse or his movements have *tride*, if they are animated, cadenced, elevated, and elegant.

Two-track work: This term has been used traditionally (and is used here by the author) to describe movements in which the horse's *forehand and hindquarters* follow different tracks, thus the "two tracks" are the track of the forehand and the track of the hindquarters. This usage does not imply that, in performing these movements, the horse's four feet are actually moving only on two tracks, as would be the case in correct movement on straight lines (the nearside lateral pair of feet following one track, and the off side lateral pair, the other). In these movements, in fact, the *horse's feet* will generally be following either three tracks (as in the form of shoulder-in prescribed for competition) or four tracks, which will not necessarily be all equidistant apart. Thus "two-track" is a generic term for the movements and exercises that are often described by another generic term, "lateral work".

Foreword

Some years ago, acceding to the urgings of a publisher friend, I committed into print a little work which was more in the nature of a student thesis than an authoritative work. My first master, René Bacharach, rightly annoyed by my impulsiveness, pointed out, with a certain coldness, the risk I was running by publishing my equestrian thoughts at an inexperienced age. I was placing myself in the same situation that had befallen Captain Saint-Phalle, brilliant disciple of François Baucher, who published at the age of thirty-two and was therefore "prematurely eliminated before he was able to give all of his worth".

Although impressed by this harsh reproof and whatever malice it barely hid, I did not turn away from my project, believing that Saint-Phalle had, after all, left behind a rather good book.

I have survived to this day, as has my good master, observing horses and relentlessly pursuing relentlessly experiences in equitation.

My encounter many years ago with my second master and friend, Nuno Oliveira, was the event of my equestrian life. It is thanks to him that I was able to carry out my most romantic ambitions and became aware of the poetry of those *écuyers*-authors of the 18th century, which had always both enchanted and frustrated me, and which finally became a reality.

It is this need to share this wonderful experience that has often made me take up my pen, yet without ever attempting to act as his mouthpiece. Rather, it is respect for his philosophy, based on the principles of the great classics, that I have always acknowledged and carried out in the training of my horses.

Nonetheless, I have never ceased wandering throughout the equestrian world, from the burning shores of the Tage or Guadalquivir to the calm northern countries, from rigorous Germany to instinctive Russia, from

Maître Nuno Oliveira, foremost equestrian intelligence of our times, a man of talent, knowledge, and passion, riding his horse Florido.

pragmatic America to academic Vienna. From each and every place I have always retained what I found to be the best – and promptly forgot the rest.

It is, however, to the original source that I continued to return, despite the turbulence inherent in a long friendship. Always, I returned to be enlightened by the greatest equestrian intelligence of our age.

The work I present here was begun simultaneously with the training of three young horses, aged 3½ years, and continued to develop throughout their schooling, until they reached 9 years of age. Photographs dealing with this period are included.

This deliberately planned concurrent training guaranteed against any possible memory lapse on my part and provided me with material on a daily basis. The diversity of the horses' personalities and genders – two stallions and a mare – nourishing this study more thoroughly than if I had been keeping a daily journal dealing with their schooling. The wealth of material their training provided was sufficient to trigger the recall of many essential facts, garnered from the training of the thirty or forty young horses long ago.

The structure of this study was conceived in such a way so as to follow rigorously, and in chronological order, the progress of a young horse from the start of training up to the execution of the classical high school airs. It is obvious that everything that the young horses will acquire during the first phases of their physical education will also enrich them should they be destined for jumping. This schooling will also confer upon them an overall superiority in respect of their balance and tractability.

To make it easier to recognize the stages of progression, I divide them somewhat arbitrarily into four periods: the time to understand, the time to learn, the time to do or execute, and the time to perfect, that is, to become a finished and complete horse.

The time to understand is indispensable in establishing some basic rules between two creatures who will collaborate without the use of words; it is also a way of verifying the young horse's perception by the way he responds to the requests and demands he receives. This becomes evident when one observes how he makes a simple turn in the corners of the *manège,* or how he responds to a lateral displacement, and continues through such matters as how he responds to the aids which signal gait changes, halts, correct bends, etc.

The time to understand is the necessary and essential time it takes the horse, who has accepted the requirement to carry the weight of a rider, to restore his natural movement while carrying the rider's weight.

The time to learn occurs when, using a language already agreed upon with his horse, the rider makes him perform lengthy fortifying and suppling exercises. The horse then learns to modify his balance with ease and to execute a series of movements which will become the more sophisticated and stylized form of his natural movements.

The time to do or execute occurs when the horse, from that stage on, can easily bring these movements together into dynamic action. This will be the basis upon which the controlled, highly cadenced movements of high school equitation are constructed.

The time to perfect will lead to further progress and the quest for perfection, but however desirable it may be, it must be recognized that perfection is seldom, if ever, attained.

To achieve this program or framework, one must be familiar with and understand certain elements in order to proceed safely and unhesitatingly in the pursuit of a goal that is both all-absorbing and difficult. One must consider carefully the equipment necessary in the schooling of a horse, as well as the choice of horse. It is important to remember the meaning of equestrian art and to define the essential objective – an equilibrium that is *rassemblé* – and also to introduce the foundations – correct position and use of aids – before approaching our four periods of schooling.

This foreword ought to have been followed by a preface written by my master. Alas, this cannot be, as he has been taken from us in such a cruel manner. While he has already given us and shown us so much, we can only admit that the final recourse in our moments of difficulty will no longer be available. We have been overwhelmed in our affection and our passion.

Preliminaries

1. Meaning and Foundation of Equestrian Art

Equestrian art is distinguished from the usual current riding practice in that it educates, rather than merely trains. That is to say, it opens out the horizons of both horse and rider, rather than passing them along a production line. In this respect, it justifies itself as 'art' in a way similar to music and dance, which do not have rigid structures or boundaries. Furthermore, as with other art forms, it is self-fulfilling: the essence of equestrian art is that it is art. The sensation, for the rider, and the sight, for the onlooker, are complete in themselves.

Equestrian art requires that the two participants, horse and rider, fuse into one entity. This fusion becomes wonderful when it is so complete that physical communication between two creatures seems replaced by the harmonious movement of single being. As with much great art, equestrian ballet has an element of tragedy, because it is based on such intimate contact and shared sentiment, which disappear once the performance is over. Like a fine ice sculpture, the work itself disappears, but the memory remains.

Origins

Until the 14th century, the horse was used merely as an instrument in the service of man; during the 15th century equitation began to be seen as a new form of expression.

The embodiment of the myth of the centaur re-appears at the beginning of the 16th century, in the kingdom of Naples. Here, Spanish Lords in the retinue of Ferdinand of Aragon reveal to the Neapolitan *écuyers* the dazzling vision of a form of equitation, the beauty of which is matched only by its efficiency. Human subtlety, combined with the natural attributes of the Spanish horse, soon reveal the beginnings of equestrian art. It is still in Italy, under the patronage of the Grand Dukes of Tuscany, that the domain of formal equitation will be explored.

The Neapolitan and Florentine Academies soon influence their neighbors, France in particular. Benefiting from vast resources, the Academies continue to blossom and become one of the expressions of classical monarchy.

This new form of equitation, forged in war, in the games of life and death, will not cease perfecting itself; a combination of art and science will evolve, to reach its highest level during the 18th century within the Royal School of Versailles. There, free from the demands of combat, it is able to adopt a final and purely artistic direction, wherein the *écuyer* is able, by means of his intelligence and skill, to stylize and render sublime the natural airs of the triumphant stallion.

A free and easy practice, which includes tact, experience and acquired knowledge, is the foundation of equestrian art. No one can be a judicious horseman if he cannot make use of his aids and cannot profit from the resources of his horse. He cannot position himself properly if he has not learned the rules which determine his posture. It is necessary for the mind to understand them fully at the same time as the body accustoms itself to them; theory and practice help each other.

Equitation becomes an art through talent, sensitivity, the fine taste of the *écuyer* and the beauty which is the result. Its dazzling evolution during the Age of Enlightenment [the 18th century] owed far more to artistry than to elaborating on definitive methods.

Breaking with Tradition

An almost general loss of artistic tradition struck Europe after the French Revolution of 1789, through the disappearance of many academies, although this had a more radical effect in France than in the principalities and monarchies of northern and central Europe.

Replacements of old ideas and the scientific evolution of the 19th century did not compensate for these changes. The different equestrian methods did, however, define common objectives, such as obtaining the confidence and obedience of the horse, controlling his temperament and muscular strength, and, when mounted, restoring his natural ease and balance under saddle. Practically speaking, it was a question of giving harmony to the horse-rider partnership by means of the rigorous use of the rider's aids to establish a common balance of horse and rider.

In France, the only school that continued to function was that of Saumur "an essentially military establishment whose main objective is the equestrian instruction of a large number of officers" (Ducroc de Chabannes, *Cours d'équitation…de Saumur* – 1827). Savante, or academic, equitation was even forbidden and its only official mission was "to establish and perfect military equitation" (Decarpentry, *Academic Equitation* – 1949). It was never given the mission to preserve equestrian art.

The *écuyers* who devoted themselves to this task, from Count d'Aure to General L'Hotte, did so as private individuals, using their own horses "to make it clear that it was a question of a personal equitation and not one belonging to a school. Saumur was obliged to envisage exclusively a war horse." (L'Hotte, *Recollections of a Cavalry Officer* – 1895.)

Regardless of the talent of certain individual and private experts, one can easily imagine the sterile nature of these studies, in that their teachings, and whatever knowledge they could hand down, were forbidden.

While the French school experienced the consequences of this sad regression the Germanic school proclaimed its resolute and unyielding fidelity to La Guérinière [François Robichon de la Guérinière, c.1688–1751], holding up his *School of Horsemanship* as the equestrian bible. Vienna and its school [the Spanish Riding School] replaced Versailles as the equestrian capital of Europe. The principal German states preserved the cult of equestrian art in Goettingen, Berlin, Stuttgart, Hanover and, later, at the remarkable school of Warendorf, where, to this day, the training of the best German dressage riders continues.

The Influence of Different Breeds of Horses on Equitation

With respect to the preservation and improvement of an equestrian tradition, one cannot ignore the importance of horses, their nature, and their breeds.

When Spanish-bred horses became less prevalent outside Spain] they were replaced in France by horses from Navarre and Limousin; they, in turn, form the basis of today's Anglo-Arabs. The Anglo-Arabs' breeding encountered certain changes in circumstances, and their production, to this day, remains uneven in terms of quality and type.

Heavy horses, crossbred with English stock, may be excellent with respect to jumping, but do not offer the qualities needed in dressage and "the options of compensation[1]" of the English Thoroughbred made it impossible for one to forget his horizontal equilibrium and his dragging gaits.

With the Trakhener, originally bred by Frederic I (1657–1713), the Germans possessed an excellent saddle and dressage horse. Just ten years after World War I (from 1928) they returned to international competition with

---

1 Term used by General Decarpentry in *Academic Equitation* – 1949.

success. The Olympic Games of 1936 witnessed their total victories in the three equestrian disciplines. Even before the ruins of World War II had been swept away, and after the loss of the entire stud-farm of the Trakhener horses – which had been appropriated by the USSR – the breeders of the German Federal Republic, without the official administration of horse-breeding farms, restored the breed. Starting with their regional breeds, with the judicial contributions of powerful English Thoroughbreds with well-grafted necks, and selected Arabs, they produced horses with excellent conformation which permitted them to succeed in all the disciplines and monopolize all the victories in dressage.

Germanic Continuity

The academic tradition of German masters, from Huenersdorf (1791) to Seeger, Seidler, Steinbrecht, Plinzner, von Heidebrecht, and Loerke (1930), formed a chain of continuous, relatively similar doctrines. This made the famous German national trainer, W. Schulteiss, say to me in 1975 that they were "Unchanged for the last hundred and fifty years and based on the principles of the former French school"; adding, with an air of affected regret, how he deplored that his team never managed to meet French riders in the international competition arenas.

It is not my intention to make a value judgement on the worth of the Germanic school and on the changes it was able to bring to its origins. Neither does it interest me to compare "the exemplary and somewhat constraining" nature of the equitation from beyond the Rhine with the "pleasing ease and brilliance of the Romanic school".[2] What is certain is that, since the end of the war, when Germany emerged ruined and France was on the side of the victors, in any equestrian confrontation between Germanic efficiency and Latin inspiration, the latter always seemed to end up in confusion.

Can one then be astonished that the German point of view, which presided at the drawing up of the rules of the F.E.I., continues to determine its interpretation?

Can one protest against the option of a "constraining submissiveness" or a "mechanical precision" when one opposes them only with horses who are hollow, irregular, and lusterless?

Let us accept frankly the supremacy of a nation in a discipline in which it has devoted, at all times, the best of its means in men, horses, and material, and recognize the fading away of our [French] nation which nourishes its self-satisfaction in its past glories, and in means that have disappeared.

---

2 Decarpentry, *Academic Equitation.*

Let us accept the heavy responsibility of equestrian authorities and the administration of stud-farms set in their monopoly, ignoring arrogantly all research and promotion which would justify their existence.

Let us have the modesty to refrain from criticizing the German manner and German horses, so long as we are not capable of adding to the seriousness of their work, this grace and lightness which was, so it seems, the former mark of equitation in the French tradition and its horses.

The Horseman and His Contradictions

The schooling of a horse consists of a precise, methodical program of exercises and placing him in certain positions which make him act and execute the various gaits and airs.

It is necessary for the rider to know and understand that, among all human physical exercises, equitation is the one that makes man face the most complex of tests. On the one hand, he works upon a base that is alive, that is sometimes unpredictable and, on the other hand, *the natural reflexes of the horseman are the opposite of what they ought to be.*

To climb a tree, throw and catch a ball, give and ward off a punch, swim, these are all spontaneous actions or gestures for which it suffices simply to work at them, in order to develop them as best one can and make them perform.

On horseback, the man placed on this moving and uncertain base is unquestionably – and for a greater length of time than one can imagine – overtaken by a certain inhibition which disturbs his motor co-ordination. Worse, his natural reflexes work rigorously against the desired effect. The young horse quivers with fear: the seat and legs of the man, who shares this anxiety, close on him, thus creating panic. The young horse, urged on, goes forward with alertness, the hand then clenches on his mouth, a sensation that he will try to remove by whatever means possible, the first one being flight...

Thus we are dealing here with the re-education of the most elementary survival reflexes, which the future *écuyer* must conquer if he wishes to attain real finesse.

The Foundations of Technique

The first element in equestrian technique is the ability to maintain oneself in a dynamic position which harmonizes with all the modifications of the correct equilibrium of the horse. The *écuyer's* body must constantly share this equilibrium, or else he must dissociate himself delicately from it, only when he seeks to vary the gait, air, or cadence.

When natural reflexes go against the sought-after effect.

This principle forms a basis which extends to all the disciplines of equitation.

The technique of schooling rests on creation through association, combined with astute channeling of reflexes and habits. With this code in mind, it is possible to indicate, without the use of force, strike-offs, halts, directional changes, and rein-backs. The initial contacts can be established in hand. The voice, touching with the whip or hand, gentle indications with the reins, caresses, and treats, create a network of communications that go beyond constraint and panic. However, the mental conditioning of the horse must not exceed this level, otherwise one moves away from true equestrian schooling into the realm of mind control and conditioned circus tricks.

The correct sequences of exercises allow one to progressively introduce the horse to the most subtle nuances. It is always a question of working the active parts, of strengthening and suppling them, in order to attain maximum harmonious efficacy; this is essential, whether one prepares horses for sport, or seeks to improve weak horses, or those with a poor conformation.

However, high school equitation would merely be a sport, or a manifestation of technical skill, if it resulted only from the application of proven techniques. It is, rather, an art rooted in talent, sensitivity and good taste, evident in the elaborate steps demanded of the *écuyer*, and in the beauty of equestrian performance.

The dazzling evolution of the School of Versailles was, moreover, a consequence of the exemplary worth of its artists, rather than the formulation of a definitive method. To convince oneself of this, one has simply to be aware of the decadence which followed, despite the uninterrupted developments of scientific methods from the 19th century to the present day.

The final argument, which justifies superior equitation and renders it indispensable, lies in the means it gives the *écuyer* to solve the overall problems upon which the rider stumbles. *While some resistances are inevitably encountered within the process, they melt away under a rational program of suppling work.* If this endeavor no longer encourages the study of academic equitation, whether or not it is related to competition, some value still exists in pure artistic creativity and in the re-establishment of the psychological and physical equilibrium of the horses.

2. Competition and Equestrian Art

The natural tendency of sensitive riders, disappointed by the dreary and boring sight of official dressage competitions, is not to take part in them. The somewhat disgraceful and annoying relationship between competition riders and their horses discourages the more modest riders who fancy trying their hand, yet retain a degree of diffidence. The sight of hands in the air, hands that carry and lock necks, legs that grip, resulting in mediocre cadences, dissuade many from entering the arena.

I have experienced this situation from the very outset of my equestrian pursuits and admit to having shared this attitude for a very long time. Was not the poetry of equitation being compromised in these very places of destruction?

I have practiced almost all the equestrian disciplines and came very close to the practice of bullfighting equitation as well as artistic equitation. Looking back from a distance, I am compelled to recognize that short-term opportunism often gets the upper hand over correct, rigorous practice – although by the term "rigorous" I am referring to self-disciplined adherence to classical practice, not to the mindless domination or constraint of the horse, which is the mark of incompetence. However, it is the case that, when one's immediate objective is to produce quickly an apparently pleasing result, one sooner or later gets caught in a trap of one's own making.

The truth is, it is as harmful to skip a pirouette at the canter on the difficult side as it is to prick or pull the horse in order to execute it. To abandon a good bend while executing difficult half-passes is a compromise which will always have a consequence. To be satisfied with deviating single lead changes will compromise successive lead changes. To allow irregular halts is renouncing the *rassembler*. "Traversing" at the canter [when

Madame M. Otto Crépin with Corlandus at the piaffe. Champion of France and European champion in dressage, World Freestyle Champion and Olympic Silver Medalist. One of the rare rider-horse combinations whose *rassembler* is indisputable.

the horse's haunches deviate by throwing themselves to the side] and trotting with ill-defined rhythm and cadence, are like singing off key…

A brilliant passage does not justify rushed extensions; a pretty piaffe does not pardon abrupt transitions.

Insofar as lucidity and self-criticism have become easy through age and experience, I have begun to react with equal hostility to the two misleading forms of dressage equitation. An angry note dealing with the misdeeds of a stifling type of dressage equitation or, on the other hand, one that is too lax, gained me a severe reprimand from the Commission of Dressage of the French Equestrian Federation and an irritated remark on the part of my teacher, considering that I had only alluded to certain pupils…

Indeed, it is by controlling my own equitation that I became aware of the washouts and the parasites who constantly installed themselves in the field and which discretion on the part of the more knowledgeable spectators, and ignorance on the part of the others, had hitherto concealed from me.

An unwritten rule exists which has it that high-level dressage competitions are generally judged by competent judges. Even if efforts are being made in this area, this is far from being true with respect to the most elementary competitions. In certain disadvantaged areas, the ignorance of the judges is a veritable barrier to serious competitors. Each time I have attended high level competitions, my own rating has more or less coincided with that of the judges. But the single important difference lies in the notation belonging to *articles 401 and 417 of the rules of the F.E.I. which stipulate "the general goals and principles" and "the position and aids of the rider"*, that is to say:

— lightness of the forehand;

— submission to the bit with neither tension nor resistance;

— animation of the haunches at the slightest request;

— the neck raised and rounded;

— gentle contact with the reins;

— a cadence that is rhythmic and harmonious;

— legs descended;

— hands low.

The rule states that the use of the voice lowers "by at least two points the mark for the movement that took place" and indicates no set penalty for serious transgressions against these other requirements.

If one were to remove two or three marks for each movement involving a transgression against one of these eight requirements, what a slaughter would occur – but what an incentive to get out of this primary and repressed equitation. Their systematic disregard for equitation ought to either disqualify these riders or bring with it a particularly severe marking. This would serve as an encouragement to riders who have a correct position and delicate aids and would be a step towards fairness.

Now that these reservations have been stated, I believe it is constructive and enriching to submit oneself to dressage tests without departing from one's ideal. On the other hand, I recommend that one works young horses, supples them, and schools them in such a way that they develop their gaits before letting them compete; otherwise the interpretations made by certain judges such as "constant contact" and "extension of the neck" will incite one to push young horses against the hand, especially if, for a while, they exhibit a dislike to take permanent contact with the bit, even if the contact is mild.

The rider who gets comments of this sort is inclined to push and hold back in order to establish contact. He will eventually end up getting resistances of force and weight, which will then compromise the raising of the neck and lightness.

I also wish to bring to mind instances of riders who possess a well schooled horse, endowed with certain qualities, but also some disadvantages arising from a conformation problem, or a gait that is naturally mediocre. One quite obviously cannot ask the judges to take this insurmountable handicap into consideration; one must simply admit that one cannot win in that particular class, but can only verify the relative quality of the work accomplished. One can then arrive objectively at the corrections that are appropriate to the inevitable poor marks and unjust comments.

Working in isolation has, as in all other expressive arts, a negative effect. However, it should be borne in mind that the judgement of a third party, friendly or not, is subjective. The views of the judges sometimes carry with them a certain weakness, often determined by taste founded on special aesthetic and cultural values, however, even views of this sort sometimes have the merit of a measure of reality.

3. Equipment

Let us now examine the various items of supplementary equipment used in equitation. Some, like the saddle, are only as good as their actual quality; others like the lungeing cavesson or the lungeing whip are to be considered only in terms of the hand that utilizes them. However, they must all conform to a quality and pattern of manufacture which permit practical and efficient use.

The Saddle

The saddle that comes from the most prestigious workshops is not necessarily the best. In an attempt to have all the trump cards on my side, I utilized these expensive equestrian "seats", the excellent leather and workmanship of which were not questioned, but I found that their conception had lost much of its purpose – namely to fit the back of the horse and receive the seat of the rider comfortably.

One can find excellent mass production saddles at affordable prices. As is the case with automobiles, they have benefited from an accumulation of experience in respect of artisan workmanship.

Once adjusted, the saddle must not touch a single point of the horse's vertebral column, otherwise it would cause serious lesions. The seat must be horizontal, with a slight depression of the padding, and must rest in the middle of the horse's back and not on the front of it. Some degree of padding, in the form of a saddle cloth or numnah, which does not compromise the fit of the saddle, will protect the horse's back and add to his comfort. One must look for the saddle which enables the seat to be as close to the horse as possible, without allowing it to slide backwards. For jumping, the flaps are placed more forward to receive the knees of the rider with shortened stirrup leathers; for school riding the leathers are adjusted longer. Extra knee and thigh rolls will serve to more or less set the leg position but they are not indispensable and, when one has attained one's balance, they will become superfluous.

Until the beginning of the 20th century, pupils were first made to sit in a French-type saddle equipped with fore-peaks (high pommel) and pads, allowing the novice to feel secure, and thus to relax sufficiently to let his legs hang down and move his pelvis. Pupils then progressed to the English saddle made of suede, which allowed a firm contact with seat and thighs, then on to an uncovered saddle when they felt sufficiently secure. Upon reflection and having observed the catastrophic seat of so many riders, one wonders whether this supposedly re-assuring progression, obtained with this variety of equipment was really necessary.

Stirrup Leathers and Stirrup Irons

At the outset, I will merely say what must be said of all aspects of adjustable saddlery: may God and saddle-makers preserve us from poorly worked leathers, from poor buckles, from loose tongues which make the slightest adjustment difficult – so that adjusting one's stirrup leathers when sitting on a horse becomes a highly risky operation! I might add that leathers and buckles can become worn and should be examined frequently. Stirrup irons must have treads that do not allow the foot to slide (non-slip bars are helpful) and they must fit the boot.

I agree with J. Pellier (*Langage Équestre* – 1889) who said: "Since holding on to one's stirrups is difficult, it is useful to accustom the pupil to make use of them from the very first lesson: half of the lesson without stirrups, the other half with them."

The Girth

This must be kept clean and supple, otherwise it will cause harm to the area where it touches the horse. It is essential to examine it before mounting and to tighten it gradually, so as not to surprise the horse and make him tense.

The Simple Snaffle; the Noseband

The best snaffle is the gentlest one; large egg-butts, large loose rings which, like side cheeks, prevent the bit from slipping sideways in the mouth. It is set as high as possible without pinching the corners of the mouth, and should be centimeter wider than the mouth. In the case of young horses, it is useful to employ a drop noseband or Flash, which fastens below the bit and thus limits the movements of the jaws which inevitably occurs with a young horse when he feels the bit for the first time. These little defenses can otherwise develop into passing the tongue over the snaffle. However, the noseband must not be too tight; it should be adjusted in such a way that one can pass a piece of sugar into the mouth.

The Double Bridle

In the wrong hands, or used inappropriately, this can be a very severe and dangerous device, acting upwards and backwards. However, it can be highly efficient when the horse has been prepared to have absolute confidence in the skilled rider's hand.

The curb bit comes with or without a port which, if it is too high, can become an instrument of torture when it see-saws forwards through the action of the reins. Its constraining force depends upon the length of the cheekpieces and a fixed curb chain. Reasonable dimensions for the upper cheeks are 4 centimeters, and 8 centimeters for the lower ones. The canon of the L'Hotte bit is slightly curved and is thus more acceptable and less dangerous. The bridoon which accompanies the curb bit is effectively a form of snaffle, but is thinner to make it less cumbersome in the mouth and can be so because the horse had initially been worked with a simple (thicker) snaffle. One adjusts it to the corners of the lips. The curb bit rests slightly lower on the bars; the lower it sits, the more severe is its action. It must never touch the canine teeth.

I use the double bridle only when the horse accepts the snaffle bit readily at the three gaits. I know then that he will not attempt to pull against the hand in which he has confidence, even if I have to take such time as is necessary to make him understand, with kindness, the effects of this new mouthpiece. One year with a snaffle seems to be a minimum before going on to the curb bit. Furthermore, returning frequently to working with a simple snaffle allows the rider to assess the extent to which his hand is accepted rather than tolerated.

The Curb Chain

This is placed flat in the chin groove and must be adjusted so that it comes into play when the lower cheeks, as a consequence of rein action, form an angle of 45 degrees to the mouth. A curb bit without a curb chain, or with a loose one, is useless and annoying.

A lip strap must be introduced as soon as one becomes aware that the horse is trying to seize the cheeks of the bit with his teeth. Let us finally note that the corners of the lips are sometimes pinched between the hooks and the upper cheeks because of the leverage action of the bit. Merely turning the hooks of the curb chain around will avoid useless suffering.

Lungeing Headgear

In addition to the ordinary stable halter, one must also possess a well cared for leather halter or headcollar, which has a well-fitting noseband with rings fixed on each side, as well as one in the center to which one attaches the lungeing line. When one places reins on the lateral rings, one has then the means of directing the first steps of the youngster, mounted, in the *manège*, initially on the lunge, then at liberty, before placing a snaffle in his mouth.

To lead and lunge certain powerful and undisciplined horses, one must have a fully furnished cavesson. One must reject two types of cavesson – first, those with a noseband that contains metal pieces that jut out and risk cutting the nose, but also avoid those with padding so excessive that it makes any action ineffectual. Thus the internal metal parts that the cavesson contains must be padded sufficiently, but the horse must still be able to feel the resonance of the vibrations of the wrist of the person who is lungeing. The noseband must fit the contours of the nose and be adjusted so that there is no play. It is important that the cavesson is placed on the bony part of the nose and not on the nasal cartilage.

When the horse becomes agitated, generally speaking, simple vibrations suffice to calm him right away, for the effect this produces throughout his body seems to have a numbing effect on him. When dealing with my stallions, I have never had to go beyond giving little taps.

The Lungeing Line

6 to 8 meters is a sufficient length. The line is clipped onto the ring of the cavesson, the halter, and even to the noseband of the bridle; but never should it be attached to the mouthpiece.

Fixed Reins or Side Reins

These can be useful when lungeing certain horses. They are attached to the rings of the snaffle and, at the other end, they pass through each side of the girth. Their length depends upon the goal one has set, but they must never be used to force the *ramener*; rather they should be used to channel more easily the neck and head of violent horses who tend to be undisciplined when lunged.

The Martingale

This is a harness that is used to hold the horse's head at a certain level by sheer force. Its use indicates that the rider is incapable of balancing and positioning the horse by means of classical suppling. Instead of preventing a horse's resistances, it can cause an accident by having the horse fall over backwards.

The So-called German Reins or Draw-reins

Attached to the girth, they pass between the forelegs of the horse, sliding into the rings of the snaffle, from the inside to the outside, to serve as a sort of double rein in the hands of the rider. Less idiotic than the martingale – since they barely have any action when the rider's hands let go of them – they still have, however, quite a constraining effect. They must only be used by very skillful riders and to remedy physiological problems. Their action must be transitory and almost always on one side at a time; the side that one experiences resistance and where flexion is sought. Their efficiency depends upon the speed with which the hand yields and takes up contact with the snaffle rein. *Prolonged actions constrain horses* and place them very definitely behind the bit.

The Chambon; the de Gogue

These are reins to be used during lungeing and must be progressively adjusted so as not to catch the horse unawares; they make the horse lengthen his neck in a horizontal position and raise his back. This is especially useful with ewe-necked horses or horses with hollow backs, as well as those who have been victims of constraint.

The Lungeing Whip

This should be as light as possible and, together with its lash and thong, should be able to touch the horse at a radius of 6 or 7 meters. It serves as an aid to the trainer who is on foot and must never be used as a punishment. It indicates, through simple contacts, the extension of gaits and the widening of the circle.

The Dressage Whip or the Riding Crop

The former is to be used as an aid, whether on foot or mounted. It must measure at least 1.1 meters so that one can, without moving the arm, touch the hocks. It must be light and supple, and its pommel must be very thin, so that it can pass from one hand to the other without disturbing the reins and the mouth of the horse. I consider the short crop, which can serve only to hit, to be quite useless, other than when it forms part of the traditional attire of the young rider.

The Spurs

The shanks should be 4 centimeters long and have no point. They serve as an auxiliary to the heels and are more precise in their signals and better perceived than the heels by the horse. They should be worn horizontally and low, so as not to damage the flanks of the horse through involuntary movements of the legs. The spur is an aid and rarely a punishment; it "asks" much more than it "attacks" a horse. The "little attacks" described by Faverot de Kerbrech must be reduced to vibrations. I admit that I was tempted three times to solve problems of impulsion with serrated spurs when I was dealing with a cold or stubborn horse. I was not successful, nor did it improve the situation. A harsh spur contracts a horse more than it propels.

4. Choosing a Horse

In itself, choice is proof of experience and the competence of the owner. This is especially so, since a good school horse is not necessarily the product of an illustrious ancestor. However, it is obvious that the perfect type with ideal gaits will always be an expensive animal. This is all the more so in that modern competition dressage is as much a competition of breeds and gaits as it is an indication of the skill of the riders. For this to be otherwise, the judges would have to be capable of adjusting their criteria with respect to the conformation of the schooled horse, his natural gaits and balance; they would have to mark in such a way as to reward work done by the rider who had attempted to correct and reduce innate imperfections, and who made improvements through reasonable exercises.

Conversely, a handicap would have to be given to trainers of horses with naturally excellent gaits and a free and easy equilibrium. I know perfectly well how complex the subjectivity of such judgements would be. This reinforces the reservations that some people have with respect to competition in the domain of equestrian art, where the luck or the scientific knowledge of the breeder are rated as highly as the art of the trainer, whose talent alone should be in question.

One can, nonetheless, find excellent subjects, who will allow an *écuyer* to practice his talent under reasonable conditions. Whatever his philosophical ideals, he must admit plainly that his chances of being placed in the competition arena will clearly be handicapped by either too small a size, a trot lacking a natural amplitude, or any other inherited imperfection; all very much outside his sphere of influence.

Let us add that the general criteria we give here also apply to the choice of the horse in other sporting disciplines, as we shall see further on.

To prepare and school a horse is an adventure which, if all goes well, lasts five to six years. Six years of daily exercises, of care, of investment of oneself, a great many disappointments, small flashes of joy or hope which, if one attaches any importance to it, make this a very risky adventure.

In the life of an *écuyer* one can usually count no more than three or four truly successful horses, so seldom do those exist who are capable of a

A horse with a good conformation.

finished performance of the complete range of school airs. One can thus understand the importance of one's decision to purchase a horse, the commitment it represents, the exercising of a horse that encompasses more or less one sixth of a man's active life.

To acquire a single horse I look at fifty. Yet, after having bought eighty these last thirty years, I have been satisfied only with one out of four or five. Of course, with the passage of time and experience helping, I have more recently bought less badly and made fewer mistakes.

One needs four to six months to know whether a young horse is worth continuing with; one needs at least eighteen months to be more or less sure that he is capable of attaining all the classical equilibria.

My principal parameters for choosing a horse are as follows.

Conformation

The horse must be athletic, sloping up from the hip joint to the center of movement of the shoulders. At 3 years of age, the development of the withers is not yet complete and one must take this into consideration in one's examination. However, the hip joint must be low, which will favor the elasticity of the gaits through the play of the hind legs.

The distance from the point of the buttocks to the point of the hip must be long, which will permit a rounded canter.

If the hocks are straight this will detract from their ability to flex elastically; if they are too close they will be subject to strain, and will provoke a cramped action of the hindquarters. In either case, the risks of a deterioration of these joints is considerable.

Too long a back risks hollowness and disturbs the *rassembler*. I prefer a short back and wide loins.

When elevated by correct movement, a long neck will become rounded and acquire correct balance. However, one must reject ewe-shaped or hollow necks as they will make the *ramener* difficult and will affect the *mise en main*.

The shoulder must be long and oblique.

The conformation and setting of the legs, which should be regular, must be noted carefully, since the legs are important for gymnastic work. Furthermore, defective conformation can, after many years of use, give rise to the appearance of various bursal and bony enlargements.

Long legs but short cannons and flexible pasterns are desirable. One must also examine the feet and, as a general rule, have a veterinarian examine the horse before purchase. One must avoid a tight [narrow] base of support, in which the hind legs, forelegs, or both, are too close to each other.

The Gaits

After having examined the horse closely in a stationary position, one must see how the horse moves at the walk, watching both from behind and from the front. One must then observe him moving at all three gaits, free of harness and rider. Whenever possible I prefer to observe the horse moving freely in a small area rather than on the lunge. Nothing will inhibit him then, and he will adopt the gaits and attitudes that come naturally to him. One must take one's time to observe and remind oneself that, while schooling will improve his gaits, it create what nature has refused to give him.

The gaits must be symmetrical, that is, regular, and their cadences must be ample and elastic. At the trot, the movement of the forelegs must originate from the shoulders and develop amply and with suppleness. The hind legs must push with energy.

At the canter, the horse must detach himself from the ground with elasticity.

Temperament

A horse's temperament is difficult to determine when one is dealing with an untrained horse or a very young horse. With such animals, uneasiness will sometimes suggest a liveliness and level of muscular activity which can change into lack of vigor at the end of a few months, after the horse has acquired confidence and ease. Energy is the essential quality, that is, a permanent desire to carry himself forward, combined with the skin-deep sensitivity which one calls finesse.

It is these qualities which the *écuyer* will use, channel, and direct against rigidity and contractions. A horse who is cold and languid, and whom one has to urge on constantly, cannot be changed and the spectacle he will present will be lusterless and mechanical. He will never reach the stage of the *rassembler* which is the cornerstone of equestrian art.

A generous impulsion can compensate for all sorts of natural imperfections. A horse who is somewhat light-framed but very ardent is better than one who is strong but cold. I have succeeded in giving acceptable schooling to horses lacking certain physical attributes, thanks to their extraordinary generosity and courage. All they needed was a more gradual schooling.

A horse's disposition must be good, of course, but, above all, it must be vibrant and generous, even warm. One can add that the rider must have the tact and the equestrian wherewithal to accommodate these qualities.

The horse must also be beautiful and expressive when he is animated. A completed schooling is a work of art, from which one cannot exclude the aesthetic aspect. To revert to my comments on generous impulsion overcoming imperfections, it is noteworthy that there are some horses who look mediocre when inactive, yet who take on a splendor in the dynamism of motion.

The Breeds

What kind of horse should one pursue? Much experience with the principal saddle horses, and a classical notion of the *rassembler*, compel me to place at the head of the list two types that are very different with respect to breed and carriage, yet which have marked similarities in key respects: the Iberian horse – the Lusitano or the pure-bred Spanish horse – and the Trakhener.

Among the former one can easily find many well disposed to the equestrian art and its execution. Many are endowed with the necessary athletic strength and exemplary gaits, so that they can compete internationally at the highest level.

While the Trakhener has a less equable temperament than the Iberian horse his gaits, sensitivity, and strength are remarkable. Undoubtedly, he is the best saddle horse. German stud farms have been able to buy back from Russia some excellent horses for breeding purposes. It is possible nowadays to see these types at selection trials as well as attending their sale at Neumuenster and other places.

The Lipizzaner has kindred qualities with the Andalusian. This breed had also, for some time, been effectively eliminated from competition because of the uncultured views of modern arbiters. However, opinions have been changing and these breeds are now able to participate in high level competitions. Our own Lusitano horse, Orphée, participated honorably at the Olympic Games in Barcelona [1992], and two pure-bred Spanish horses went to Atlanta [1996].

In France, those in authority have always shown a lack of interest in the dressage horse and placed all sorts of obstacles in the way of the importation and breeding of foreign horses. It is left to chance, a statistically weak option, to find a horse who possesses all the essential points mentioned earlier. The Anglo-Arab: let us content ourselves by saying modestly that he is no longer what he used to be! The Selle Français [French saddle horse] bred for jumping is surely the best in the world… so long as one does not compete at jumping or dressage against foreign horses who are better schooled – perhaps more capable of being schooled – because they have a natural balance that is more suitable.

The English Thoroughbred, with his tendency to put his weight on his shoulders, with gaits that tend to drag on the ground, is often rigid and not very athletic, and is sometimes temperamental. He feels more at home when moving on a straight line when his body is stretched, rather than *rassemblé*, executing lateral movements and the high airs. General Decarpentry attributed to him the aptitude of finding "devices of compensation", which is sometimes accurate when he does not use this aptitude against equitation! He is, furthermore, used less and less in dressage.

The rules of competition have, unfortunately, been formulated with these horses just mentioned in mind, giving preference to their type of gait to the detriment of the *rassembler*. Even if our chauvinism suffers from it, we must acquaint ourselves with what the North Europeans (Germany, Denmark, Sweden, Holland) are producing, resulting in a remarkable genetic selection begun some years ago. Seductive types with a remarkable equilibrium, powerful, but without being heavy, elegant and endowed with gaits of a rare amplitude and a regularity. At the large annual sales, I have seen champion rider from the dressage and jumping disciplines fighting over the same horses!

Each year in Belgium, Holland, and Germany, competitions occur when selections of stallions take place with the purpose of keeping the best ones. For example, in Utrecht, Holland, these trials occur in February. It is an occasion for contemplating the best products of Dutch breeding. All the original stocks are represented, from Lipizzaners to Hanoverians. Six to seven hundred horses pass before a jury, but also in front of many spectators seated in the tiers, passionately interested in this exhibition; however, one sees no horses being ridden. About forty of them are admitted to a three-month stay in the state establishment, where they will be broken in and recommended either for jumping, harness racing, cross-country, or dressage. In June, the final selection will keep the twenty best stallions, who will cover mares in view of the general public for the benefit of their owners. From among the horses who were not kept in the first or second selection, it is possible to acquire some excellent ones. A similar system occurs in Germany. The associations of breeders, whether Hanoverian, Holsteiner, Westphalian, Oldenburg etc., are remarkably well organized and possess commercial centers where, several times a year, they regroup the best horses chosen for reproduction and sale.

Russia and the former Republics of the Soviet Union, still have seven million of the world's twelve million horses. They have annual sales of some six hundred horses at international auctions, but this selection is neither bred to type nor evaluated rigorously. It is now no longer possible to buy these horses on the actual breeding farms. Nevertheless, I have seen there some beautiful types of dressage and sport horses. In general, the types are more or less close to the Arabian, and also to the Trakhener and Hanoverian.

Too many poor purchases during one's equestrian career can compromise it seriously, especially with respect to schooling. The active life of a rider is relatively short. Between maturity and the time when the first physical problems overtake one, there are altogether only three or four dozen years. It requires six to eight years to really complete the schooling of a horse; before that, one succeeds and fails in a large number of attempts, which take up as much time.

If it takes a competent horseman three to six months to judge the general qualities of a three- or four-year-old, that is because, at times – especially at the end of his fourth year, when one approaches the mysteries of an *rassemblé* equilibrium – serious difficulties appear.

While working at the gaits, a negligible flaw in the conformation of the horse's legs can lead to a wavering at the passage or a dissociation of the diagonals at the piaffe. A lack of strength in the haunches, which had never interfered at a medium canter, can give rise to pirouettes that are arduous and lusterless. Closely set forelegs knocking into each other when one executes the half-pass will always compromise a good cadence on two tracks, and a balanced halt.

Books on equitation, old and modern, usually give the naïve reader the impression that only his mistakes prevent him from imitating the models presented in pictures. This may be true for cooking recipes, or even when one is learning a musical instrument at an elementary level – if the materials and the instrument are of normal quality, then there is no possibility of failure for the energetic apprentice. But it is quite another matter when one is dealing with a living being. All the great masters were familiar with the absolute failure of certain movements or airs with a good many of their partners. It is not mere chance that many masters seldom mention more than one or two horses with whom they were completely successful, from among all they trained.

5. Objective: the Rassembler

In these preliminaries devoted to the study of schooling the horse, I have presented at an early stage the physiological and philosophical facts which I deem necessary to consider jointly before throwing myself into this difficult and passionate adventure. The *rassembler*, which represents the ultimate balance of the ridden horse, could have been presented in the latter part of this work. I believe, however, that it is difficult to construct and develop profitably the work that we have begun without giving prior consideration to the end result.

Every time the horse opposes with force or inertia, rigidity or heaviness,

The *rassembler*: the air
of supreme majesty.
N. Oliveira on Euclides.

we will know that we are distancing ourselves from our goal, either
through our own clumsiness or our own passivity.

Definition of the Rassembler

The best image one can give of the *rassembler* is that of a wild animal
ready to pounce upon his prey: he is consumed by a vibrant force which
takes over every part of his body, which puts him into a state of readiness
which he can instantaneously activate in his move for the kill.

In equestrian disciplines involving jumping, the horse – even if not
assisted by the rider's aids – attempts to gather or collect himself in front
of an obstacle in order that he can, through establishing the appropriate
posture and balance, use his physical forces effectively to clear it. This is
a matter of natural and spontaneous *rassembler*.

In high school or academic equitation, one can define this *rassembler*
as a state of superior equilibrium obtained through the physical enhance-

ment and suppling work which make up the school exercises. This is the objective, the ideal, of all *écuyers*; that which we will pursue methodically as the study develops. The *rassembler* is achieved through flexion of haunches and hocks, carried forward and engaged, which produce the lightening and raising of the forehand and provide the energy necessary for impulsion at all times and in every direction. The correct *rassembler* allows for the distribution, at will, of weight and force between the forehand and the hindquarters. A shortening of the stride and bringing the hind limbs closer to the center of gravity assures the maximum mobility in every direction, making possible the harmonious and rapid variations of gaits and speed and the execution of the airs, and produces the brilliant elevation and extension of the limbs.

Conceptions of the Rassembler

The rassembler was highly valued and sought after by all schools of equitation and was fully achieved in the 18th century by the *écuyers* of the Royal School of Versailles. Just as a dancer maintains his light and airy equilibrium which allows him to detach himself from the ground without apparent effort, so the school horse, at all times, preserves, with no apparent effort, his leaping rhythm; the flexibility and regularity of his cadence. Every step, every beat, every stride contains in itself the easy transition towards the appropriate equilibrium that follows. The erroneous ideas about the *rassembler* arose through forced compressions of the horse's frame which encompass an abusive engagement of the haunches and prevent the correct deployment of the hocks, which, in turn, provoke a hollow back and a refusal to engage. This misfortune never occurs when the *rassembler* arises, without force, from a progressive program of lateral and longitudinal suppling: circles, voltes, serpentines, figures of eight, the shoulder-in, the half-pass, etc. These allow the horse to rediscover, under the rider, the optimal level of his natural balance by engaging his strength through the consistent deployment of energy from back to front.

Maître Oliveira said to me one day: "When I get on a colt for the first time, I already have the *rassembler* in mind." This does not mean that he sought it already at the breaking in stage, but that he was already preparing the youngster for it during the very first lessons. It is not a matter of forcing but, by means of sensitive touches, influencing the balance of the young horse in such a way that he will, years later, arrive at the *rassembler*.

The *ramener*, which describes the placement of the horse's head as close as possible in the vertical position, is only one element of the *rassembler*. It makes no sense without it. The erroneous principle of pursuing the ramener in isolation actually causes havoc; yet *almost all school horses are introduced to the ramener without concurrent work towards the rassembler*. The result is then a sad resorting to draw-reins, to which is added mouth damage by the bit. We are thus seeing what Colonel Podhajsky stigmatized as the false *rassembler*, provoked by traction going from the forehand backwards; a compressed equitation.

The definition of the *rassembler* indicates that only one form of it exists for each horse, just as there is only one correct equilibrium in a given position. François Baucher [1796–1873] wished to define a new kind of *rassembler*, which would efface that of the School of Versailles. He first recommended a maximum drawing together of the hind legs and the forelegs (the image of the chamois on a rock); fortunately, he abandoned this in his second method, only to pick it up once more by the raising of the neck with direct actions of the hand. This only provokes a hollowing of the back and hinders the impulsion of horses who have not been suppled in the classical manner.

Captain Beudant, *écuyer*, a direct intellectual descendant of Baucher and of Faverot de Kerbrech wrote: "The *ramener* is not indispensable to the equilibrium." (*Dressage of the Saddle Horse* – 1938); he added that it was not an error to imitate the horse in a state of liberty, even when we are dealing with school equitation. He admitted that the complete *ramener* gave the horse "all of his splendor" and underscored that one was dealing with "a *ramener* wherein the neck actually becomes higher so that the nose can be lowered but without lowering the poll".

I hope that each and every one understands that the *rassembler* is not a means used in dressage; rather it is a state of being for the horse. Consequently, no one will be astonished when I withhold describing it further.

The Rassembler of the Rider

I want to speak unambiguously about something that appears important to me and that the great authors did not stress sufficiently: a horse can hold the position of the *rassembler* only if the rider collects himself; this is a position which unites each part of the rider's body and establishes optimal muscular tonicity, a deep seat and a stable center of gravity.

There are some airs which cannot really be executed without the *rassembler*, that is, all those that demand the *descente de main et de jambes* – which means a momentary discontinuance of any action of hands and legs, namely, at the passage, the piaffe, the transition from one to the other and, above all, the true school trot or *rassemblé* trot, which has virtually disappeared nowadays, but which we will discuss later.

An equilibrium that is *rassemblé* is the true and only distinguishing mark that authenticates artistic dressage.

6. The Rider's Position

The position, that is, a posture that has been worked at and acquired is, together with tact, an essential quality and the foundation of high school equitation. Upon it depends the equestrian development of the rider, as well as the schooling of his horse.

The position is not merely a matter of aesthetics and style; it assures maximum stability, security and balance of the rider, and permits such modifications of the seat as are necessary to promote and accord with the movements, airs and gaits required.

When unity with the horse is complete, and there is no instability in the hands or legs, the rider is able to apply even the basic aids in a subtle way that reflects the finesse of equestrian art.

When the horse is moving in a relatively uncollected manner in the slower gaits on flat ground – such as may be the case when going for a hack – his center of gravity will generally be located just a little behind his forelegs. On the other hand, the center of gravity of a *rassemblé* horse, especially in airs such as the levade, may shift right back towards his hind legs. It is easy to imagine, especially in the latter case, how important is the relationship between the rider's center of gravity and that of the horse. Displacements of the seat to give weight aids are carried out by varying the inclination of the rider's torso, its inflexion or light twist in the region of the pelvis but never by sliding the seat in the saddle.

As schooling progresses, increasingly refined weight aids can be introduced, which signal adjustments of the horse's center of gravity backwards, forwards or to the side, as required. At this level of subtlety, one can attain perfection in the art and true equestrian happiness. The use of hands and legs is then of only subsidiary value. The rider's position is now the determining factor for the equilibrium of the ridden horse.

It is easy to take an ideal position at the halt, but to move from this static equilibrium to a dynamic one, on a horse in motion, is another matter and is the great concern of sensitive equitation.

The movement of the horse has a constant influence on his center of gravity, and thus upon his balance, and he must therefore make adaptations to his position in order to retain his equilibrium. Thus, as we have noted, at a certain level the principal aid is the astute and finely controlled adjustment of the rider's weight in the saddle. This continual modification is, essentially, impossible to describe; it can only be felt.

The outstanding Captain Beudant (*Dressage du Cheval de Selle* – 1938) gives a wonderful definition of the movement, that is, of the air executed by a schooled horse: "It is the effect that is produced by the action (of the rider) on the position (of the horse). Passing from movement to inaction is the effect of the position (of the rider) on the action (of the horse)." We understand how much we must have control of and, above all, limit the movement and position of our body, to be able to influence correctly the position of the horse and make this weight aid the superior one, so that it reduces reliance upon the others.

The difficulty the novice has lies in adapting his position when, at the slightest movement, it must vary and fuse into the dynamics of action. The concept of equilibrium married to movement clarifies the words: suppleness, finesse and relaxation, which occur again and again in the writings of those who have pursued the study of equitation into all of its nuances.

Montfaucon de Rogles, *écuyer* of the *Petite Ecurie du Roi* at Versailles, describes the state "of the beautiful posture of the man on horseback" when he says: "All that one had said assumes a horse at rest whose movements will soon disturb this equilibrium in more ways than one. The effects of these destructive causes of the beautiful position and even of the equilibrium can be anticipated or fought efficiently, either by *this solid and curved line which the lumbar vertebrae form, or by the play of these very vertebrae, or by these two combined.*"

Rider's posture. A carriage that allows the joints to function, while remaining close to the horse's center of gravity which is in continuous motion in the gaits, exercises and airs.

The correct position.

Establishing the Position

Upon what does one sit? You have certainly been told about the ischia, these bony protuberances; try to seat yourself upon them and look at yourself in profile... no... Sit deeply in the saddle, on the triangle formed by the anterior perineum [lower front aspect of the pubis] and the ischia [seat bones]: a seat that is largely open. This is your "base" stated anatomically and the creator of the "curved lumbar line" – that is to say, when correctly seated on the perineum and ischia, the lumbar vertebrae are pushed out slightly and the pelvis is a little tilted.

How to sit? The torso and head upright and free from undue tension as though one is standing erect upon one's legs.

The shoulders must not be hunched; they must be drawn back somewhat, but not to the extent of being rigid. The upper arms hang, without tension, vertically down the sides of the body, the forearms are raised some 45 degrees from the vertical, the hands close to each other at the level of the withers.

The waist is pushed forward and the pelvis tilted downwards without displacing the seat and disturbing the line of the arms, which are placed slightly behind the rider's sides (the curved lumbar line is now created).

The thighs are flat, hanging freely, which ensures that the weight is correctly placed in the seat.

The legs hang down by their own weight in a way that is free from tension, the inner side of the calves having a light contact. Gripping is not tolerated. The feet follow the legs, toes slightly raised, turned towards the inside without locking the ankles. The stirrups carry only the weight of the feet, thus avoiding the absorption of the jolts transmitted to the stirrup leathers by the movement of the horse's back, jolts that are borne unconsciously by many riders who put too much weight on the stirrups.

This posture allows the rider's joints to function efficiently and further absorb those movements that have already been absorbed in part by correctly positioned loins – "the loins should be bent and firm to resist the movements of the horse" (La Guérinière, *School of Horsemanship* – 1733).

Control of the Rider's Position

A vertical line that runs from the nape of the neck must just touch the first and the last vertebrae and, eventually, the spurs. A vertical line that falls from the knee must just touch the toe. One must be seated on the perineal-ischial triangle described earlier.

Working at the Position

The lunge in the hands of the *écuyer* relieves the pupil from being concerned with the direction and regulation of the three gaits, eliminating all related problems. To let go of reins, placing the hands on the thighs, and quitting the stirrups, all the while retaining the exact position one would have with stirrups, is an excellent exercise. A pliant stick placed behind the elbows, across the lower part of the back indicates the correct posture of the lower back in the lumbar region.

M. Irbinger, the former *écuyer en chef* of the Spanish Riding School, confided to me that, at the age of sixty, he had one of his *écuyers* lunge him from time to time. He wanted to preserve the flexibility of the lumbar muscles, the undulating movements of which regulate the breadth of the strides, especially at the canter.

So long as the functioning of this lower section of the back is compromised, one cannot apply oneself to the pursuit of *rassemblé* movement. The correct posture, which requires the disappearance of total contraction and any clutching with legs on the rider's part, can be examined on the lunge, where one is free from the problems of maintaining direction and impulsion. One places one's seat forwards, holding the pommel of the saddle firmly with one's hand, at the trot and at the canter. At the canter, one follows perfectly the rocking movement of the horse, which one can then increase or reduce at will.

So long as the smallest portion of the back of the seat rises at the canter, then the supple movement of the loins is not employed efficiently and must absorb the movement of the horse's back while, at the same time, regulating it.

7. The Aids

The aids should be examined only after the rider has determined and adopted the correct position; indeed, the same aids applied to different positions have different results, even opposite ones.

The aids are the means by which the rider can communicate to his partner the general effect and the quality of the movements expected of him. Their finesse and frequency establish a two-way code of communication, in that the signals from man to horse are conveyed by the same means as those that pass from horse to man. For example, when the horse is asked to become light by means of a vibration of the rider's fingers, there should be a response, namely, a relaxation of the jaw which detaches softly from the hand upon which it had weighed heavily.

Delicate aids which are correctly given– *hands without legs, legs without hands* – produce light and precise horses; awkward and brutal aids produce hesitant and pulling horses.

The aids are first the seat, then the leg, the hand, the riding whip, the heel, the spur and the voice.

The Seat

The seat is the part of the body permanently in contact with the horse by means of an intermediary saddle. It is the perineal-ischial triangle spread out in the center and in the front of the saddle, extended by the inner part of the thighs, and down to and including the knees. *It is when the seat finally becomes a means of contact rather than merely an agent of good posture that it becomes the most important aid.*

Further to this, so long as the crude basic posture of the seat is established through a gripping with thighs and legs, the seat is neutralized as an aid; a musician cannot both clutch at and play his instrument. The same holds true for hands and legs. Authors have not sufficiently emphasized the fact that these can only serve as means of communication when they cease to utilized as so much ballast.

When pliability of the rider is evidenced by flexibility of the rider's back working in accord with the movements of the horse's back, either limiting or amplifying them, then the seat suffices as the means of transmitting the directions of the rider. Any modification in the distribution of weight in the seat displaces the center of gravity of the horse-rider combination. Of course, it is never a question of sliding in the saddle, but of increasing or lightening the weight in one area or another by lateral or longitudinal inflexion of the loins, or by drawing back the inside shoulder – in a volte, for example.

Engagement of the lumbar vertebrae, together with a gentle, enveloping movement from the inner sides of thighs and calves, bring about, in a suppled horse, the flexion of the joints and raising of the back which leads to the *rassembler*. The same engagement, directed forward and facilitated by the wrists (which, while still preserving contact, move forward with the pelvis), brings about an extension of the gait. Weight placed on the inner part of the saddle, in the direction of the required movement, forms part of lateral displacement. For example, with a left shoulder-in, the left buttock assists the movement of the horse's haunches, by pushing them in the direction of the shoulder-in. It is now easy to understand why the rider who still has to cling to the saddle in order to stay in it must curtail his ambitions to participate in superior equitation.

The Hand

The hand indicates. To do so, it must be solely devoted to this task. Is this evident? Perhaps, but even so, it is better to be explicit. Indeed, how often have I noticed, while lungeing experienced riders, that they are destabilized when they abandon the reins.

The first effect of the hand is to direct and position. When the reins are held parallel, they keep the horse straight. When one of the reins is lowered in a more or less pronounced way, on the intended side, without pulling back, it flexes the neck without twisting the nose, and, if given light support by the opposite rein, it indicates to the horse that he must not "fall" on to the inside shoulder: it makes the haunches follow the tracks of the shoulders and prevents them from falling to the inside. The outside rein prevents exaggerated bend in the horse. When executing a half-pass, it allows the haunches to come forward while more or less holding back the shoulders. At the shoulder-in, it allows the shoulders to go forward in the direction of the movement by moving towards the outside, or regulates their movement by coming back to the base of neck.

The hand also determines the position which the rider decides to give to his horse on the basis of the level of his development.

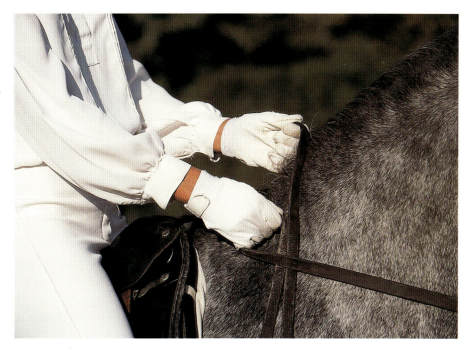

The inside hand low, maintaining the position of the nose, while the outside hand determines support of the forehand and the level of the poll.

a) *The inside hand, always held lower, determines the angle of the nose.* It prevents the opening of the angle of the head and neck, and the raising of the poll. It must remain still and serve as a point of contact to which the actions of the outside rein relate. Only the fingers of this hand can move on still wrists.

b) *The outside hand, more elevated, determines the extent to which the poll is raised.* By means of vibrations or half-halts, it prevents any falling onto the forehand, overbending, or lowering of the neck.

These positions and actions of the inside and outside rein must be achieved with a length of rein and degree of contact that signify lightness.

The second effect is to slow down or halt the horse by raising the outside rein in an upward movement; this is the half-halt or the halt.

The third effect is to free the horse by moving the wrists forward as though one were seeking the straightening of a gait or a *"descente de main"* wherein the horse preserves his balance. This movement must be measured but gentle. That is to say, it must retain a consistent contact with the horse's mouth, at no time transmitting to it any of the movements originating in the horse's back – which must be absorbed by the rider's own seat and back.

The hand can oppose with equal force, but should never over-react to, resistance in the horse's mouth. It must yield as soon as the mouth yields.

31

To the definition of the fixed hand, "which should suffice to all" (Baucher), I add the importance of mobile or gentle fingers, for, indeed, really fixed fingers would be intolerable to the mouth. *The action of the hand is really the action of the fingers and not that of the wrists, and even less the action of the arms, for the latter would be pulling.*

The fingers take, yield, play with the reins on the side that is required to yield but they must never pull. At the beginning of any schooling session, the hands must be placed as low as possible.

Raised Hands and their Problems

While the classical authors, whether past or contemporary, are very precise when referring to the rider's position and to the placement of the aids with respect to the horse, they are more reticent when it comes to any reference to the precise position the hand must take, contenting themselves by simply stating that the position should be low.

Instructions given by the F.E.I. produce riders who hold their hands high. They begin a change in direction by raising the inside hand even higher than the outside hand, which provokes simultaneously a loss of impulsion, a lateral tilting of the nose, and a hollowing of the horse's top line.

The loss of impulsion occurs because raising the hand provokes the half-halt and the halt. Oscillating one's hand to one side makes the horse's nose deviate to that side. A hollowing of the vertebral column occurs because raising the hand provokes a tendency in the horse to throw back the poll and hollow his back.

And because the spontaneous reaction of the novice is to raise his arms at the slightest unexpected movement of the horse, this increases even further the horse's instinctive reaction to escape the hand, resulting in immediate loss of control. This reaction is especially evident in riding school horses and those used for pleasure riding, who have never been properly trained. Such animals have escaped the deadly recommendation of item 3.243 of the French Equestrian Federation's manual: "Yielding by means of German reins [draw-reins]" which, while it has been established as a system, is as bizarre and distorted as attempting to put a baby to sleep by administering opium.

It is evident that horses put through such treatment by new, unreasoning converts are definitely either behind or above the bit. And when it comes to competitive riders – even with those competing on an international level – one sees only raised wrists clutching reins that are likewise taut and raised.

Horses who get this kind of treatment sometimes have noses that are vertical, and often behind the vertical; their jaws and polls are locked and their movements are frozen into a mechanical rigidity. These types either execute a poor passage and piaffe or are incapable of doing them at all. They have usually been fitted with draw-reins and a "serrated snaffle", which gives them a rhythmic oscillation of the head when they trot! They never dare throw back or raise their heads, but will permanently pull their heads downwards; hence these raised hands, suspended, taut, and, as a corollary, renouncing lightness.

I have always wanted to understand everything, even extravagances. And so I will explain to you the structure of this one.

When one pulls the reins downwards, the horse frees himself by pulling upwards; when one pulls the reins upwards the horse tries to find relief by pulling downwards. Thus, through the use of draw-reins, one locks the poll. To set it in position, one raises the wrists firmly upwards and the horse, used to reacting against the hand, will pull his poll – downwards!

The Leg

The leg is used as an extension of the seat to achieve impulsion; the leg also complements the hand to achieve direction.

The efficacy of the leg aid depends upon it eliciting an immediate response and ceasing to act once the response has been made. This absolutely proscribes the idea of legs clutching at, or glued to, the flanks, since discernible aids are never then felt by the horse. The legs act simultaneously or separately according to the purpose intended. One must use the inside of the calf and, if absolutely necessary, the heels, with or without spurs. Vibrations, or individually distinct "taps" are always more efficient than using pressure.

The Whip or Crop

To serve as a useful aid, the whip or crop must be at least 1.1 meters long and able to reach any part of the horse without the rider having to displace his wrists. The whip complements the leg and serves as a substitute during work in hand. It indicates rather than corrects. One must use delicate taps on those areas of the horse which the rider cannot reach with his legs. The whip is an indispensable tool to the horseman. It is difficult to understand why the masters have classified it as an aid, whereas General Decarpentry does not mention the spur as one; however, in France, the whip is generally forbidden during competition, whereas the spur is permitted! [*Translator's note: rules regarding use of whip and spur may vary from country to country and depend upon type and level of competition.*]

The Spur

The spur extends the heel and gives it a more precise action. With its simple, rounded shank, it acts with greater precision and is more easily felt by the horse.

Conceived in this manner, it is useful. But when used with a pricking or cutting rowel, it is always harmful and only serves to satisfy the rage or the impotence of the rider. In this shape it ought to be forbidden, but it is, alas, practically institutionalized. [*Translator's note: rules in some countries require that, if spurs have rowels, these must be blunted.*]

The Voice

The voice is important because, used astutely, it is unlikely to contradict itself, or invoke negative responses, in the way that incorrectly applied physical aids may do. In this respect, it has particular value when dealing with worried or nervous horses, who fear the effects of hand or leg.

Not only does the voice calm, but it can also give directions. It is during work on the lunge that a code of communication is established. The voice is then replaced by contact aids, then by associated reflexes. However, it is considered unseemly, and is even forbidden in competition, undoubtedly because it is too "cerebral".

Use of the Aids

We will discuss this matter in greater detail when dealing with the various airs and exercises. Here, it suffices to repeat that they must be simple and used with discretion and that one must not lose oneself in complex and foggy notions. There are diagonal aids and lateral aids, but no combination of aids can be predetermined since the same exercises on the same horse can, within a few seconds and during a greater or lesser contraction, become reliant upon the application of a dominant lateral or, contrarily, a strong diagonal aid. It is also true that there are certain complicated combinations of rein aids that have perverse effects and which we prefer to ignore.

On the other hand, I consider it essential to clarify certain fundamental elements which govern a good relationship between the rider's hand and the horse's mouth, and between the rider's seat and the horse's back. Adjustment and co-ordination of these different means of communication are of such importance that they justify these precise statements.

The "Pre-setting" of the Aids

Let us first state certain essential truths:

1. the arms must be placed alongside the body;

2. at no time should they be pulled backwards, for that means pulling reins;

3. the reins must be adjusted to a semi-tension, that is, to the weight of the leather;

4. should there be any resistances of weight or force, the fingers must take up and yield as appropriate, to nullify the resistance;

5. the legs are an extension of the seat, components that indicate and set the balance;

6. the horse must be forewarned before commencing an exercise.

All of these combined requirements come under this heading "the pre-setting of aids", that is, *to anticipate the position of the hands on the reins and even that of the seat in the saddle without necessarily modifying the action* (the equilibrium) before starting the new exercise. Here is a simple example: I am on the track on the long side of the *manège* and decide to turn and go to a center track, keeping the horse parallel to the long sides, not allowing the haunches to veer when leaving the track or returning to the track.

Before leaving the track, I execute two strides, then I:

1. Advance the hand on the inside rein a little, but without taking any other overt action.

2. Sit – but without displacing myself – slightly more on the inside of the saddle, balancing this seat aid by supporting the horse slightly more with the outside rein.

I leave the track and:

1. I lower the inside hand, vertically, vibrating with the tips of my fingers. I advance the outside wrist slightly, which facilitates the bend, limiting it to the necessary minimum.

2. The weight of my inside buttock has slowed down the movement of the inside hind leg and facilitated the turn.

"Pre-setting" has avoided the following: pulling back the arm and acting with a direct rein in order to turn both head and neck, thereby minimizing traction on the mouth, loss of balance of my torso, and reduction of impulsion; it has also avoided the lateral twisting of the horse's nose, which an opening rein would have provoked.

One must definitely not put oneself in the position of having to act both backwards and upwards in order to turn all or part of the horse. This would, undoubtedly, occur if both hands were at an equal distance from his mouth at the moment when one asks for a flexion. It would be worse still if both hands were directed backwards, whether the reins were loose or had contact, for the pommel of the saddle would prevent one from lowering one's hand without moving it sideways.

It is simply a question of giving the inside hand, through anticipation, the position which allows it to act with a simple vertical lowering and a light vibration of the fingers.

Extensive observation has proved to me the efficacy of such a "pre-setting", which avoids all lateral or longitudinal traction in order to turn the head and shoulders. This acquires special importance when executing the shoulder-in and the half-pass, where premature actions of the inside hand would provoke a "break" in the neck and have a series of undesirable consequences.

CHAPTER ONE

The Time to Understand

1. First Contacts

The new youngster has just arrived. He is 3 years old. He stands in a stall and the best years of his life are now over.

This could be quite different if those who take on the responsibility of acquiring and schooling a horse possessed a minimum of good sense and training.

Important factors, that is, decisive ones, pertaining to the behavior of a horse to be ridden, are his equilibrium, his temperament, and his gaits. He will be profoundly affected by the contacts and experiences he has in the stall and, later, by those he has with his rider and the rider's aids on the terrain chosen for his breaking in.

One must make a great effort to imagine and understand *the tremendous shock this essentially emotional being experiences when he is removed* from the pasture and the foaling box where he was born and, after a harrowing journey, taken to an unknown place which ends up between narrow partitions. Jostled when being loaded and unloaded into a new and noisy environment, everything contributes to making his reflexes react with anguish and him wanting to flee.

To avoid or at least to diminish his traumatic experience, we should understand that it is in the stall and around the stable that his breaking in begins. The experience I have had in breaking in and schooling ninety youngsters of seven or eight different breeds, all stallions, indicated to me the diverse reactions each one had with respect to their environment, how they had been initially raised, and the kind of treatment they had received earlier in the stable. It also revealed each one's temperament.

Everything that happens around him and to him will affect a young horse's memory and his behavior. Even if it is possible for him to recover from some harm done to him, bear in mind that a horse will never forget the action that caused this harm and that, years later, this same tactless action will continue to create panic and anxiety. One must not try to interpret what occurred earlier and its consequential effects as evidence of cowardice on the horse's part, but consider his reactions to be the result of an accumulation of a vast number of experiences.

I will add that the behavior of the horse, based on the human contact he has had before being ridden, does not permit one to make too hasty a judgement about his reactions.

I have worked with very confident and friendly horses who, thanks to an intimate and pleasant background accepted and even sought the bit, when worked in hand, but then reacted vehemently to the girth and the weight of the rider. On the other hand, I have seen colts who were practically wild and hard to handle – one even trying to bite the whip – who then behaved very calmly under saddle.

This simply means that the behavior of a young horse on a social level has no correlation with any future behavior when physically constrained by humans and that the breaking in is composed of two different parts.

In the Stall

Speak to the horse in a gentle voice as you approach him. Place your arms alongside your body and allow him to sniff you. Raise only your forearm to let him smell your hand. Offer him a natural treat, a carrot or an apple. As long as he is unaware of sugar do not give him any, for its mineral composition will make him anxious.

Try to caress him on the shoulder, then extend the caress farther back. Avoid making him turn around you in the stall. Should he try to avoid you by doing so, place yourself at a right angle to his left shoulder and gently extend your left arm to bring him to a halt; then once more take up your attempt to approach him and tempt him with a treat.

Should he become anxious when you place the halter on him, show it to him first, caress him with it, then slowly slide it around him.

If you first have to tie him to a ring in the stall, place between the ring and the halter a thin piece of string, which will break if he panics and pulls away. This way, an accident is avoided.

Always start out caressing him from the shoulder, then gently continue caressing him towards the head and the haunches, even reaching down to his legs – but stay out of their reach. Keep on talking to him in a soothing voice. But, regardless of what happens, your movements must be slow. Show no nervousness. Go through the same ritual when you first enter the stall with the manure fork and bucket. The use of a currycomb and brush should follow the same procedure as with caresses.

Continue this way progressively with grooming and washing down. Should he refuse to be touched on certain parts of the body, do not insist right away. Try again the next day and tempt him with a treat.

Each day, try to win a little more of his confidence. A more solid base is thus formed. Beware that a move that is too sudden can cancel out many weeks of work.

From the Stall to the Schooling Ground

Selecting on the basis of the temperament and strength of the horse, put on him a halter or cavesson that fits correctly (see Equestrian Equipment). I reject systematically anything that constrains a horse's mouth. Place a helper safely behind the youngster, for he will most likely stop once or twice; pulling him by the head will only make him step back and bring about a repetition of this behavior at the same spot. Place him in such a manner so that if he rushes, he will pass your shoulder and not jostle you in the back. Never place yourself facing him when asking him to advance. If, later, you proceed to the *manège* without your helper and he refuses to pass through a tight passage or a doorway, you must use what is known as "a whip on the chest" which we will mention later (see pages 62, 233).

2. Breaking In[1]

The choice of site will be: a *manège*, a dressage arena or, if neither is available, some area with well-marked boundaries, with ground that is firm and even. An enclosed area of 20 by 10 meters will suffice – if necessary, this can be constructed by the use of a few light stakes linked together by colored ribbons to control him. If a purpose-built enclosed arena is too extensive, one should reduce it in the same manner, since one must prevent the young horse from venturing too far out.

Equipment

A leather halter, or cavesson, a lungeing line of 7 to 10 meters, a surcingle, a neck strap (to keep the mane in check), a snaffle, a lungeing whip, a schooling whip, chalk (to mark off a schooling area as necessary), and a little pail with slices of carrots and apples.

1 M. Henriquet, *Le Débourrage du Cheval*. Prest. Edit. Connaissance du Cheval, 1986.

The Personnel

These consist of the *écuyer* – the master of ceremonies – who is responsible for handling the lungeing line; a helper, who will ride the horse; and, for a few days, two additional people, who will eventually close half of the *manège*, to assist at the mounting block and control the first steps taken by the horse ridden on the lunge.

In the Manège

The *écuyer* holds the lungeing line in his right hand at 20 centimeters away from the horse's head. His arm must be supple; the left hand holds the coil of the lungeing line. The helper, lungeing whip or schooling whip in hand, follows close at the horse's haunches. Go around the *manège* in each direction at a quiet walk. Speak to the horse, caress him, and execute circles at each end of the track.

The youngster is now familiar with the *manège*, which he has covered in all directions; the *écuyer* then places himself in the middle of the circle and releases 5 or 6 meters of the lungeing line; the second additional helper replaces the *écuyer* at the horse's head; the third helper continues to accompany the young horse near the haunches on this circle of 10 to 12 meters, with the *écuyer* at the center.

The *écuyer* moves the horse forward by voice and gesture, first at a walk, then at the trot. Help on the part of the assistant is necessary until the horse can move without difficulty at the *écuyer's* command, and without trying to whip around or go backwards.

It is in the *manège* that problems surface that are sometimes unavoidable: resistances always tend to increase there. Thus it is here that the third helper, when he no longer needs to follow the youngster around the circle, can intervene to close the fourth side of the square if this has not already been done.

All the while, the *écuyer* calls for halts, the walk, the trot, as well as generating calm and stimulation (see: Aids, the voice, page 34).

The use of all these helpers initially may seem excessive, but this is necessary for only a few days if the *écuyer* and his chief helper are competent. At the end of eight days, two helpers in total should suffice, then only one from the beginning of the third week.

Each year, we break in ten to twelve colts, who work regularly and calmly and are mounted in the arena during the fifth week. Some of them, returned to pasture from July to November, are then ridden again without any difficulty.

On the lunge: the lunge line reduces the effective size of the open arena and allows one to control the circle.

Fitting the Girth

As soon as the youngster accepts caresses and being touched on all parts of the body – usually during the second or third day after he has been put at ease on the lunge – it is time to fit a simple surcingle, which is akin to fitting a light girth without the weight of the saddle. The horse should be halted, and treats given, mainly by the *écuyer*. Helper No. 1 fits the surcingle carefully, that is, he slides it along the horse's sides as though it were a caress; he then passes it over the horse's back to helper No. 2, who then passes it back under the body to helper No. 1, who calmly buckles it and adjusts it so that it cannot slide around. The *écuyer* maintains calmness in the horse by means of his voice, giving a treat, and vibrations of the halter or cavesson.

The helpers having let go, the *écuyer* stands aside for, at times, it is at this moment that the youngster discovers that he has been girthed and leaps off. The *écuyer* puts him on a circle, calms him, but, should he try to halt or refuse to go forward, makes him do so by touching him gently with the lungeing whip. The *écuyer* also makes sure that the girth does not have to be re-tightened.

Once the youngster is relaxed and reassured, protective boots may be placed on him at the end of the session.

The Saddle

When the youngster no longer reacts to the surcingle, he can be saddled. After some beneficial lungeing in each direction, to relax him, the *écuyer* halts the horse, faces him, and has a bowl filled with sliced carrots and apples brought to him. The noseband is loosened so that the horse is able to chew properly; helper No. 1 places himself facing the horse's flank on the off side, while helper No. 2 brings the saddle, with stirrup leathers looped, and the girth loose. He lets the horse sniff the saddle. The two helpers stroke the horse's back and shoulders while the *écuyer* gives the horse a treat.

Helper No. 2 then caresses the horse's shoulder and flank with the saddle. If everything has been carefully prepared, the worst that the horse can now do is rush forwards or backwards when he feels the saddle. If the former occurs, the saddle should be removed and vibrations with the cavesson should be given, perhaps even giving sharp, quick jerks with the wrist. One notes that the cavesson, used with tact, can render the young horse completely immobile much more effectively and with less harm than the use of any kind of mouthpiece. The horse must never go past the *écuyer*. If he is violent, only the cavesson can make him stay in place. When he has settled, take up once again contact with the saddle and the treats.

The second possible problem is that the horse may back quickly. In this case, the *écuyer*, the helper on the off side and the helper carrying the saddle, all follow the horse as he backs, placing treats under his nose until he stops and eats. The interrupted activities are then taken up once again. The horse will very likely try to back again, but he will do so less and less. Horses have a natural dislike of backing and the taste of apples will, sooner or later, make him stop.

Placing the saddle on the horse will then be repeated. Helper No. 2 holds it vertically over the youngster's back, lowers it, and places it gently on the back, while helper No. 1 gathers the girth, passes it under the horse's abdomen to No. 2, who then buckles it moderately, yet firmly, so that it cannot slide around. The *écuyer* who, in the meantime, has allowed the horse to stuff himself with treats from the bowl, steps aside immediately so that the horse can go forward, which he may often do, arching his back and sometimes even leaping forward. All these actions must take place away from any walls, so that no one can be squeezed into a corner should the horse react violently.

The Snaffle

One can now place a snaffle under the cavesson. No reins should be used at this point. It is done only to get the horse used to the presence of a strange body in his mouth. It is a good idea to buckle a drop noseband in front of the snaffle, which is adjusted in such a way that the horse can eat slices of carrots. It will also prevent the tongue from slipping over the snaffle, which can happen when a young horse crosses his jaw to push away the bit with his tongue.

The horse is now saddled and bridled and circles on the lunge in each direction. This lesson takes place with the stirrups hanging freely. The helpers are always ready to assist the *écuyer* should the horse try to leave the circle or go beyond it.

One interrupts work on the circle four to six times to make a change in direction, returning to a walk and making two circles in walk before and after each direction change, the former especially to prevent the horse from stopping abruptly opposite the *écuyer* holding the lungeing line. Such halts would quickly become a way of resisting; it is impossible to control a horse who is no longer level with the one who is lungeing him.

Mounting

When a change of direction occurs, the *écuyer* calls the horse to him and rewards him, while the helpers caress and stroke along the horse's entire body, tap on the saddle and knock the stirrups about. Then, one on each side, the helpers push down on the stirrup irons in an attempt to get the horse to accept the weight of the rider as he mounts. It is also necessary for the helper facing the left stirrup to jump up and down several times, legs together, and to stomp on the ground, in order to accustom the horse to being dismounted without fear.

When nothing frightens him any more, the second week is the time to give him a lesson on being mounted. The situation is similar to when the saddle was placed on his back, with the same disposal of the team, unless the helper on the mounting side, who formerly carried the saddle, will be the one mounting.

The helper on the off side of the horse will hold down the stirrup-iron to compensate for the weight of his team-mate who, after lengthening the stirrup-leather as much as possible, will place his foot in the stirrup on his side and take hold of the mane with his left hand, the saddle with his right hand, all the while putting more weight in the stirrup. Each time the youngster fusses and stops chewing his carrots, the assistant will take his foot out of the stirrup, only to place it back again. He must avoid putting the point of his foot into the abdomen of the horse, allowing only contact on the tibia; the rest of the movement is executed by means of his arms. After a maximum of three lessons, the helper will hoist himself up, his abdomen on the saddle, torso and both arms on the off side, and both legs, out of the stirrups, on the mounting side of the horse. He will slide to the ground as soon as the colt becomes agitated, then mount again in the same manner, for as long as it is necessary, until everything is accomplished in a calm manner. In this position, somewhat unusual, yet safe, the mounted helper will stroke the horse on the shoulders, flanks, croup, where helper No. 1 has usually stroked the horse, thereby accustoming him to be touched in those very areas.

Flat on one's stomach across the horse's back, so that one can slide off in an emergency without getting hurt.

De-dramatization

All phony attempts to replace the rider on the saddle by using a sack of sand, or the use of a stool to facilitate mounting, are forbidden: centrifugal force will displace the former and the horse will jostle or knock over the latter, provoking panic. Useless constraints and violent means are only repaid by resistances which may sometimes last a horse's lifetime. It is of paramount importance that all activity occurs in complete calm and silence, interrupted only by calm, reassuring voices. Everyone should know exactly the role to which he has been assigned, and that, at no time, is the disorder of the young horse to be penalized by the slightest blow, which would only aggravate matters. *Rather, everything should occur in a way which de-dramatizes the agonizing situation* – we will use this word again later – in which he finds himself.

Let us return to our valiant helper whom we left lying on his abdomen on the saddle, across the horse who, at the time, was chewing carrots. He will continue in this rather uncomfortable position as the horse takes his first steps. In the meantime, another helper has passed a second lungeing line through the cavesson and places himself at the right shoulder of the horse, while the third helper is standing behind, and the *écuyer*, who is on the left, lungeing line in hand, signals the movement. Should the youngster refuse to budge, helper No. 3 touches him lightly with the lungeing whip and talks to him and then he moves forward and goes around the *manège*, shepherded by all members of the team.

On the Horse

After two more lessons like the aforementioned one, and after forty minutes of lungeing and changing direction, the time has arrived when one can sit astride the horse. If everything goes according to plan, and the necessary time is taken, so that everything flows well, nothing unpleasant should occur. From the horse's point of view, no new sensation has so far been felt with respect to the rider, who is lying across the saddle and who is already touching the horse's flanks with his hand. Well framed by the *écuyer* and helper No. 1, gorging himself from his bowl of carrots – which is, for him, the most important aspect of the whole ritual – the young horse will allow himself to be ridden without difficulty. It goes without saying that the mounted helper's right leg will avoid hitting the horse's croup and that placing himself on the saddle will be done gently.

Going around the *manège* at a walk, the mounted helper holds the mane with his outside hand; with the other hand he holds the reins, which have been fixed on each side of the cavesson or, better still, of a well-fitting halter which has replaced the now redundant cavesson. For the moment and for a few weeks, no rein is to be attached to the snaffle that is already in the horse's mouth. A strap placed around the base of his neck keeps his mane in check.

One circuit is ridden on the right rein, then a change of direction on the diagonal, and a circuit on the left rein. After this, execute a few large circles then a few strides at the trot, supported by a helper on foot, as

The first steps, astride.

the youngster may sometimes hold back or rush forward – behavior which must be accepted as natural and corrected only with gentleness.

From now on the important role is put into the hands of the helper on horseback, who assumes a supple and responsive seat, free from tension yet ever ready to adjust and respond to the rather violent accelerations, typical of all lively youngsters. Such actions must be absorbed by the rider's posture, leaning back (without pulling on the reins) if necessary, but not gripping harshly with the legs.

The *écuyer*, holding his lungeing whip 5 or 6 meters from the horse, places himself in the center of a circle and a helper on the ground initially accompanies the horse around the circle, then withdraws. From now on the mounted helper, together with the *écuyer* in the center of the circle, share the direction and impulsion of the horse.

Prior to him first being ridden, it is useful to have already accustomed a horse with the contact of a whip or a long crop against his flanks to make him go forward without frightening him. The mounted helper will make sure that the horse goes forward by means of his seat or whip. He can do this with greater synchronization than can the *écuyer* with his lungeing whip. The role of the *écuyer*, especially that of his lungeing whip, now decreases progressively and becomes merely one of giving assistance and security (which eventually ceases), and giving advice to the helper. The aim now is to go at the walk, to halt, to trot, to execute some more circles and halts, not seeking the canter at first, but accepting it if it occurs.

One must begin teaching the aids for forward movement by means of the whip, but without force. One should not hesitate to use the whip to assist the leg if the horse does not respond. However, it is important to touch the sides of the horse, and not the haunches, with the whip. To support the forward movement, the reins, attached to the halter, must take and yield to avoid constant traction. While a strong rein contact may initially cause the horse to accelerate in an attempt to evade it, this will cause even more traction, and the movement will be hurried and resistant, not the true forward movement required.

Now that the youngster is able to circle calmly on the lunge at two or three gaits, halt, then move off again when the helper indicates it. This time, the *écuyer* leads him to the track of the *manège*, accompanying him around the *manège*, lungeing line semi-taut, making him walk straight, turn at the corners and execute circles and simple figures on each rein.

Free at Last

If all goes well, one can now free the horse/rider combination from the lungeing line, but if the écuyer has experience and tact, he will remain in the *manège*, lungeing whip lowered, in valuable partnership with his assistant. As a simple consequence of his relationship with the horse and rider, he will help his assistant in the execution of directional changes and elementary figures, remaining close at hand and, if not actively assisting in turning corners, at least going to the end of the *manège*.

It is now time to fit reins to the snaffle – although these will, for a while, double with the halter reins, before replacing them. It should be noted that, while this step will introduce greater precision, it will also bring about greater risks.

It goes without saying that, at this stage, the trot will be a rising trot in order to spare the horse's back. It is essential that the mounted helper continues using the same voice commands as the *écuyer*, who has accustomed the horse to recognize at least ten commands which facilitate the aids. Halts, strike-offs, walk, trot, canter, slowing-down, acceleration, relaxation, are among the commands which can be spoken, and these limit the emphasis upon the physical aids, which can cause a certain amount of tension. I have often noticed that some of my horses – the most sensitive ones – stiffen easily but immediately relax when I speak to them.

The rider of the young horse should now immobilize his hands on each side of the shoulders, for it is at this stage that horses who have been constantly bruised in their mouths by highly raised and unstable hands, start violent head-tossing and hollowing their backs. This way of neutralizing the hands does not exclude extending them out to prevent the horse from falling in, or lowering them vertically along the shoulder to make him turn: the main thing is returning the hand to the neutral position as soon as it has acted. It is at this point that one must pay attention to the straightness of the horse's body with respect to the track, and that he maintains a proper flexion on circles, even if one occasionally tolerates a poor turning at the corner. One must already be attentive to clean strike-offs, precise halts, and the stretching out of the natural gaits.

I have known too many riders, smitten with delicate movements, who fall into a kind of lusterless and languishing riding at this stage, becoming blasé in their approach. I have already explained this when I discussed "the time it takes"; it is not easy to program in advance the time it takes to break in a horse; and this applies to the whole of schooling. However, to prevent some of my more demanding readers from getting ahead of schedule, I would suggest it is probable that, with an average horse, the period between the first lesson and the first outdoor ride, accompanied by a calm horse – and after an hour of relaxation in the *manège* – takes from six to eight weeks.

At what age can one begin to break in a horse? The ideal time to do this is in the March/April period of his third year, then to put him back in the field until the first cold weather sets in; then begin riding him again – which can take a mere forty-eight hours of re-introduction.

To begin riding a youngster before he is 3 years old is to deliberately compromise his growth and his health. One must have seen the skeletons of 2-year-old Thoroughbreds – supposedly a breed that is more precocious than others – to verify the existence of bony lesions brought about by premature work.

The Breaking In of the Horse by the Rider

I would like to stress how important it is for the rider who wants to undertake a career in dressage or equestrian sport, to serve, himself, as an assistant in breaking in a large number of youngstock. He will then have learned how to connect but without gripping on tightly, to experience sudden spurts and starts without reacting, and to move the horse along without constraint.

Of paramount importance also is the competence of the teaching personnel at Riding Clubs, who are often the only teachers with whom their members have contact; it is for them to show those who have just acquired a young horse how to saddle him. *Is it not incredible that instructors who have never participated in the breaking in of a young horse, are given diplomas?* If this situation were addressed, it is possible that we would then avoid this procession of violent and brutal aberrations, starting out with the twitch, or a group of humans holding on to a foal just to saddle him, or even the use of a hobble. These horrors escape the attention of those associations whose function it is to protect horses because they occur in areas involving people who have been officially invested with the function of teaching.

It is common knowledge that a horse never forgets anything, good or bad. If I have been able to make clear that a little knowledge, a little elementary psychology and friendship, can bring about confidence on the part of this marvelous companion, then the objective has been achieved.

3. Work on the Lunge

We will see when we study the breaking in that three-quarters of this essential phase in preparing the horse occurs on the lunge. The lunge will remain an indispensable means to the *écuyer* and to the serious rider for other uses: relaxation before work and making a beginner feel secure when placing him in the saddle.

During the breaking in period, lungeing provides the means of exercising the youngster daily, of controlling the cadence of his gaits, suppling him, establishing the beginnings of the codification of the aids, and regulating and channeling impulsion. Furthermore, beyond the breaking in phase, it allows one to assess the gait variants on circles and straight lines.

The Necessary Equipment

The equipment needed for lungeing consists of a light cavesson or a well-fitting halter, a good lungeing whip, and sometimes a pair of side reins or a chambon.

The area should be a closed one, which prevents any attempted flights to the outside or associated behavioral disorders. In the matter of a wilful youngster or a poorly trained horse, the assistance of a helper who walks alongside the *écuyer* with a lungeing whip will forestall half-turns or violent changes of direction.

When and why does one use side reins? They are used only with troublesome and difficult horses; or horses who are violent. They are never used to position the head of a horse but only to control the horse better. Adjustment must be carefully and progressively observed. A chambon is to be used only for naturally ewe-necked horses, or those who have

With a horse already well schooled one can verify the good effects of work on the lunge. Here, the development of the trot.

become so as a result of heavy hands or hands held too high. These horses, at the slightest contact with the lungeing line, throw their polls back, hollow their backs, and drag their hind legs. A chambon, progressively adjusted, makes them lengthen the neck first downwards, then horizontally, and persuades them to raise and relax the back. Usually, side reins and the chambon are adjusted equally on both sides. Shortening the inside rein when the horse has a false outside bend does not rectify flexion, rather it will often accentuate it by bringing about a resistance to the constraint placed on the horse.

Finally, something I will never condone: one must never lunge a horse using a snaffle ring; one must only lunge using a halter or a cavesson. The young horse will experience nervous and uncontrolled moments and unforeseen attempts to escape; if lunged from the snaffle, each time these occasions arise he will traumatize his mouth, even if the hand functions skillfully, and this will only result in problems of the tongue and grinding of teeth.

Getting Started

This session begins at a walk, along the track going large. On the left rein, standing at the horse's left shoulder, the *écuyer* holds the lungeing line in his right hand about 10 centimeters from the horse's head. The lungeing whip is in his left hand, tip back and, should the helper be absent, agitating it judiciously near the tail enables him to make the horse go forward.

One turn around the track at a walk, one turn on a circle of 12 meters diameter, then have him come to you and caress him. After having placed the lungeing line in the left hand, make the horse go forward, extend the left forearm and gradually slacken the line; stimulate the horse by clicking the tongue and, in a very controlled movement of the lungeing whip, lower it towards the haunches.

It is a good idea to get the horse used to walking straight along the track, accompanying him level with the saddle and 3 meters inside, and proceed from the straight line to a circle, and so on.

The Aids

At a walk on a circle, gradually allow 5 or 6 meters of lungeing line and hold it without slack but with no significant tension with the horse walking perpendicularly to the lungeing line. Use voice commands such as "walk on"; "move" if he slows down; later "trot", "canter", or "easy, easy" to calm him, and go back over the gaits with the same commands but using a steadier and more measured tone.

The horse is now between the hand and the leg, that is, between the lungeing line and the whip. The latter should always be lowered and pointing towards the tail when the horse is asked to go forward; it is pointed towards the girth to touch him, or to keep him on the circumference of the circle. If the horse does not move forward when the lungeing whip is slightly raised, or when the voice is used, touch the horse quickly and briskly, ideally on the girth and not under the tail. Any actual impact with the thong of the whip should occur seldom but, if it is used, it should be brief and efficient; repeated little smacks irritate and provoke disorders and stubbornness.

When standing in the circle, the *écuyer* must pivot around his right leg on the right rein, and left leg on the left rein; whether going to the right or the left, he must pivot in place and not run after the horse. He must keep his arms close to his body to give them the maximum of firmness.

It is good practice to describe a succession of circles with different tangent points on the long side of the *manège*. To do this, in order to retain his relative place at the center of each circle, the *écuyer* must displace himself along a parallel line in the *manège* to allow the horse to go large by 3 or 4 meters between each circle. He should also stretch out the arm that holds the lungeing line in the direction of the horse's movement, and avoid placing himself in front of the horse.

An efficient combination of vibrations with the lunge line and the position of the lungeing whip gathers the trot into a form from which the passage will develop.

To change direction, first the lungeing whip must be moved from one hand to the other, then passed behind one's back and temporarily tucked under one's arm. The horse is then asked to approach while the line is being vibrated and rolled up. As the horse is halted, he is given a piece of sugar, and turned at the shoulder onto the other rein.

Mistakes

Never set the hand to oppose a provoked impulsion. This means that when one solicits an increase in impulsion with the lungeing whip, one must choose the moment when the horse's outside shoulder finds itself against the wall, then one yields a little with the line and achieves a veritable *descente de main*. The use of a taut lungeing line can bring about a weight increase on the line and a veering of the haunches towards the outside, rather than an extension of forward movement. At the trot, between two circles progressing down the arena, the *écuyer* can obtain the first extensions of the trot if, using large steps, he places himself at the median line, level with the haunches held at the wall. These extended strides are promoted by the engagement of the inside hind leg (which occurred in the circle) and developed on the straight, then recovered [shortened again] on the following circle.

If the horse falls inside on the circle, one can enlarge it by pointing the lungeing whip and sending the thong towards his shoulder, while undulating the line.

If he pulls towards the outside, take and give some of the line, vibrate it but not to the extent of yanking on the horse's head or causing discomfort.

Horses who become unruly and disunited while being lunged at the canter are the victims of excessive tension on the lungeing line, combined with the effects of centrifugal force and excessive action with the lungeing whip, which forces them to place weight on their outside lateral in order to retain balance.

Incurvation and Cadence

After a few weeks, the young horse who has established a sound equilibrium at the trot and canter can be placed on circles that have a smaller diameter, from 12 to 10, 8, then 5 meters and enlarged once again from 5 to 8, 10, 12, that is, in the form of a spiral. One should note that circles of 8 meters should be executed at a gait no faster than a slow trot, and those of 5 meters are executed only at the walk. If the *écuyer* is skillful and uses the corners of the *manège* to "contain" the horse, he can gain

Between hand and lungeing whip – here a substitute for the leg – the horse executes the piaffe.

cadence, suppleness and, to some extent, achieve a *rassembler* in the unmounted horse.

At this phase, by returning the horse to the walk, and by playing with the lungeing line and the end of the lungeing whip, one can obtain a few good strides at the shoulder-in, which one can exploit later when working in hand.

Finally, it is by means of vibrations on the lungeing line attached to the cavesson that one can obtain the absolute calm necessary when mounting. With a horse who has already been broken in, the lungeing line is indispensable.

4. Work In Hand [2]

The idea of working a horse to tire him before he is mounted by a novice rider, or to relax him for more sophisticated riders, is as old as equitation itself (Xenophon). To *prepare* a horse by working him in hand, without the additional constraint of a weight, is relatively recent, since it was in the 19th century that Baucher and his disciples developed it, raising it to the level of a method. Before this, the single pillar around which the horse

2 M. Henriquet, *Le Travail à Pied*. Opiprest. Connaissance du Cheval, 1987.

turned in order to bend him in the 16th century, or the double pillars of the 17th century, used to perfect the *rassembler*, together with the lunge-ing line and long reins, were all attempts to prepare the horse for the rider.

The Importance of Work In Hand

Suppling exercises for the young horse, or for the re-schooling of a spoiled horse are of unquestionable importance. However, even though exercises in hand diminish the risk of falling off, they are not any easier to do prop-erly than mounted work! In fact, if exercises in hand are poorly executed, they can even degenerate into a tussle between man and horse, ending up in the desperate running away of the latter, followed by greater problems. As with so much in equitation, explanations of work in hand, whether written or oral, are insufficient if they are not based on authoritative demonstrations and practical experience given to the pupil by the master. However, the benefit derived from correct work in hand is formidable and we have already touched upon this in discussing the breaking in stage, when the mere presence of a man seated on his back can be a time of great trauma for the young horse.

We have already tackled the ways one can reduce this problem and we will discuss it again later. But, regardless of what work one undertakes, the horse will always feel more at ease when he moves on his own than when he carries 15 percent of his own weight on his back.

The advantages one gains when working in hand is seen in the following:

1. The establishment of a code between horse and rider; a code which will be used later when the horse is mounted, but which will not be eroded by the horse's concern and uneasiness which always occur in the initial stages when a rider sits astride.

2. By a reduction in the tension and muscular contractions that derive from carrying the rider's weight and from awkward movement when suppling exercises are introduced in the early stages under saddle. If the exercises are first learnt in hand, they are more readily acquired and are then performed with greater facility under saddle.

Baucher's Work In Hand

Before discussing the progressive steps I usually take when working in hand, I feel it is necessary to present the essential suppling preliminaries which Baucher, Faverot de Kerbrech and their principal pupils discuss, namely, flexions of the jaw and neck. I will not give an appreciation of their relative merit but simply say that, if the slightest equestrian gesture requires knowledge and finesse, then flexions of the jaw and neck demand the competence, experience, and tact of a master. They are essential when horses are very much handicapped because of their conformation, or because of the clumsiness and tactlessness of people who have ridden them previously. They are indispensable to the method of Baucher, which ignores the shoulder-in, itself a complete flexion of the ensemble of the horse, jaw and neck included. Baucherism believes that "it is always a matter of these areas which contract first when a horse attempts to resist the aids" (Gustav Gerhardt, *Manuel d'équitation* – 1859). These flexions aim at making the jaw, head, and neck yield to the actions of the bit.

The Baucherist School proposes first:

— preparatory flexions, which allow one to show the horse what is expected of him through the mobilization of his mouth and neck when contacted with the hand;

— direct flexions of the jaw;

— lateral flexions of jaw and neck.

The aim of all these flexions is to obtain a light, two-way rapport between the hand of the rider and the mouth of the horse. These flexions are described by Baucherist writers (Baucher himself, Faverot de Kerbrech, Gustav Gerhardt, Charles Raabe, Etienne Beudant, etc.) with certain minor variations.

It is obvious that the *écuyer* who adheres strictly to the supplings proposed by these masters cannot school a horse without these "preparatory" flexions, as General Faverot stated.

The basis of all these methods depends upon exercises involving lateral flexions and circular movements. It is impossible to avoid this, for whoever controls the curvature of the horse, regulates his equilibrium – but to each his own flexions!

The School of Versailles proposed the shoulder-in, mounted, which mobilizes and flexes the horse's whole body within the movement, through lateral displacement. Baucher, on the other hand, works each part separately in a stationary position.

I have, for a long time, applied both methods. With horses who have a normal conformation and disposition, I adhere more often to the lateral displacements of the shoulder-in, which requires less skill and subtlety.

In the course of the last thirty-five years of work, I have observed, in France and elsewhere, work done in an attempt to supple a horse, beginning with Iberian riders of the bullfighting type, passing through German and Russian Olympic champions, up to the last Baucherists; but never have I witnessed any of them going through the whole range of flexions of the jaw and neck and ending solely with them, that is, without executing the shoulder-in as a complete schooling of the horse.

Baucher's flexions.

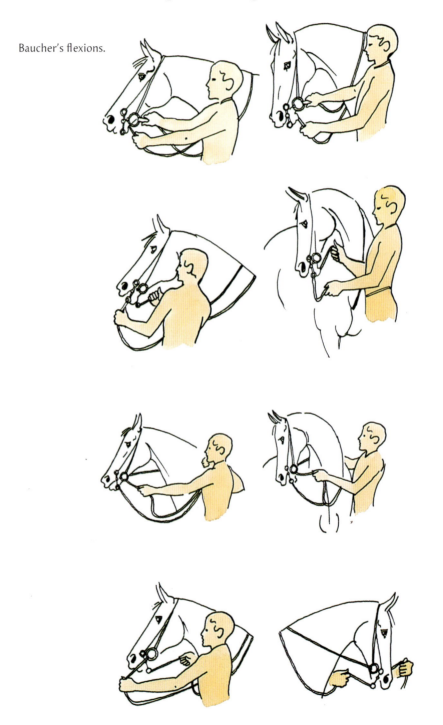

Nonetheless, I repeat that, with certain poorly conformed horses and those who pull, some flexions of the jaw done by an expert hand can only be an advantage in laying the groundwork, and this process will always be less horrendous than the use of those abominable bits which have a cutting effect and which, in addition to the use of draw reins, are being institutionalized: barbarism is gaining ground…

Progression

The following is the least complex progression of work to accomplish and can be taught to a pupil with a young horse in about ten lessons.

Walking Straight

The first thing one does after lungeing a horse in each direction is to lead the horse to the track, on the left rein, shoulders and haunches straight, with the left snaffle rein and the lungeing line of the cavesson in the left hand, lungeing whip and right rein in the right hand. The cavesson is to be vibrated to spare the horse's mouth should he bore on the hand; the snaffle should suffice if he has understood.

Halt the horse straight and parallel to the wall, using equal contact on each rein. First attain first immobility, an even halt, that is, with the legs evenly placed, as soon as possible. Caress him, have him move forward

In hand. The halt should be straight and regular.

In hand: the position of the inside hand. The outside hand (in this case, the right one) holds the right snaffle rein.

Walking straight in hand.

by touching him, then raise the whip, placing it where the rider's leg is positioned.

Halt again after a few steps, first by means of a light opposition of the fingers, then by voice alone; then have the horse move forward through the voice and raising of the whip.

Once this is work is achieved satisfactorily, do the same thing in the other direction.

Voltes

When everything goes well, and halts and strike-offs are light and even, one can achieve the same thing on voltes of 6 meters diameter, in each direction. One needs sufficient tact on each rein to prevent the haunches from veering. Head and neck must remain in the normal position and relatively fixed. At the slightest sign of disorder, straighten the horse, re-balance him, then send him off again. Should the horse bear strongly on the hand, voltes are the solution, before straightening him again and putting him back on the track.

The Shoulder-in

When the horse has understood what is expected of him, the time has come to acquaint him with the shoulder-in.

With the first straight and light halt on the left rein, have him come to you, moving laterally with his forelegs, shoulders in. This is achieved by making the horse step forward once, simultaneously pulling the shoulders to the inside of the *manège* with the inside (left) rein. Then, still standing opposite the horse's left shoulder, give him some light contacts with the outside (right) rein, while holding the haunches with the left rein on the girth; this quickly makes the horse take a few lateral steps.

From now on, whether on foot or mounted, the inside rein (in relationship to the bend of the horse), will play the main role in maintaining the bend. The outside rein, acting more or less towards the inside, will retard the displacement of the shoulders and thus give the haunches time to move forwards.

The first steps of the shoulder-in may bring about a certain amount of contraction; should this happens, one should not force the issue; rather one should put the horse into a volte around oneself and, retaining the bend, take him back to the track at the shoulder-in, and begin again.

It is important not to position the horse's body at too great an angle to the track, but to maintain it at an angle of 30 to 35 degrees. One must halt him frequently at the shoulder-in and, with a *descente de main*, allow him to relax, become calm, then take off once again, properly flexed and light.

At every halt, verify the engagement of the inside hind leg. Turning

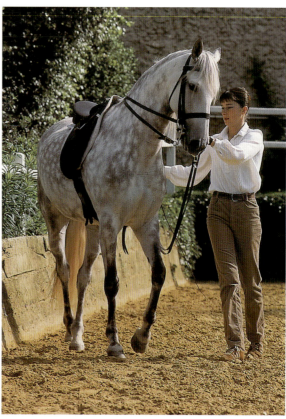

ABOVE LEFT Work in hand. The shoulder-in on the diagonal.

ABOVE RIGHT Work in hand. The shoulder-in at the track.

corners will bring about a maximum of crossing of the hind legs. Therefore, gently hold back the shoulders slightly before reaching the corner to allow the haunches to make an arc of a quarter of a circle in the corner. One can then put him on a circle and begin the shoulder-in. Make sure that he walks laterally, advancing slightly. When executing this exercise in hand, the hands have the same action as when mounted: the whip replaces the legs to direct as well as to stimulate.

The Half-pass

When the previous exercise has been executed with ease, in each direction, the moment has arrived when the horse can proceed to the half-pass, which follows the shoulder-in. However, there is this difference, which poses an additional difficulty, namely that, with the half-pass, the horse turns his head and his incurvation in the direction of the movement, whereas in the shoulder-in, his head and the inflexion of his body are inverted in the direction opposed to the movement.

It is relatively easy to go from the shoulder-in to the half-pass, but a little more difficult to maintain it. When one reaches the end of the long side in the position of the shoulder-in (for example, shoulder-in left from H to

K), one goes beyond the corner, slows down, takes the horse off the track as though one were turning towards the center line of the *manège*; one then brings forward the left hand which, until now, held the bend of the neck to the left, and brings the neck and the shoulder to the right, adjusting the rein on the same side. The whip, which is in the right hand, touches the flank of the horse telling the haunches that a lateral displacement from left to right is required. The left hand slows or frees the shoulders.

Then, giving a greater or lesser bend by means of yielding or taking up the reins, and with the whip at the haunches, one leads the horse on the diagonal to the opposite wall; one can then proceed in the same manner croup to wall.

BELOW LEFT Work in hand. The half-pass, head to wall.

BELOW RIGHT Work in hand. The half-pass, croup to wall.

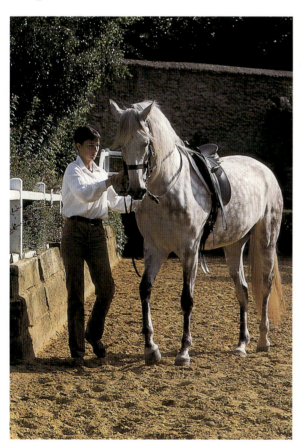

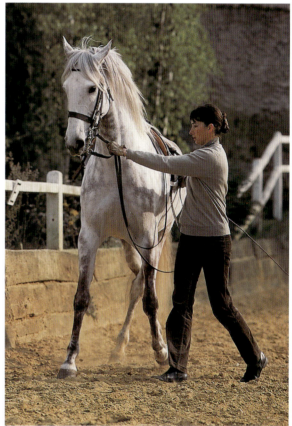

The Rein-back

This movement can be taught in hand as soon as the horse is able to halt in the position of the *rassembler*, that is, when the forelegs and hind legs are united and engaged. One places oneself in front of the horse, takes hold of the snaffle reins near the rings, raises one's wrists vertically, and holds the reins firmly but without jerking them until one attains a step backwards. Then, in hand, as when mounted, make sure that the horse steps back on the appropriate diagonal: right rein = right foreleg, left hind leg; left rein = left foreleg, right hind leg, and so on. If the horse takes crooked steps, straighten him by means of a light inversion of neck and shoulders. Never use the whip on the chest, for this is an aid to achieve a forward movement. However, if there is any hesitation in moving backwards, one can tap the forelegs at the knees with the whip. When the horse has understood this movement, one has him execute it after replacing oneself at his shoulder.

Pirouettes

An easy lateral displacement of shoulders and haunches is both the end and the means of these exercises. This displacement can be perfected in hand by means of reversed and ordinary pirouettes.

With respect to reversed pirouettes from left to right, the horse is bent in such a way that he will see his haunches coming to him and his whole body will pivot around the left foreleg which will mark time. Place yourself at his left shoulder, give the bend with the right rein, fix the left shoulder in place with the left rein, tap the flank of the horse to displace his haunches The ordinary pirouette from left to right is executed around the right hind leg, which marks time. The whip prevents the haunches from

BELOW LEFT Work in hand. Reversed pirouette, from right to left.

BELOW RIGHT Work in hand. The ordinary pirouette, from right to left.

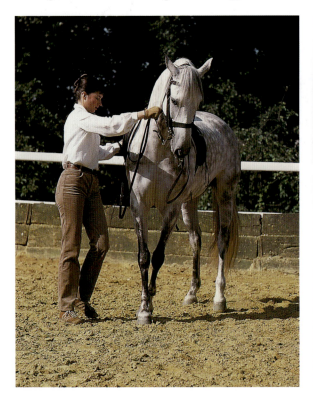

veering; the hand produces the displacement of the shoulders. It is of the utmost importance that these two exercises are initiated and executed step by step, interrupted frequently to caress and reward the horse. Trying to introduce several steps of the pirouette at a time can only create panic and lead to failure.

When all these exercises have been executed calmly and with rigorous attention to detail it is possible to take up again walking straight, in hand, with halts and strike-offs, and executing the shoulder-in and half-passes at the trot. The trainer can accompany the horse at the trot, without himself running, which would only excite the horse and bring about disorder; it suffices for him to walk with large steps and slow down or interrupt the exercise as soon as the horse accelerates.

Once the halts, rein-backs and strike-offs from halt are executed with ease, and the trot is light and straight, the time has come to ask of the horse those exercises with a slight diagonalization, [jumping from one diagonal to the other] which will serve as a prelude to the piaffe.

Work in hand: extended trot. The mare actually executes this extension with a light vertical flexion.

The Piaffe

Halt the horse in the position of the *rassembler*. Let him stand still for three seconds, the left hand holding the lungeing line that is attached to the cavesson, while the right hand holds the whip horizontally, covering the flank and the haunches. Now raise the whip. The hand holding the lungeing line, which is placed under the lower jaw, vibrates gently to prevent the horse from going forward; the whip is gently activated to make him move in place.

Hand without whip, whip without hand will produce the first diagonal step; halt the horse right away by means of the voice, placing the whip on the horse's back behind the saddle. For the horse who has been well prepared and schooled in hand, this is a signal for him to stop work and halt. Reward and repeat once more on each rein.

In certain cases, side reins can facilitate and maintain the *mise en main*.

A horse, prepared in this fashion, will be easy to handle and immediately receptive when first given the aids, mounted.

The rider initiated in the piaffe via these exercises will perceive more readily the correct measure and frequency of aids to be given, and the

Work in hand; the piaffe. Here, with the guiding rein of the cavesson.

advantages of applying them with gently. Finally, the relationship between man and horse will become more intimate as the days go by, and confidence in each other will become reciprocal.

When should one begin these exercises? Right away, when one is dealing with an adult horse; otherwise, as soon as a young horse has been broken in – that is, assuming one is dealing with reasonable people, with whom the breaking in begins at the age of three and a half, and *manège* work at the beginning of the fourth year. This is when one begins suppling exercises, in hand. Since they are rather constraining, they should not exceed twenty minutes in duration, interrupted by rest and treats. After working in hand for a month, followed each day by relatively relaxed work at the three gaits, or going for a hack, one can, without being too demanding, start to ask for the same exercises, mounted, for a few steps.

5. Mounted Beginnings

We have progressively broken in our young horse and two or three months have passed since he came to the *manège*. Ideally, we would now return him to pasture until the cold weather sets in, so that he could profit from the rich summer grass to complete his growth; we would then take him up again in late fall/early winter and place him quietly once again under a rider when, after two or three days, we would find him as we had left him.

But, if we do not have this option, we must continue to exercise our young pupil, that is, we must ride him daily.

The best formula up to the age four is to continue his schooling along these lines: five minutes of work in hand; thirty minutes of calm mounted work in the *manège* and arena; thirty to forty minutes hacking.

After the preliminaries, which we have outlined with care, we enter the first phase, which I call the time to learn. Why the time to learn? Because experience has shown that, for true communication and understanding to occur, *it is necessary to establish between pupil and teacher a system of coherent conventions* – a codified language. Without this, taking into account the mental age and inexperience of the youngster, initial contacts would only be a series of clashes between disparate beings.

We shall try to remove from our equestrian gestures all that could hinder clarity and efficacy. As we have seen, this is only possible by acquiring a perfect balance in the saddle, from which posture our signals, the aids, will be executed with a maximum degree of accuracy and precision, their timing and intensity reflecting the demands of the moment.

The time to learn will replace the time to understand when the young horse, now familiar with the simple and elementary exercises, is able to execute, with regular and cadenced gaits, some semblance of the school airs. A few years later, the time to perfect will finally arrive, when the work, heretofore executed merely as a sketch, will, day by day, take on more precise contours.

The First Steps: the Trot and the Canter

Today, we have lunged our pupil. Then, working in hand, we have asked him for a few steps of shoulder-in, interspersed with halts and gentle strike-offs in each direction.

Now, we are in the saddle and the horse has been provided with a simple snaffle. We go to the track at a walk. Although the reins have contact, they are long enough to allow the neck to stretch without constraint. We follow the track with the horse's vertebral column parallel to the wall.

We turn smoothly through the corners, without riding them too deep, and change the rein across the diagonal three or four times, being sure to follow a straight course.

Let us now begin the trot, that is, the rising trot, for relaxation, covering the same path as we did at the walk. One must be careful to hold the axis of the horse's body parallel to the wall of the *manège*. At first, one must not hesitate to lower the outside rein somewhat to the side, to prevent the horse from leaving the track and going to the inside of the manège. This slight opening of the rein must be done with a lowered hand, that is, level with the withers, so as not to bring the neck up and back. While this will create a slightly false bend, it is preferable to the inconvenience of having a horse rush into the middle of the *manège*, and is it a temporary resort, which will diminish progressively. To keep the horse on the track, the inside leg must be maintained on the girth, but the outside leg should not grip. Above all, do not pull on the inside rein; instead be satisfied with a vibrating action of the fingers on this side, which will, in the first instance, limit the false bend and, after a few weeks, determine the correct bend, when the outside rein, maintaining contact, is no longer deforming the bend of the neck towards the outside.

After having changed rein several times at the walk and the trot by means of precise diagonals, turns down the center line, and across the *manège*, return to the walk and add a circle which has already been marked out. It is a figure of a minimum of 12 meters in diameter that the horse must cover, adapting his bend to it, which is actually the purpose of the exercise. At this stage, the circle can be performed accurately at the walk by channeling the horse between light contact of the reins and legs, which serve to guide him. A slight movement of the wrist, the vibration of a leg, will keep the horse on the correct arc of the circle on which he travels. It is important to make reference marks in the *manège* and never rely on one's intuition. Using reference marks is a means of controlling the perfect geometry of the figures. It is then not difficult to describe accurate circles if one simply uses delicate aids and does not make the horse stiffen by asking him prematurely to modify his "horizontal" outline.

Placing one's own shoulders parallel to the shoulders of the horse will help bend him. To this simple work at walk, add circles of 12 to 20 meters diameter at each end of the *manège*, then in the center, always making sure that the circles are completed where they started. One must also be concerned with the regularity of the walk, which must be maintained on an equal and constant basis, whether the horse is going in straight lines or on curves. This rule must be adhered to during the entire period of schooling, whether the horse is going on one track or on two tracks at the three gaits.

The aids used on circles to achieve the horse's initial balance must not be forceful. They should indicate but not be coercive, as the following example shows. On the left rein, to circle to the left, gently open out the left hand 15 centimeters downwards, pivoting the whole pelvis - torso placed in such a way that your shoulders are parallel to those of the horse. The rider's dorsal muscles are in the vertical, lumbar vertebrae engaged; the inside leg is on the girth serving as an axis, the outside leg is 5 centimeters farther back to guide the haunches on the curve. The outside rein compensates for a possible excessive effect on the part of the inside rein by moving to a horizontal position without being raised, thus preventing the horse from turning suddenly to the inside of the circle.

At first, be sure to distinguish between the actions of hands and legs. Always proceed by means of touches that either indicate or rectify. If one acts on both reins simultaneously one provokes head tossing and attempts to run off on the part of the youngster, who feels cornered. The same holds true for leg aids: use vibrating touches but never overt pressure that provokes opposite reactions. Try this out on horses who are tied up: press both hands on their flanks to try to steady them and you will see that most of them will oppose and resist you. But touch their sides with a few light flicks of the fingers and they will obey you.

Never forget that, as soon as a horse begins an exercise or leaves the straight line, *the bend that is required has a braking effect which must be forestalled by an increase in impulsion.* At this point I say that one must never sacrifice impulsion to the execution of an exercise, neither should straightness on a straight line, nor inflexion on curves, be sacrificed in the preparation of a specific air. Should this happen, abandon the exercise and proceed straight and forward.

Asking for Impulsion

Impulsion is engendered by a forward impulse of the rider's braced lumbar vertebrae, accompanied by an enveloping action of the seat, followed by a vibration of the upper part of the calves. At the current stage, it is not a question of using spurs; rather, by using the whip behind the leg (but not on the haunches or croup), can one supplement the previous indications, should they not have been clearly understood. But take note: whether it is the action of the legs or the whip that finally elicits the response, one must simultaneously advance the wrists to let the horse move forwards. This is the *sacrosanct* concept of Baucher: *"hand without legs, legs without hand"*, which everybody knows but nobody practices.

On which side should one use the whip? This is a matter of circumstances. If, on a circle, the horse lets his haunches fall either out or in, touch the area where the mistake was made. In this connection, so as not to worry the horse by changing the whip from one hand to the other, for a few months I carry a whip in each hand, which allows me to perfect what Maître Oliveira called "the silken passageway of the aids".

How intensely should one use the whip? Use the kind of stroke you yourself can receive without feeling actual pain. This can range from a caress to a sharp smack, but never make a mistake as to the intensity required by circumstances, that is, neither too soft or too sharp.

Gait Transitions

Throughout the entire life of the horse one must, at all cost, avoid the humdrum of daily routine. In the same spirit as the martial arts, which high equitation resembles, the horse must always be ready to understand and respond instantaneously to all requests of gaits, direction, equilibrium, and airs demanded of him. This concept applies from now on because of the attention one pays to the transitions between gaits, even during the early phases of the horse's education.

From the halt to the walk, the walk to the trot, to the canter, and the converse, whatever the sequence, the transitions must be requested carefully and performed obediently. It is not yet a question of obtaining speed or fluidity of transition, which the *rassembler* brings about progressively. One must make allowances for the young horse's foibles, but accept no overt inattention or clumsiness when it comes to transitions. Let us not forget that, throughout the breaking in period, we have initiated the horse to the voice and that he recognizes words such as "walk", "trot", "canter", "there" (in place). Always forewarn him by means of your voice when you re-balance yourself, whenever you ask him to do something.

Likewise, he has been accustomed to the whip during work in hand; do not hesitate to use it either on the sides or behind the leg at the slightest reluctance to perform a forward transition.

As the horse progresses, as his back becomes stronger and less tense, and after having used the rising trot for a while, you can begin trying the sitting trot.

Take advantage of a circle at the trot, which will slow him down and give him cadence, and go from one trot to the other, making maximum use of the absorbent quality of your lumbar region so that you do not jar the horse's back, thus provoking rigidity. Return to the rising trot each time you feel that contact with the horse's back is lost because it has begun to contract and become rigid. This feeling of discomfort on the back of the young horse will disappear from year to year and he will gain strength, become more supple, and acquire a better balance to a degree one would never have anticipated.

Halts

The notion of the halt, that is, for the horse to stand quietly in place, is not at all obvious for a young animal made restless by this living weight on his back, which overwhelms and disturbs him and makes him push forward. At times he will stop as a consequence of muscular contractions throughout his whole body, and he will tremble without moving forward when asked to do so. At other times he will refuse to stand still when asked to halt and, instead, will rush forward against the hand.

It is at these times that a soothing voice will be of paramount importance. Sometimes one must wait until the end of the lesson before first asking him to halt on the track, for if one returns to the middle of the *manège* to ask him to halt, he will try to seek refuge there during the working period. Progressively, however, by means of voice and hand, one can halt him several times during the working period.

The action of the hand with respect to halts is much less pronounced than those riders believe, who act as though their biceps have to stop a mass of 600 kilograms, hurled at 10, 20, even 50 kilometers per hour.

It is not customary to say that the horse is a thinking being, who suffers. But should you take the trouble of putting yourself in his position, that is, *explaining* to him what it is that you wish, then, where the strength of six arms cannot halt him, a repeated closing of the fingers, accompanied by an easing of legs and a gentle voice (all too often neglected), will achieve the result in two or three sessions. As soon as the halt is achieved, the hand yields (the wrists advance by a few centimeters), which rewards and confirms the halt.

This method of communication with the horse's mouth avoids thrusts of the head and forcing with the hand. My old horse *Miguelista* who, for many years has been executing all the school airs and who halts, haunches flexed, from a full canter with only a slight vibration of my fingers, will do two circuits of the *manège* with a beginner astride who pulls with all his might, legs gripping and shouting frightened "whoas"…

The Canter

This is the gait that is the most agreeable to beginners as long as the horse does not thrust his head forward too much, and goes on a straight line. The canter is more exhilarating than the walk, less agitating than the trot but, like a racquet, throws into the air seats that are welded to rigid backs. A young horse cantering in an arena often throws himself onto his shoulders and loses his balance when entering corners. This gait creates additional problems because of its speed, provoking in each corner and on each circle a centrifugal force, which tends to unbalance the horse/rider mass, if neither have the experience and technique to compensate for it.

The horse, losing his balance, will try to regain it by going onto the outside lateral or, more often, by disuniting on the outside hind leg. This will prevent him from falling over, but will make him fall back into trot, which, as a corollary, will bring with it an intolerable pounding of the rider's behind. This type of broken-gaited canter has the same kind of disunity as when the horse is being lunged incorrectly at the canter: the lungeing line restricts the horse at the head, while the haunches are chased towards the outside by the lungeing whip. Thus the horse is forced to disunite in order not to fall.

The canter is the fastest of the school gaits, but it is also the most exhilarating for the young horse and the one wherein he is the least sensitive to the commands of the rider until he has he has received the proper schooling. At this three-beat gait, the horse is supported in succession by a hind leg, a diagonal biped, and a foreleg. He prepares himself for this with the very first exercises at the walk and trot, from which he acquires a new equilibrium. At these gaits, the young horse is more inclined to concentrate and is more receptive to being taught.

At the very first lessons in the *manège* we can canter without giving the horse an imposed carriage. Lengthen the trot on a circle, preferably when his outside shoulder is restrained by the wall; then give the signal to canter, supported by the voice.

Striking Off at the Canter

Whether we are dealing with a beginner or a schooled horse, the principles for the equilibrium are the same, only the level of collection varies. One must sit more on the outside buttock in order to release the inner side, that is, the leading shoulder. That is where the futility of the following question arises: must one signal the strike off with the inside leg (with respect to the bend of the horse) or the outside one? There is only one ideal set of balancing aids for the strike-off at the canter. When on a circle, the inside hand, motionless and level with the withers, indicates a very moderate inside flexion; the outside rein supports the outside shoulder and prevents the horse from falling to the inside. The inside leg, placed gently on the girth, anticipates any deviation of the haunches and "takes along" the inside hind leg, the outside leg instigates the strike-off by a twisting forward movement.

With certain young horses or poorly trained horses, one can encounter difficulties striking off on the correct lead. A provisional but infallible method is to invert the bend of the neck slightly towards the outside at the moment of striking off in a corner, to release the inside shoulder. Keep your hands scrupulously low and your legs in place. Any sudden disorder of the aids will bring about an involuntary return to the trot.

In your work in the *manège* you will include two or three brief sessions at the canter. Sustain the regularity of the gait by gently driving with the lumbar region, an action supported by the outside leg which, pushing from back to front, serves as a metronome and regulates the canter. Remain in the saddle without gripping with the calves, since these have a role requiring them to be permanently free.

Should the horse rush too fast at the canter, put him into circles, supporting your outside aids with very little inside rein and leg.

With these simple methods, in conjunction with suppling at the walk and trot, the basic canter can be either slowed-down or opened out, the haunches putting forth all their propulsive force, the forehand being raised, thus achieving the wonderful sensation described by Steinbrecht: "that each forward thrust of the canter already contains the next stride". Remember, also, that a horse is not taught to canter by continuous and lengthy cantering but, rather, by numerous strike-offs which are on the correct lead and straight, first from the trot, later from the walk and the halt.

Now that we have terminated our gymnastic sessions in the *manège*, the pupil is relaxed and mature enough to go for a short hack at the quiet gaits to discover the outside world.

Should you be accompanied by another horse at first? That depends upon the temperament of your youngster. Some become quite excited at finding a fellow by their side; others feel reassured. If you are accompanied, be sure that the other horse is ridden by a serious rider, and that the horse is not given to sudden reactions, which would only be transmitted to your youngster.

Here, then, is an outline pertaining to elementary work applicable to horses aged three to four. You can add to it a few small natural obstacles when riding outside, or place some cavalletti in the *manège*, or use varied terrain at walk, to improve both balance and self-sufficiency.

We will now approach the second phase, that is, *the time to learn*, which will include the first lateral movements and lead into the whole series of exercises which will develop an improved balance.

CHAPTER TWO

The Time to Learn

OUR PUPIL IS NOW completing his fourth year. He has acquired a certain mental and physical maturity, but one cannot say that his development is complete. A horse, regardless of his breed, is really only an adult when he has reached the age of six; his understanding and perception are only complete at that age.

At present, he is able to move easily around the *manège* at all three gaits, on straight lines, on diagonals and circles, in a more or less horizontal balance; that is to say, his neck is scarcely higher than the extension of his vertical column, but his poll is supple. Hands quiet and low have not disturbed his mouth and he does not move his head in an upward direction, which would indicate that he is irritated by the slightest contact with the reins.

We will begin with a series of exercises which will prepare him, little by little, to acquire a more sustained equilibrium by strengthening and suppling all those resources which form his joints and muscles. It is the flexibility and interplay of his whole body that will determine the cadence and rhythm of all the gestures of his limbs.

One hour's work in the *manège*, interspersed with moments of relaxation on a long rein, will make up most of the time devoted to pure gymnastics. A hack of half an hour will complete the work joyfully.

1. The Notion of Contact

This important question is one of the most delicate. The way the concept is commonly understood and the instruction, usually erroneous, which emanates from faulty conception, are responsible for the deterioration of equestrian practice.

For example, very debatable equestrian instruction recommends, without gradation, a search for "tension with the hand". The horse must "run after the bit". As for dressage juries, even when it is a matter of elementary tests, they never fail to approve young horses who are insufficiently stretched. Without wincing, they will witness the spectacle of riders at all levels bracing themselves on the mouths of their horses.

A free and measured contact proceeds from delicate and prolonged work. It is not imposed by force, but allows the horse to seek a light support on the bit, similar to a child seeking the hand of his mother.

According to various disciplines and forms of equitation, a serious analysis of the relationship between hand and mouth leads one to distinguish between a large range of tensions. When it comes to racing, for example, one of the world's best jockeys, Yves Saint-Martin, told me that when he sat properly over the horse's center of gravity, he never felt the weight of the horse. This is obviously quite contrary to the ideas we have acquired when we use racehorses for other disciplines without adapting their equilibrium to their new functions!

The Concept of Contact

This has evolved together with changes in the objectives of schooling. In the first historical phase (the one that prepares for close combat), as well as that of the School of Versailles, with respect to artistic equitation in the 18th century, the objective has always been lightness, which one can define as merely contact through the weight of the reins.

Horses involved in bullfighting, when handled by such masters as the Spaniard Don Alvaro Domecq or the Portuguese José Nuncio, totally share the initiative with their rider. This eliminates any hand-mouth contact other than that evident in the weight of the reins. Communication is made through the weight aids of the seat and a common objective: confront, then avoid the bull.

I remember my confusion when I was riding a fabulous horse belonging to the great Nuncio, and faced a training bull. I urged the horse towards the adversary, keeping him well within the reins; he contracted as he charged at the canter, only to turn around 3 meters from the bull. Nuncio, smiling, merely said to me: "Begin again and yield", and the horse, with a superb shoulder-in, brushed against the bull and I was able to touch his shoulder symbolically.

The horse involved in competition dressage, and his rider, are under the control of the judges, who are more implacable than the bull, taking off marks at the slightest irregularities. Already, at his second competition, the dressage rider will secure his horse tightly in the steely channel of his aids.

Goodbye grace, brilliance, lightness and, above all, the *rassembler*. That is why racehorses and combat horses are lighter than today's dressage horses.

At the School of Versailles, lightness was the touchstone of brilliance and rhythm, a sign of artistic equitation. It was still insisted upon in the 19th century by the Baucherist School and, at the dawn of the 20th Century by General L'Hotte, who insisted upon "perfect lightness, whether the movements were simple or complicated". Competitive equitation, with its imposed sequences and figures, had its beginnings in 1912 and expressed a worthy objective in trials that evaluated the relative qualities of the competitors.

General Decarpentry exhibited an incredible optimism when he announced, in 1936, the blossoming "of the poetry of equitation, thanks to the artistic influence of the Fédération Equestre Internationale". He participated in the drafting of the F.E.I rules, especially those of article 401, which defined the general principles as being simply a question of "harmony", "ease of movements", and "lightness", "the horse seems to perform by himself", "his submission to the bit without tension or resistance", "he must be in hand" with "a light and gentle contact with the bit", etc.

Alas, the good general did not foresee the perverse effects brought about by the intrusion of heavy horses into the arenas and, on the competitors' part, the need to maintain a constant pressure to carry on, in rapid succession, and with no breathing space in between, with the federal trials.

Faced with the stark reality of competition, the wonderful article 401 resembles today a fairy tale reserved for credulous adults and children. It is obvious that, to accord with the criteria required today, which have nothing in common with article 401, one must hold the horse tightly and push him forward with a hypertension which explodes the notion of "poetry in equitation". The technical contacts I have with dressage riders at the highest level have made it possible for me to understand these problems better.

In this very spirit, let us try to redefine a notion dealing with contact that is realistic and practical rather than theoretical.

Definition of Contact

Contact is communication through the adjustment of the reins involving a relative lightness – a few hundred grams, never a dozen kilograms – which permits a dialogue between the seat, back and hand of the rider and the mouth of the horse.

Contact is never an intense hold or traction on the bit, a relationship between hand and mouth that is to be condemned. Such a relationship with the bit begins when the horse is allowed to lean on his shoulders, letting the rider carry his head, and develops into traction through contraction.

In all such instances, there is no longer an equitation involving equilibrium. The opposition that a rider brings to these resistances, whether of inert weight (the horse simply leaning on the bit) or of overt force (active traction of the mouth) destabilizes him or forces him to brace himself. Communication has been severed.

Communication exists only when there is gradual contact, in proportion to and regulated at the level of the horse's schooling, that is, accepted without resistance.

The optimum contact is the weight of the reins only. This is proper for the horse who adopts the *rassemblés* airs, as, for example, the jumper who goes forward and flexes his haunches to store up power before going over an obstacle.

To make things doubly clear, so that young riders do not experience the deception – which struck me at their stage of competition – I repeat that the delicate relationship that exists with the horse's mouth is in accordance with the quality of the rider's seat, his use of aids, and the suppling of the horse.

Graduated Steps Regarding Contact

First Stage

We must take it for granted that young horses, regardless of their breed and the quality of the rider, never accept willingly in their mouth this foreign object, the bit. The movements which are communicated to the mouth by the hand, add to their sense of disquiet. As a result, they often try to back away from the hand to avoid contact; head-tossing also occurs and, if the hand becomes too repressive, they begin to resist and try to break away.

One or more years of schooling with a quiet and steady hand and light fingers are needed to establish an initial contact that is steady and light. This is essential to re-establish the natural gaits of the young horse when mounted.

Second Stage

This corresponds to the *time to learn* and *the time to do*, that is, the time of doing gymnastic exercises, focusing on the development of transitions.

Going from one movement, or gait to the other, extensions, shortenings, and the stabilization of a gait will, at this stage, bring about a revival of the gaits and a decrease of tension corresponding to the transfer of weight from forehand to hindquarters or vice versa. While it is widely understood that, when extensions are poorly controlled, transfer of weight from the haunches to the forehand can bring about an excess of weight on he shoulders, it is not so readily appreciated that an excessive transfer of weight onto the haunches can, in effect, "squash" them and annul their activity. Overburdening either end of the horse in such ways will translate into tensions or contractions, at times quite severe and, in the circumstances, inevitable. Who would dare declare never to have experienced moments when he felt the weight of several kilos and a lack of contact at a few strides.

Although these manifestations of tension are to some extent inevitable, one must not permit them beyond certain limits. Rather, one must become aware that when, during this period of schooling, the horse shows confidence in the hand, contact will be infinitely more pronounced during an extension than during a period of stabilization which follows a return to the "working" gait. Tension will even diminish further when one goes from a "working" gait to the cadence of the *rassemblée*.

While one must accept these variations of intensity, one must immediately counter every action that forces the hand, or requires contact to be relinquished, with half-halts or halts.

Third Stage

Here we are dealing with the *rassembler* belonging to *the time to perfect*. One can admit intellectually that, if the rassembler is completely attained, then the amount of contact required for all the exercises, airs, and gaits will from now on be constant, amounting to some hundreds of grams. *A transition from the piaffe to an extended trot, haunches remaining flexed*, should be executed *with the neck in a constant position* and with the same lightness.

In this respect I do not believe that I am in disagreement with the F.E.I. definition which states that, at the extended trot "the rider allows his horse, while retaining contact, to lower and lengthen his neck" but, as I stated clearly, only if the *rassembler* has succeeded completely!

Finally, when you work with or present young horses, do not let yourself be influenced by premature recommendations of tension on the bit which coaches and jury members will make. It is at this stage that perversions in equitation begin. One then goes straight towards resistances which compromise the development of lightness. That is where the deadly cycle begins to take hold.

2. Exercises at the Walk

It is when at a quiet walk that the horse is most receptive to new exercises and movements: and it is with impulsion, at the trot, that the best result can be obtained. Since the canter provokes exuberance, it is not the gait best suited to the introduction of new exercises: even those that are appropriate to the canter, such as lead changes and pirouettes, can easily be worked out at the walk or the trot. By this I mean, for example, that excellent control and balance promoted and retained in halts and strike-offs to walk and trot will lay the foundation for correct halts and halt to canter transitions, which are the cornerstone of lead changes.

Present-day Germanic trainers (and also the Spanish Riding School), do not execute any lateral movements (for example, shoulder-in or half-pass) at the walk. The reason for this is that, beyond the Rhine, they are convinced that these lateral movements, if executed at the walk, would lead to a loss of impulsion, and that it is at the trot that the horse should be introduced to these movements. In my opinion this is totally erroneous for two reasons. First, with some excellent young horses – especially sensitive and nervous ones – lateral movements at a moderate walk are excellent ways of calming them and balancing them. Second, and more generally, at the walk it is easier to make clear to a young horse the complexity of a shoulder-in and, above all, a half-pass. We have been present when German champions initiated young horses to lateral movements at the trot; they contracted terribly when exposed to these new movements, which they did not understand and fell into a way of going that was incoherent and destructive.

We affirm that these exercises, executed at the walk, and always respecting the non-opposition of hands to legs, do not in the least interfere with impulsion; only the use of force with hands and legs extinguishes the courage of the horse. Furthermore, with a young horse who is just learning this work, the amplitude of the crossing over of the limbs will always be greater at a slow and majestic walk than at the trot which, after all, is a skipping gait, whereby the horse can more easily avoid doing the movement.

Basic Exercises

The purpose of exercises on two tracks is twofold: to straighten the natural inflexion of the horse so that he can hold himself straight on straight lines and correctly bent on curves, and to improve his equilibrium and agility by increasing the functioning of certain muscles in the dorsal region and those in his limbs which only work in lateral displacements. The pirouette flows out of the half-pass which, in turn, flows out of the shoulder-in, which, itself, gets its preparation on the circle, the volte, and turning corners.

It is in this order that we shall follow our study. We estimate that, after a year of elementary work, our pupil will be able to execute correctly, in each direction, and with the correct curvature, circles of 12 meters in diameter at all three gaits.

His balance is still natural, that is, it is characterized by a slight raising of the neck; his gaits are ample but not exaggerated, confining themselves to developing the propulsive force of the hind legs. Progression towards a more stylized or sophisticated equilibrium, one, begins now.

This equilibrium is indispensable to the dressage rider, necessary for the sports rider, and useful to all who simply hack. To the first group it brings its finality, to the second one, all the possibilities of re-balancing, and to the latter comfort and security.

Before introducing the volte and after having, from the very start, rounded off the corners of the *manège*, that is, tolerated the horse to go somewhat obliquely from one side of the angle to the other by bending naturally, we will now introduce the first elements necessary for suppling the horse towards the *rassembler*.

Turning Corners

It is in this very strategic section of the *manège* that the *écuyer* will begin the first elements of his method of establishing the horse's equilibrium. Taking a corner will now require the horse to turn into its arc totally while maintaining, step by step, the hind legs in line with the forelegs. The horse's body bends into what constitutes the arc of a circle which is approximately 6 meters in diameter, that is, the diameter of the volte which we are preparing. But if the horse is directed by aids that are too pronounced, he will try to escape by veering with his haunches.

To place a horse into a corner, as one comes to it, *the inside hand is held low, the rein is set in such a way that the vibrating fingers of this lowered hand bend him; at the same time, the outside rein is adjusted slightly,* opening the outside wrist a little, but not to the extent that it interferes with the bend established by the inside hand. This rein, together with the action of the inside leg vibrating at the girth, will make the horse's shoulder enter the corner. The outside leg remains neutral, unless its use becomes necessary to stimulate the impulsion.

Turning corners must be performed carefully at all three gaits. At the canter if, in spite of an acceptable seat and aids, the horse tries to evade the corner, touch his inside shoulder lightly, with the whip held vertically.

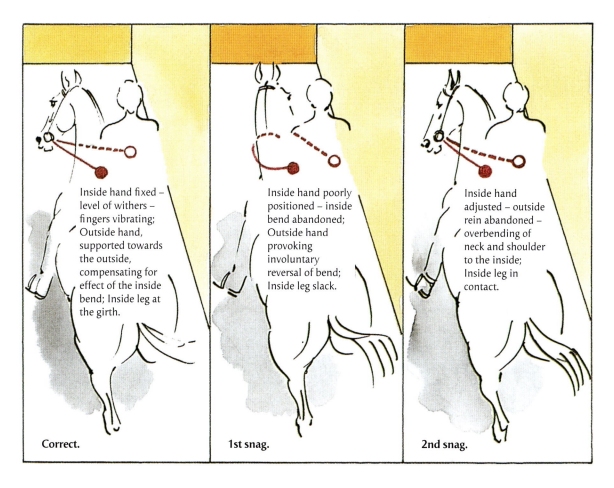

Inside hand fixed –
level of withers –
fingers vibrating;
Outside hand,
supported towards
the outside,
compensating for
effect of the inside
bend; Inside leg at
the girth.

Inside hand poorly
positioned – inside
bend abandoned;
Outside hand
provoking
involuntary
reversal of bend;
Inside leg slack.

Inside hand
adjusted – outside
rein abandoned –
overbending of
neck and shoulder
to the inside;
Inside leg in
contact.

Correct.   **1st snag.**   **2nd snag.**

This is the first lesson in preparation for the volte, the 6 meters diameter of which are the equivalent of four well executed turns into a corner, without the "moral support" of angles. It is the touchstone for suppling work, directional changes, and the rider's discipline.

Turning the corners.

Having done circles, we shall be able to include voltes in our work. One begins them at the walk, preferably at the corner where the horse learned to bend. For the volte, as for the circle, a geometric outline must be used and the figures must end where they began.

The Volte

It is useless to attempt the difficult airs of the high school if one does not perform, rigorously and correctly, the simple exercises which serve as their basis.

One way to be accurate is to trace with one's eyes the line of one's course a few meters in front of the horse, taking a succession of references on the ground he will cover.

On the volte, the horse executes a circular movement on a single track with a lateral flexion that corresponds to the circumference of the circle. The lateral flexion of the vertebral column determines a more pronounced load upon the inside hind leg, and thus requires greater flexibility of this limb and more activity on the part of the outside hind leg, which has a larger path to cover.

This attitude of the horse is enhanced by the position of the rider who, while remaining upright in the saddle, pivots his pelvis so that his hips and shoulders adjust to accord with those of the horse, and places more weight upon his inside seat bone, the intention being to put the balance of the horse/rider partnership towards the inside.

The inside rein determines the bend, the outside rein and leg limit it; the inside leg at the girth fixes it. Support of the outside rein and the influence of the inside leg towards the outside will make the volte bigger. The action of the inside rein and the outside leg towards the inside will reduce it. One must increase the size of the voltes on the rein in which the horse finds greater difficulty in bending.

Enlarged and reduced voltes in the form of spirals of 6 to 12 meters in diameter serve as excellent exercises.

Because of its small diameter, and the requirement to move with an impulsion and cadence that are sustained and regular, the volte compels the horse to flex without any resistance to the rider's hands and legs. This flexing, indirectly induced, brings with it the natural raising of the neck and back and the lowering of the hindquarters and promotes the suppling of the inside hind leg.

When one works in a space limited by walls, one must beware of letting oneself fall into the natural tendency of the horse to cling to the wall, which destroys the geometry of the figures.

When a horse is placed on circles and voltes, one is able to change direction by means of two demi-voltes within the figure. The demi-volte is also the figure by which a horse leaves the track along the wall on a semi-circle, which takes him back to the wall, on the opposite rein, on a straight line, forming a sharp angle with the track. It becomes a reversed demi-volte when one leaves the track on an oblique straight line to join it once again by a half-circle, which brings us back on the opposite rein.

The circle (having a circumference of 12 to 20 meters), the volte and the demi-volte are executed at the three gaits on one or two tracks – the latter at the half-pass (renvers and travers positions), the shoulder-in and the counter-shoulder-in. As described by Baucher, the ordinary demi-volte is the demi-volte on two tracks with the croup towards the center; the reversed demi-volte is the demi-volte on two tracks with the shoulders towards the center.

Thus our work has progressed from a more rigorous turning at the corners to voltes, giving the horse a strengthened cadence and equilibrium, increased the demands imposed upon him, demands which become even greater when we tackle lateral displacements. In addition to a period of rest at the walk with loose reins, in order to help the horse sustain these new, rigorous exercises, we must return frequently to a free, extended walk, the poll level with the withers.

Gait Transitions

Transitions between the various gaits must be understood *as part of the gymnastics which increase the power and energy*, and as a psychological element which holds the horse always ready to move from one cadence to another without ever allowing him to go to sleep at the routine gait.

One must not confuse the sought-for variations of stride length in the horse's gaits with an increase in the speed and frequency of steps, which are the instinctive means a horse uses in order to protect himself from effort.

Transitions are made from one gait to another on circles and are also performed within each gait.

When starting to work at the trot, it is ideal to work each morning, on each rein, at five or six transitions from the working trot to the walk and back to trot. This is requested by means of light half-halts at the trot, followed by 3 or 4 steps at the walk, then a return to the trot that is light and rounded.

The same transitions are made from the canter to the trot, always with half-halts, 3 or 4 strides at the trot and strike-offs at the canter. One must not use the hand to oppose upward transitions from the walk and the trot to the canter.

After having worked for a while at the trot, executing relatively tight figures, one asks the young horse for a more progressive and sustained extension of these same figures, but performed larger, then introduces a relaxation of his resources [joints, muscles, etc.] which a well-directed horse feels as a freeing of his energy. On the other hand, when starting out from an extended trot on a straight line, if one slows him down with a volte and a signal with one's fingers, but without one's legs, the horse quickly understands that he must adjust his equilibrium by raising his back and flexing his hindquarters.

At first, and each time one senses that the back becomes hollow during a lengthening, go to the rising trot to spare the horse from bumps from the seat. General Decarpentry recommends doing these variations of gaits while on a hack with the aim of exploring a veritable gamut of trots. They must, however, be frequently interspersed with work in the *manège*. I believe it is useful to add a personal observation. For a long time I have watched our dressage riders working their young horses for hours, at a fast trot, on their shoulders and, by the riders supporting their horses' weight on their hands, this confirms a state of imbalance upon which most Selle Français horses, whose confirmation is unfavorable to dressage, are already teetering.

I believe that wisdom dictates that one should place equal importance on both sides of the scale, that is, never stretch out more than you are able to gather together again and, always defer the limits of extension, on the one hand, and the *rassembler*, on the other.

At the canter, the young horse will lengthen himself instinctively going around the *manège*; but before he loses his balance through over-excitement, it would be better to take him onto a circle, supporting him through outside lateral aids, the inside hand low and immobile. When he has become steady and regular again and his flexion is correct, it is a good idea to end this lesson at the canter, allowing him to stretch, reins considerably lengthened; continue on the circle, let his neck lengthen, and let this stretching extend through his back, but do not let him lose his lateral bending on the circle.

The rider must remain seated, torso straight, keeping the horse on the circle by means of the lateral effects of very long reins. This exercise will miraculously calm even the most excitable horses, who will desist from bolting as soon as the hand no longer constrains, but, rather, leads them onto the circle. It is likewise necessary to play skillfully between the outside rein, which prevents the horse from "falling" into the circle, and the inside rein, which maintains the correct bend. This action is known as *la descente d'encolure* at the canter.

Extension of the Stem of the Vertebral Column and the Descente D'encolure

Here, we are in search of a double goal. The first is to counteract the tendency of the young horse, now mounted and with a bit in his mouth, to react negatively when his still relatively weak back gives way under the weight of the rider. To this negative reaction – a basic hollowing of the back – may be added the ewe-shaped inversion of his neck, provoked by any concern or discomfort created by the hand and bit. The handling of a somewhat sensitive young horse in this posture requires almost impossible feats. He will do his best to break away from the hold of the rider and leave, star-gazing [above the bit], in any direction.

Besides avoiding this scenario, the other (permanent) goal, is to assist the horse who has gymnastic potential to become either a dressage athlete or a jumper.

However, other horses who will benefit from this work include those who are too long, who have soft back muscles, low shoulders or weak hocks. These horses can attain a better way of moving under a rider if given the necessary muscular strengthening by being worked in such a way as to obtain an extension of the neck that is low and forward.

Extension and lowering of neck occurs progressively. Here, the first phase. Poète, 4 years.

Right inflexion of neck and shoulder as with the counter-shoulder-in, encourages relaxation and extension. Poète, 4 years.

In the 18th century, horses used for war or the *manège* were of Iberian and Oriental breed, their *rassembler* was natural, their back short, the neck arched, which made the *mise en main* easy. In general, nothing justified a remaking of their natural equilibrium. This explains, in part, why one does not find in any analytical work of that time a description dealing with the vertebral column and its muscles. It is only towards the end of the 19th century that one becomes aware of the importance of the functions assigned to the stem of the vertebral column, thanks to the Baucherist School, which emphasized the neck flexions. The types of horses used at that time were more long-limbed, with more horizontal necks.

Today, great trainers and international champions agree on the need to extend the spine and lower the neck. Alas, their mode of operation is often the most pernicious, through the use of those ill-starred draw-reins, also known as German reins, the secondary effects of which are catastrophic and irreversible. If horses are worked in these, their polls will, indeed, yield and lower themselves, but their necks will "break" and overbend through the increased use of these draw-reins. The head will never be raised but will also overbend, weighing heavily on the rider's hand.

This reaction explains why so many riders, when competing, hold their hands up in the air, pulling upwards on the reins. Contact is merely a constant weight; head and neck are literally carried by the riders' arms in order to avoid them caving in. Under such a permanent constraint and a phony equilibrium, lightness is merely a dream and the perversity of draw-reins is obvious.

In the excellent work of the veterinarian Dr. Pierre Pradier, *Mécanique Equestre et Equitation*, published by Maloine, I discovered the best definition outlining the reason for achieving the ideal extension and the sensitivity to perceive it. "A horse who seeks a contact which progressively eludes him, without ever overbending or throwing himself against the hand, and stretches his head downwards and forwards, widens the head-neck angle without modifying the cadence." It was with Dr. Pradier, himself, that we worked successfully with respect to this important preparatory phase.

Preparing for and starting to work at the extension of the neck begins at the walk, but regardless of the gait, it must always be controlled. If the purpose is to stretch and raise again the neck, then the seat must be light at the trot, and at the canter it must barely brush the saddle.

The lateral bend attained on the circle when working on a single track will favor the flexion and the longitudinal extension. The transition to the shoulder-in on the circle, the rider's inside leg seeking the engagement of the horse's inside hind leg and contact with the outside rein, will bring about an elastic extension of the neck and back, insofar as the horse, at that very moment, has contact with the outside rein, which will "progressively slip away" (P. Pradier).

This work will occur at the three gaits, making use of the shoulder-in as well as the counter shoulder-in along the walls of the *manège*, which will bring about the desired yielding, but without the horse advancing of the axis of the track.

Dr. Pradier stresses the fact that flexion will reduce tension of the vertebral column. Therefore, one must frequently straighten the horse with the outside rein and try to maintain the extension of the vertebral column and the lowering of the neck on a straight line. One must at first accept some imbalances, while at the same time helping the horse to overcome them through changes of direction, transitions between gaits and also transitions within the gaits themselves, without any modification of the stretched position.

As the horse refines his understanding of the aids signaling extension, he will become more sensitive and learn to follow contact with the hand that eludes (that is, gives), as easily as the one that takes up again. It is this perfect accord of the aids that will lead to the *rassembler*, that is, to the immediate mastery of going from one equilibrium (that of collection) to the other (that of extension).

3. The Shoulder-in

The shoulder-in is an exercise on two tracks wherein the horse moves laterally after having been correctly flexed and without any part of his body being more bent than any other. The convex part of the curvature leads the lateral movement. The forehand precedes the hindquarters, so that the angle formed by the horse's shoulders and the track is between 30 and 40 degrees, however, if the angle were greater, the horse would be unable to cross his legs without hitting them or tripping.

Shoulder-in can be executed at the three gaits, but it is at the canter that it is most delicate, for it then places the horse in the balance required to introduce lead changes. If, for example, one is executing shoulder-in at the canter on the C–E or A–B diagonal, with the outside shoulder disengaged by the bend on the inside, and the horse is pushed towards the outside, the conditions are in place for encouraging a change of lead in the young horse.

The usefulness and essential aim of shoulder-in lies in the flexion of the haunches and shoulders, with the inside fore and hind legs moving over [crossing] their outside counterparts. As a result, the inside hind leg is engaged towards the center of gravity, causing the haunches to flex and

A slight angle at the shoulder-in, left, at the trot with a young horse.

the shoulders to become free, naturally raising the forehand and having a suppling effect on the whole horse.

For the moment we shall limit ourselves to working at the shoulder-in in the simplest manner, that is, the one which will permit us to counter at all times the false flexions which the horse will try to adopt in order to evade responding to the aids, which will hold him straight on straight lines and correctly bent on curves: this being the shoulder-in on diagonals going from the center of the short side to the long side.

Lateral Displacements on Diagonals

At a walk on the left rein, I follow the outside track at the first corner of the short side: I move along the short side to some 4 or 5 meters from the second corner. I then turn my horse to the left, aiming to move to an inside track situated 4 meters from the wall of the next long side and parallel to it. I maintained a very slight flexion of the horse to the left when he left the short side. I take advantage of the natural attraction that a wall has on horses (try to keep your horse 2 meters from the wall without him clinging to it) and allow him to return to this wall, moving laterally, parallel to it, maintaining a slight general bend.

From the precise spot where I left the short side to the one where I rejoined the long one, I covered a diagonal, keeping the horse parallel to the long side, except that I held his shoulders slightly in front of his haunches.

Why do we execute this exercise, one that is almost similar to the shoulder-in but which does not appear in reference books? Because it is easier for a young horse to perform and understand this exercise, first, because of the attraction to the wall, which makes it possible for us not to have to push the horse laterally; second, because one can vary the angle formed by the diagonal with the wall one rejoins, allowing the young horse to advance as much as possible as he moves laterally – if one rejoins the wall at the end of the *manège*. On the other hand, the movement can be ridden so that he is barely advancing, if one rejoins it only a few meters after the corner.

My friend and co-disciple, Dr. Guilherm Borba, Director of the Portuguese National School of Equestrian Art, believes that we are dealing here with a lateral mobilization rather than with a shoulder-in which, to him, is executed along the wall with a flexion and a *rassembler* that are more pronounced, the horse forming a wider angle with the wall. This lateral mobilization, shoulder-fore, is, indeed, an early phase of the shoulder-in, which one asks of the horse initially, because one wants to constrain the horse as little as possible, yet still be able to obtain a light general flexion. I see little difference between the two movements; furthermore, I do not wish to add to the already existing controversies which have troubled readers of equestrian journals for decades.

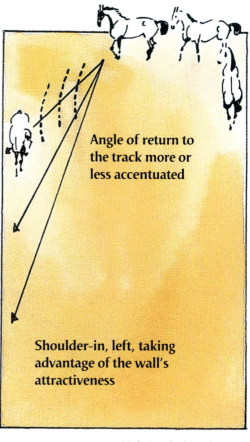

Angle of return to the track more or less accentuated

Shoulder-in, left, taking advantage of the wall's attractiveness

Utilizing the horse's attraction to the wall with lateral displacements.

The Usefulness of the Shoulder-in

Of course it supples the horse. It also teaches the horse to yield or to hold his haunches at signals given by the legs and, likewise, yield or hold his shoulders to signals given by the hand. And yet there is much more that is important: it serves both to straighten the horse who goes crooked when on a straight line in order to evade the aids, and to bend him correctly to keep him on a circle.

Whoever you may be, sports rider, dressage rider, or one who goes merrily on a hack, try to remember the circumstances of those incidents which put you in opposition to your horse during a ride; observe, film, the defenses of the horse who wants to evade the direction indicated by his rider. Such a horse will always try to bend in the direction opposite to that asked of him and, the moment he has succeeded, rider failure is assured. Neither strength nor violence will allow the rider to re-establish the movement forward in the desired direction. At best, whether at the walk or trot, if he refuses to bend correctly on the segment of the circle he is covering, he will bend excessively to the inside, while pushing his haunches to the outside, or, conversely, invert the bend to the outside, while pushing his haunches to the inside. At the canter he will invert the bend when turning a corner, which will enable him to throw himself back on his inside shoulder and, ignoring the aids for the canter, he will fall back into the trot or the walk. When facing an obstacle, the lateral swerving with bend will be irrepressible. At worst, refusing to bend in the direction asked by the rider, the horse will throw his inside hind leg inside the circle and brace himself on it, only to whirl around or to rear. It is at this point that I share the reflection made by Guilherm Borba, unrivalled horseman, who does not hesitate to say: "I am afraid of riding a horse who has not been worked at the shoulder-in."

The highlighting of the shoulder-in during the 18th century marked an advancement in the utilization of the war horse which was as important as the use of the stirrup. Its obvious omission by the Baucherist School caused a missing piece of the schooling jigsaw which their multiple flexions never replaced and explains why Baucherism fell out of favor.

The Theory behind the Shoulder-in

Attempts have been made to redefine this exercise but they have only succeeded in making it more difficult to understand, complicating the procedure and misleading its execution.

If this movement is not one of the easiest to execute, it is one that is relatively simple to understand. I believe that a return to the basic source is imperative. Let us look at the definition given by La Guérinière, who describes it with his customary simplicity: "The line of the haunches must remain close to the wall and that of the shoulders away from the wall at a distance of about a foot and a half to two feet", that is, the outside shoulder of the horse must be held 55 to 60 centimeters away from the wall, depending upon the need for suppling. The more the angle is accentuated, the more must the gait be slowed, so as not to force the horse's movement. "One must turn his head and shoulders slightly towards the inside of the *manège*...He must be asked to walk forward along the wall, helped with the inside rein and leg...but when one turns onto a new track this must be done with the outside rein, bringing the hand to the inside"; by slowing down the shoulders, this half-halt on the outside rein enables the haunches to turn the corners, pivoting around the inside shoulder.

This outside rein is important, even when going on straight lines, actually directing the shoulders and regulating their moving away from the wall. It acts, through contact, on the base of the neck (the contact rein) or, alternatively, by moving away from the neck (the opening rein), to adjust the degree of shoulder-in as required. Gustav Steinbrecht insists upon the predominance of the outside aids.

"With a well-proportioned action of the outside rein and leg to the inside leg, a correct effect of opposition must be given if one wants the gait to be regulated and not to degenerate into falling to the side. The rider is then forced to work his outside rein and leg more vigorously and even use his weight with greater strength towards the outside."

The means are clearly outlined and emphasize that progression, that is, the widening from one to two tracks, must be measured and obtained centimeter by centimeter, until the redistribution of the weight on all four legs occurs: "Position the horse just as he is placing his inside legs in front of or beyond his outside legs."

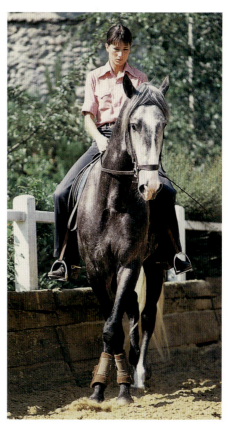

Left shoulder-in at the walk with a young horse. Orphée at 4 years.

General Decarpentry, whose *Academic Equitation* could be used as a reference work to undo today's pathetic methods, deals with the shoulder-in in less than fifty lines, placing himself under the auspices of La Guérinière, Du Paty de Clam, Steinbrecht, and Gerhardt, who are unanimous with respect to the technique of the procedure. He describes clearly how this movement is in accord with the masters of the 18th and 19th centuries. He is even briefer when discussing the means: "The inside heel must move forward and the outside rein leads the forehand."

Colonel Podhajsky states that the Spanish Riding School adheres to the manner of execution and the ground rules of La Guérinière. He specifies that the forehand is positioned to the inside by a half-step, that the inside foreleg moves in front of the outside one, and that the inside hind leg engages itself farther under the mass towards the center of gravity.

It is obvious that a certain amount of unawareness or a lack of culture is evident when one has to settle once again questions that three centuries of equestrian art have answered with ever-increasing refinement. The same could be said when one claims to add something new which is nothing more than the personal formulation of a technique that is already well-expressed.

Execution of the Shoulder-in

It is begun with a volte in a corner of the *manège*. When the horse returns to the track in the corner, the rider can profit from the natural incurvation the horse acquired from the volte he is just leaving, keeping his hindquar-

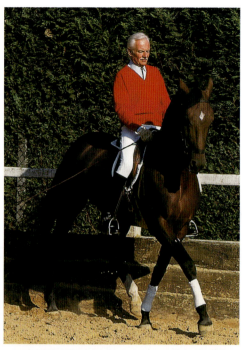

ters at the tangent point, and the forehand parallel to the tangent, that is, to the track of the hindquarters.

The gap between the two tracks of the shoulders and the hindquarters, that is, the moving away of the shoulders towards the inside, must be increased gradually.

The rider retains the incurvation of the horse and the shoulder-in position by means of a light twisting of his hips that are positioned parallel to the shoulders of the horse. He moves his pelvis a little in the direction of the overall movement without ever actually displacing the seat from the axis of the horse. The inside rein, adjusted, assures the bend; the supporting outside rein limits it and leads the shoulders, or slows them down as appropriate. The inside leg, at the girth, serves as an axis around which the horse bends; the outside leg, placed slightly behind the girth, contributes to the incurvation and impulse. The rider's hips tend to mirror the lateral movement and the weight of the inside buttock is set in the same direction, but these subtle effects must not disintegrate into collapsing, leaning, or any overt displacement of the seat.

The aids act by means of delicate touches, followed by *descentes de main et de jambes*. All extraneous movements must be avoided. At first, one must content oneself with a few steps. When the horse contracts, he must not be forced into the shoulder-in, but should simply be ridden straight forward and then be put on a volte. Then, when he finds himself at the tangent point of the volte to the track, try the shoulder-in once again.

Control of the quality of this exercise depends as much on the harmonious bend and the amplitude of the crossing of the legs as on the overall yielding and the rhythm of the gait.

LEFT ABOVE Right shoulder-in at the trot with a young horse. Ultra, 4 years.

LEFT BELOW Right shoulder-in at the trot with a young horse. Everton, 4 years.

When one terminates the shoulder-in, one allows the horse to straighten out without forcing him to do so, for this would be a mistake actually countermanding what one has just asked of him. An additional amount of impulsion together with equalizing the reins and straightening the neck will suffice.

Today's conception of the shoulder-in is linked to the mediocrity of contemporary equitation. The shoulder-in is practiced only seldom and is considered a minor exercise, which one completes rapidly. More often it is obtained by a combination of so-called "intermediary" reins: traction on the inside rein towards the outside haunch, the spur pricking the inside flank, provoking a rigidity and a lateral swerving of the horse. The overall inflexion is replaced by a "break" in the neck: the correct flexing of the joints of the limbs is impaired and the crossing of the limbs degenerates into a tendency for the inside lateral limbs to hit the outside laterals.

The Counter-shoulder-in

La Guérinière forbids lateral movements head to wall, be it in connection with the bend brought about by the half-pass or the shoulder-in. They can be disastrous when executed by an ignorant and brutal rider if the space between the horse and the wall is insufficient. In this case the clumsiness of the rider will push the horse's head into the wall. Modern equitation has abandoned the counter-shoulder-in. Executed by poorly given aids, the stubborn horse would overbend, head towards the wall.

The shoulder-in puts the horse on his haunches, whereas the counter-shoulder-in tends to put him on his shoulders. However, both of these movements fully exercise the horse's adductor and abductor muscles.

The counter-shoulder-in begins, for example, after a demi-volte at the end of the track, which brings one tangentially back to the track, the horse flexed, with his convex side in the direction of the movement, head to wall.

Purely in terms of locomotion and on straight lines there is no difference between the counter-shoulder-in and the shoulder-in. It is at the turning of corners and on circles wherein the difference lies, shoulders pivoting around the haunches with the counter-shoulder-in whereas, with the shoulder-in, the haunches turn around the shoulders.

When we are dealing with a young horse who, when executing the shoulder-in, tends to force the hand towards the inside of the *manège*, a counter-shoulder-in, begun at the start of a demi-volte, is effective in that the wall serves as a screen which will incite the horse to slide sideways along it, if he is positioned somewhat obliquely.

This is not a matter of using the wall as a brutal way of forcing the horse to walk laterally – besides, his head would have to be held at more than 50 centimeters from the wall and the angle formed with his body and the wall, would have to be less than 35 degrees.

The counter-shoulder-in is done at the walk and the trot. If, at the canter, one wants to relax the neck and shoulders, one inverts the bend towards the outside – for example, when one canters to the left, the

Counter-shoulder-in.

neck bends to the right. However, in this case we are not dealing with a counter-shoulder-in. Steinbrecht, when he says that this exercise "is the air I prefer", classifies it in what he calls "the counter-lessons". These he considers an extension of the corresponding simple airs, with an inversion of the direction of the movement, and says that "the difference with the simple lesson lies only in the turning".

Right shoulder-in leaving the volte.

What Must be Heeded at the Shoulder-in

Obviously one cannot review here the thousands of possible mistakes and their consequences with respect to this exercise. I will therefore limit myself to underscoring the most common ones, some emphasizing a systematic desire to apply false principles, others certain reflexes which, even if they are natural and spontaneous, are no less contrary to correct action.

The first point concerns the action of the inside rein. It acts towards the inside rather than as a downward movement, in order to place and regulate the bend, and to position the shoulder-in in accord with the outside rein. Once this has been attained the hand, which is perfectly set, becomes very quiet. Should the bend be lost, *the fingers of this hand – not the arms – take up and give several times to re-establish it.*

But what is it that one encounters so often? A traction on the inside rein insufficiently adjusted or, if you prefer, pre-set. It may even pass over the withers: a vicious rein of opposition acting upwards and towards the outside. If, as a result, the horse's head is pulled to the outside, the horse will move in that direction. Should this happen, the outside hand comes to the aid of the inside hand to prevent him from falling into the inside, which would bring about a total loss of impulsion; then a touch with the inside spur to re-establish it, with a twisting of the nose towards the inside, etc.

Second, the action of the outside rein: assuming that it has been pre-set, it accompanies the inside rein to position the shoulder-in. With elbows beside the body, both forearms should be brought towards the inside.

But what happens often? This outside rein, which is a rein of paramount importance, serving to carry the shoulders in and keep them there, often tends to be irresolute in its effect, because it is not pre-set. As a result, especially when going to the left (in which direction necks generally flex too readily), the horse's neck "breaks" and the rider merely obtains a ridiculous looking head-in, for the shoulders have remained on the track; the movement has failed.

Third, the inside leg: on the girth, the inside leg forms an axis around which the horse bends. It also has a directional role and, to some extent, a partial impulsive force. It is frequently assumed that this inside leg is more efficient in keeping the haunches on the track, and consequently it is placed too far back. As a result, the haunches are pushed back towards the wall and the bend inverts.

Fourth, the outside leg: this must be placed slightly back and must direct the haunches with the same gentleness as the arm of a dancer leading his partner. It perfects the bending of the horse. But what does one usually see? Either an outside leg rigidly compressed against the horse's flank, which halts the lateral movement, or a "floating" leg which "lets go" the haunches, resulting in their hitting the kicking boards. The impact sounds one then hears are the result of errors of the rider, not the horse.

Fifth, the positioning of the rider's pelvis and torso towards the inside place the shoulders parallel to those of the horse. This position is so effective that it alone suffices to obtain the shoulder-in with sensitive horses. Yet one often sees riders pivoting the torso in the opposite direction. The problem with the shoulder-in is that, through errors, it brings about contractions of the rider. The torso is bent forward, thighs and knees climb up, when one must, rather, unload the horse's shoulders and channel him to the utmost.

Here, then, is a description of the most common errors and, believe me, I have far from exhausted them.

I could not end in good conscience if I were not to point out the abuses of the shoulder-in as lateral movements in general. I am speaking of suppling exercises which are indispensable, but, nonetheless, constraining; which should be considered a means and not an end. Inexperienced riders are convinced that the more they do them, the more supple and light will their horses be; others believe that the shoulder-in, especially at the trot, will bring them additional comfort when, in reality, they are just breaking down the trot.

One must seldom work on two tracks for longer than a third of one's time; above all, one must return frequently to working on a straight line in order to verify one's eventual improvement. One must be wary of abuses which could destroy the spontaneity of the horse in his forward movement.

The Different Figures Executed at the Shoulder-in

The figures one executes at the shoulder-in and at the counter-shoulder-in proceed from the straight line along the wall to diagonals, from work on the center line to circles and voltes. Turning the corners at the shoulder-in is first executed at the walk, since one must keep the shoulders almost stationary, while the haunches mark a quarter rotation. At the counter-shoulder-in, one retains the haunches while the shoulders cover a quarter of a circle.

Executing the shoulder-in and counter-shoulder-in on circles at the walk requires a certain level of skill on the part of both rider and horse. Indeed, as in the case of turning corners, but even more so, one must regulate the movement of both the forelegs and the hind legs to different cadences and amplitudes of strides, since both will describe circles of different diameters.

One executes these figures at the trot. Then, as one progresses, and when the horse has perfectly absorbed the mechanics of these lateral movements, one executes them at the canter. We will return to this.

4. Manège Figures

At the stage we are at, we shall work initially only at *manège* figures on one track, although we already have the shoulder-in behind us. Nothing stops us from attempting it a little earlier; in fact, that will even reinforce your conviction of the usefulness of the shoulder-in!

Try to execute, at the trot, a serpentine composed of four loops, or a spiral, before having suppled your horse in a systematic way at the shoulder-in. If you obtain an equal and harmonious flexion without the horse veering into the loops on both right and left.

Tell yourself that you own a future Olympic champion. One is allowed to dream...

All these figures that follow will allow you to guide your pupil without the support of walls in directions that he could not foresee.

You will first try to evaluate the kind of therapy he will need. You will then test the benefits of suppling on two tracks by using the same *manège* figures with an increased ease and accuracy.

I have worked extensively more than eighty horses of ten different breeds between the ages of 6 months and 10 years. This was necessary in order to understand the wide differences in aptitude from one horse to the other, which now seems to be infinite, bringing about new and varied difficulties, whose combinations still pose uncharted problems.

When dealing with a newly acquired horse, I tackle these figures at the three gaits, first on one track then on two tracks, which allows me to size up the difficulties that have to be solved, and the potential talent. It is in this manner that I try to diagnose the situation and introduce the correct exercises.

It is by returning to these procedures that I size up the accuracy of the treatment and the progress attained.

Before approaching these exercises, one must be totally familiar with their basic "ground-plan". When you get involved with them you must set precise references and run through them resolutely. Finally, never forget that constant quest for lightness by means of frequent yielding of hand and legs: take up and yield immediately...

For those strong and passionate souls, this will never be boring. It is a game that must be won by means of the body and the mind.

Before starting this work, it is assumed that voltes, circles and demi-voltes are more or less executed correctly.

Manège figures. *continued on page 98*

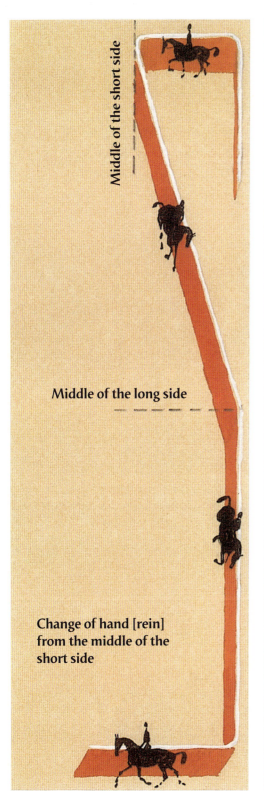

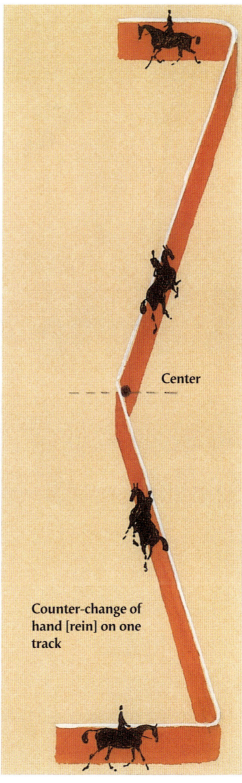

Middle of the short side

Middle of the long side

Center

Change of hand [rein] from the middle of the short side

Counter-change of hand [rein] on one track

Manège
figures.

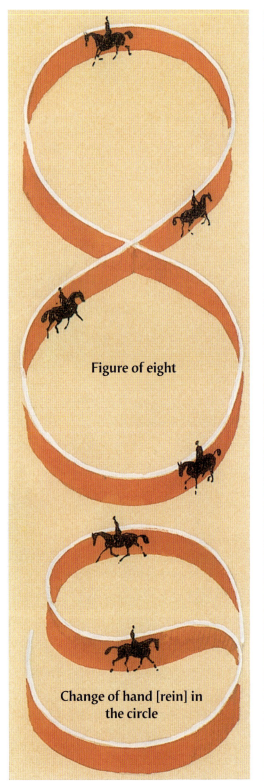

Figure of eight

**Change of hand [rein] in
the circle**

Serpentine

Spiral

The Figure Eight

The figure eight is the first exercise to be undertaken. We have seen that circles, in order to be geometrically correct, must finish at the very spot where they began. The figure eight contains a change of rein where the first circle finishes, and then starts another of the same dimension, which will also end where it began. Identical inflexions on each rein, regular cadences, and no veering indicate success.

Going in all Directions – a Mêlée

Originally this term meant that one was walking without any order. It evolved from a succession of turns to the right and to the left, in an orderly and a disorderly manner, wherein one avoids going straight on the tracks. As usual, the inside rein limits itself to indicate turning, the execution of each turn deriving essentially from the resilience of the outside rein serving as support.

Changes of Hand [Changes of Rein]

Change of Hand Starting from the Center

From the middle of the short side, one returns to the middle of the long side. This requires a change of inflexion as one leaves the track, another one when one returns it.

The Counter-change of Hand on One Track

After leaving the second corner, one reaches the center of the *manège* where one departs again for the third corner.

Change of Hand on the Circle

This is accomplished inside the circle by an "S". At a given point, one describes a small semi-circle which brings one back to the center of the circle where one changes hand by reversing the bend of the horse and making another small semi-circle, which takes one back to the circumference of the large circle.

The Serpentine

This is composed of three to six loops, starting with a loop from the middle of the short side and continuing in the form of back to back figures that extend just beyond semi-circles of equal radius, thus forming pear shapes, and terminating in the middle of the opposite short side. At first one chooses a fairly wide radius of about 7 meters; this is reduced as suppling progresses. When the horse is familiar with the counter-canter, covering the serpentine at the canter is a remarkable exercise.

The Spiral

One starts out on a wide circle of 20 meters diameter, decreasing it to the size of a volte of 6 meters. The inside rein indicates the flexion. The outside rein limits it and regulates the reduction of the circle to the volte through successive spirals. The inside leg holds the correct bend of the horse, the outside leg and outside rein prevent the haunches from falling out. One does two turns on the final volte, then enlarges, in order to return to the circle by means of the spiral.

The more the size of the circle decreases, the more one flexes the horse by engaging the inside hind leg; the more it increases, the more one reduces the flexion of the ensemble.

At the walk, I reduce the spiral to a minimum in order to arrive at the pirouette around the inside foreleg, the horse remaining flexed towards the inside; I then increase the spiral, going back to the circle, where I rejoin the track at a shoulder-in, retaining the same bend.

5. Halts, Strike-offs at the Walk, Trot, Canter

The Halt

The halt is the immobile posture of the horse on all four legs. At the beginning of his breaking in and during the months that follow, one must attain this stationary posture from all three gaits, after asking for a few satisfactory strides, even if the halt is not completely straight and the placing of the legs not quite regular.

During the breaking in period, first on the lunge, then mounted, the young horse became used to slowing down and halting at voice commands. This should be maintained, for it forewarns the horse and has a calming effect on him. However, the voice alone is not always sufficient and the intervention of the hand or, *rather the fingers*, will be necessary.

It is equally necessary to be familiar with and understand that the signal that the hand gives to the bit (already called a breaking device by the Romans) is not necessarily comprehended and interpreted as such by the young horse; this will occur only after a period of education and patience.

Taking man's simplistic logic into consideration, the halt is the hand's action of holding back to immobilize. Actually, this action produces the opposite effect on an animal not used to it. He considers this obstacle that passes through his mouth as an undesirable shackle which he wants to sever through force.

During the initial phase, the halt must be requested by means of a succession of closing and opening of the fingers, underscored by the voice, and even by rewarding with a treat given by an assistant on foot.

To keep one's fingers tight incites the horse to force open the confinement he feels. Always *"take up and yield"* and, above all, never forget to slacken the legs at the same time.

To become annoyed because the young horse does not understand, to use force to halt him right away, only brings about, in the case of an energetic animal, defenses which will begin with a sudden stepping back to rear or buck. Of course, one always manages to immobilize a horse, but to achieve it in this manner, as with all other exercises, will only get the kind of results in keeping with the means employed.

The first halt is simply immobility, obtained without demanding any further requirement other than its execution at any point of the track, that is, not giving in to something easier, which would be to allow the horse to halt in the middle of the *manège*, which he will always try to do. This first halt is known as the *free halt*. At the end of two or three months, however, *the halt must be regular*, that is, the horse must stand straight from shoulders to haunches in relation to the track, and the forelegs and hind legs must be placed together, straight and united.

This posture can be acquired by a good rider to a level appropriate to the youngster's progress during the first year of work. At a more advanced stage of schooling, *the halt must be rassemblé*. This will be *l'arrêt d'école* [the school halt], to which we will return later.

If you are inclined to make an enriching observation, have fun watching riders halt their horses on the track of a *manège* or a dressage arena. Most of them are immobilized by veering their haunches towards the inside of the *manège*, and push out the hind leg on the same side. This posture is not innocent: as your training experience evolves, you will discover that it indicates a refusal on the part of the horse to accept his rider. It is a defensive attitude which you will find amplified in the case of a horse who wants to evade his rider, or who is going to rear, or simply refuses the *rassembler*.

Thus you will have the key to the presentation of a rational technique of schooling a horse which will strengthen the rider's control of his partner.

We have seen how to teach the young horse the principle of the halt by first demanding immobility over and above the regularity of the position. We can now teach the young horse the correct halt.

A *rassemblé* halt. Fandango. The position is correct with the exception of the rider's feet, which should be parallel to the horse's sides.

Before obtaining the halt, the horse must be further activated by a forward movement of the pelvis. To obtain the halt, the rider's legs must be passive, the fingers must be gently closed with a more pronounced support with the outside rein, in conjunction with the firm engagement of the inside buttock towards the outside. These aids will make your horse place his inside hind leg under him and more or less take on the position of a shoulder-in than a haunches-in. Release your fingers at the very moment your horse halts.

The Strike-off

This is the most important moment with respect to the quality of the gait which will follow it. If the total balance is not correctly established at the moment of the strike-off, it will never re-establish itself during the movement itself. That is why one says that *the last stride of a gait must contain the first stride of the next gait.*

Although a voice command is forbidden when competing, one must not fail using it to forewarn young horses. It suffices to make a light noise with tongue or throat which can be imperceptible to the most sensitive of human ears.

From the Halt to the Walk

To accomplish this you must engage the lumbar vertebrae, a signal prolonged by a leg vibration. At the same time advance the wrists by virtue of the sacrosanct Baucherist principle: *"hand without legs, legs without hand", which must dominate your equestrian actions.* Should the horse not go forward right away, give more animated vibrations with the legs, as well as a rapid touch behind the leg with the dressage whip, while advancing the wrist so as not to offend the horse's mouth – never touch the horse on the croup or thigh, which would make him kick out. An important word as to how to act with the legs which is easier to express by a gesture than with the pen! One hundred percent of the riders who have received their training today will continually hold their hands in the air, calves gripping the horse's flanks when not hooked around the horse's abdomen, knees open, heels raised. These gripping calves, used when starting out or giving impulsion, can only produce "overpressure" of the legs, which the horse cannot distinguish from the usual pressure.

To make clear the way legs must act, I place myself facing the rider and ask him to imagine that my arms are legs. I let them fall along the sides of my body, gently and without tension. I move them away from my body and then slap them back vigorously, whipping my hips as though I were using two inert lashes. At the very moment after they hit, they remain totally quiet, that is, after the "attack", as before it, they still do not grip. This is first done without spurs, for the importance of this action is the complete passivity of the leg before and after its use, whether or not it is backed up by a touch with the whip.

Then, if the horse is endowed with a normal sensitivity, it suffices to arch the lower back slightly and start with a driving seat for a brief moment to bring about an impulsion or an over-impulsion.

It is *impossible* to act with finesse with legs that grip, be it to indicate movement or impulsion.

From the Walk to the Trot

One must forewarn the horse with respect to his mental make-up and his equilibrium. The little noise made with the mouth, together with a caress with the leg given by bending the knees, are sufficient to forewarn and unleash the trot. If one wants a balanced and energetic trot at the very first strides, the last step at the walk must be especially pronounced, even somewhat shortened. If, at the moment of the strike-off, the haunches drag and the neck stretches out and down with little vigor, then the first strides of the trot will be listless. At this point it is not a question of asking for strike-offs that are *rassemblé*, but one must see to it that one obtains a sustained cadence. This can be achieved with a minimum of emphasis at the walk. If, at the first request, the horse does not go immediately and positively from the walk to the trot, then try once more, touching him briskly behind the leg with the whip.

For the moment, a halt from the trot will be done by returning from the trot to the walk by voice command as well as the fingers (but without legs), and the halt from the walk will be as we have already discussed it.

At the medium trot with Ultra, 4 years, seeking contact which is neither heavy nor forced.

From the Trot to the Canter

Striking off at the canter is initially asked for from the trot. One must place oneself on a circle at the trot and ask for a strike-off the moment the horse rejoins the track and the outside shoulder is held by the wall, which will prevent him from falling out of the circle. When we have an energetic trot, the aids are as follows: the inside hand at the withers assures a slight inside bend, the outside hand offsets the effect of the inside hand, which could let the horse enter into the circle. It supports the horse's forehand *more by moving aside horizontally rather than vertically*. But the effect of the one hand must not reverse the effect of the other; it is a question of tact. The same holds true for the legs: the inside leg at the girth prevents the horse from "falling" into the center of the circle, the outside leg, slightly back, acting with precision, moves forwards, starting off the canter, helped by the voice – with which the horse is already familiar from when he cantered on the lunge.

All these aids would be to no avail if the position of the rider's torso and seat were not impeccable, otherwise, any attempt at a strike-off on the part of the young horse would be impossible.

A natural but poor movement by a beginner (but, unfortunately, still prevalent with many more seasoned riders), is the forward projection of the shoulders, the rear section of the seat leaving the saddle, together with a mighty kick on the horse's flanks with both legs.

The result is an overloading of the horse's shoulders which should, on the contrary, be freed. If this happens, then one has a strike-off that dis-unites the horse's outside foreleg, brought about by the action of the rider's inside leg which, at this stage, should remain quietly at the girth.

The rider's torso must be upright – and parallel to the shoulders of the horse, that is, turned towards the inside of the circle; the seat must be engaged to a maximum and the strike-off requested by the rider's outside hip, extended by his outside thigh and knee. The whole, we repeat, should act from the outside to the inside.

An explicit picture that emerges, is that this outside lateral aid (outside hand/ rein/ leg/ hip) must act as an elastic wall, which checks and sends off the horse's body from the outside to the inside, thus compensating for the devastating effect that centrifugal force exerts, and establishing bal-ance on the correct lead without meeting resistance.

I see many riders cantering with no difficulty outdoors, but incapable of executing a strike-off at a canter on a volte of 6 to 8 meters in the *manège*. Outside, at the trot, in a rush, and moving on a straight path, the balance is on the shoulders, thus the horse goes quite literally from the trot to the canter so as not to fall down!

This same rider, his nose close to the horse's neck, buttocks in the air, hands waving, legs gripping, *will never be able to strike off* at a correct canter on a small circle and, even if he does, his position will disturb the centrifugal force for which the horse will have to compensate – as we have observed at the lunge – by striking off on the outside leg, which is erro-neous and disuniting.

If it is felt that I am being too insistent about this problem, those who think that way should try out an experiment, asking all their friends to participate. They should count those who are be able to strike off correctly and make two circuits at the canter on a volte of 6 to 12 meters in each direction; then compare the positions of the winners and the losers.

I, myself, sometimes find it difficult to strike off in the classical way, on the correct lead, one of those unfortunate victims of the realities of equitation.

Here is the remedy: at the moment of striking off, slightly invert the bend of the horse's neck towards the outside by lowering the outside hand, but without allowing the haunches to move too much to the inside. Having done this, you disengage the inside shoulder of the horse and facilitate immediately and correctly the strike-off on this foreleg. As soon as you have begun to canter, first on the circle then on the straight line, re-establish the correct bend, by bringing the inside hand to the withers. Each day, reduce the inversion of the bend of the neck until you have re-established a sense of the normal aids.

Later on, as we progress, we will study striking off at the *rassemblé* canter from the walk and the halt, but we can, as of now, begin to introduce our pupil to the equilibrium required for the counter-canter, which is somewhat worrisome for him.

6. The Counter-canter

The horse is executing the counter-canter when, on a turn or circle, he leads with his outside leg. This canter is sometimes called a "false" canter, but this is incorrect because many free and balanced horses use it to compensate for the destabilizing effect that centrifugal force exerts on them when they turn rapidly.

One can introduce it when the horse has acquired a minimum of cadence at the canter.

Here is a procedure I have worked out as I observed the psychological reactions the horse experiences under certain conditions at the canter.

When a horse strikes off at the counter-canter without the rider having asked him to do so and, wanting to exploit the situation, the rider makes him continue, the horse will stiffen and immediately become disunited. On the other hand, if one tries to interrupt the situation by holding him back a little, he will tend to take a few strides more before returning to the walk.

Exploiting this contradiction, I leave the track at the canter on the true canter lead, on the diagonal, to the opposite side, encouraging the horse with my voice to continue the canter. A few meters before reaching the opposite side, when the horse shows concern at finding himself at the counter-canter, instead of pushing him I calm him by voice until we go into the trot. By progressing at the rate of one stride each day, I quickly reach the first corner of the *manège* at the counter-canter. Sensing by the tone of my voice that the halt will soon intervene, the horse does not contract and even accepts doing two or more strides. Knowing that he will have to halt, he spares himself the effort of changing lead or becoming disunited. In a few weeks he will turn the four corners of the *manège* at the counter-canter. The position of the rider is of prime importance; by stressing it, he must maintain the position he had at the canter on the correct lead.

For example: I am executing a canter on the correct lead to the right, right hand at the withers, left rein supporting, cadence given by my left hip and leg. The horse's neck has a slight bend to the right when I start onto the diagonal. When the horse reaches the opposite track, I take care not to reverse my aids, but, rather, to reinforce them by turning my torso slightly to the right. When I turn the corners of the *manège* at the counter-canter, I maintain the bend, the action of the outside leg (in relation to the bend), the flexion of my torso towards the right and the position of the hands – except that I advance my two wrists in order to free the forehand and not impede it. In a word, I maintain my position but am discreet with my aids so as not to contribute to the trouble that may naturally arise when I turn the first corners at the counter-canter.

It is important to reach the opposite track as soon as possible before reaching the corner so that the horse's body is parallel to the wall. This is already the beginning of the half-pass at the canter, which is not very difficult even for a young horse.

Nothing is more absurd than arriving at the counter-canter perpendicular to the opposite wall, which assumes that the young horse is capable of executing a quarter of a reversed pirouette at the canter to take up again the track parallel to the wall at the counter-canter!

Equally absurd is the rider who arrives at the counter-canter on the bisection of the angle which the corner of the *manège* forms; negotiating this would really be an impossible feat!

Certain authors berate those who do not scrupulously observe their theories. I try not to do this, but believe me that to transgress against the wisdom of the points made here will haunt you, maybe even when you attempt lead changes.

The counter-canter is useful for exercising the hind legs, to work at attaining a straight canter in the case of horses who throw their haunches inside and to obtain a slowed-down canter which, thanks to the wall, limits the escape of their haunches. It is absolutely essential to lead changes, for how could a horse who has just managed for the first time to go from a true canter to a counter-canter by changing his lead in the air maintain that gait, if he were not already balanced in the counter-canter as well as in the canter on the correct lead? Furthermore, his uneasy canter would make it impossible for him to return to a canter on the correct lead by means of a second lead change.

Contractions and Balance at the Counter-canter

The uneasiness that a young horse experiences to a greater or lesser degree at the counter-canter brings with it a certain number of contractions and anxieties which are evidently more pronounced when reaching corners.

When the young horse has just been initiated into the counter-canter, he feels at times the need to balance himself, especially at the corners, and thus leans on his shoulders. It would be a serious error at this stage of work and at this moment to try to re-balance him on his haunches by blocking with one's hands or attempting to send the weight back onto his hindquarters by means of half-halts.

The only way of solving this problem at first is to give his neck a maximum of freedom just as one is entering the corner, while retaining the outside bend. This is achieved by advancing the wrists, after having given impulsion again with the hip and leg opposite to the leg on which the horse is cantering.

Another silly and frequent occurrence at the start of the counter-canter is an unsolicited return to a trot or a disunited canter, all provoked by the awkwardness of the horse…or the rider. Here are two solutions. Either begin once more by taking up again the true canter, then take the diagonal to go on to the counter-canter, taking care of the horse's balance and one's aids or, with more advanced horses, striking off straight from the walk to the counter-canter.

Here, too, two strategies can be used: the first is to execute a half-pass at the walk that is parallel to the wall, then, still in the position of the half-pass, strike off at the canter on the correct lead before reaching the end of the diagonal, which would put you back into the counter-canter as you reach the track. The second strategy, which is best used with horses who strike off easily from a walk to the true canter, is to take up a slightly accentuated position of croup to wall, or renvers. The outside rein – with respect to the bend – is supported, outside leg is slightly placed back, inside hand is at the base of the neck, fixing the bend, inside leg is at the girth and, eventually, the whip behind the outside leg. If, at the strike-off, the rider remains seated without pushing his torso forward, and if the co-ordination of his aids is correct, this manner of striking off at the counter-canter is superior. One must, of course, straighten out the horse at the very first strides of the counter-canter on the track.

Since we have not yet studied the half-pass, one assumes that the croup to wall is, as yet, unfamiliar; but we shall get there. If your counter-canter is attained with difficulty, consolidate your canter on the correct lead while waiting to begin the half-pass.

7. Rotation of the Haunches

In the course of this first stage of the horse's schooling, one can find one-self confronted with a more or less pronounced resistance with respect to the horse's haunches when they are asked to yield. It is precisely when one finds oneself in a particular "situation", that is, in a lateral movement on the diagonal of the *manège*, or executing a shoulder-in on the track, that the horse's opposition to an insisting aid will be felt.

To cope with this resistance by using force with the leg or the spur will only bring about the loss of the horse's incurvation and a deviation of the whole horse. One must therefore try to solve this particular problem, which is really simple. The first thing to do, at the beginning of one's work, and after having lunged the horse, is to take up once again the shoulder-in, in hand, as has already been discussed.

Should work in hand prove insufficient, *one must then have recourse to a rotation of the haunches mounted*, that is, activating the haunches by making them turn around the forehand. This is the yielding of a single leg at a reversed pirouette, executed with the most natural bend, namely, that of the shoulder-in, wherein the horse does not see his haunches coming towards him, as is the case with a true reversed pirouette, rather, he sees them leaving…

With respect to the bend of the horse, the outside foreleg turns around the inside foreleg, the latter serving as an axis.

One halts the horse in the middle of the *manège*, his limbs set, united on the same line; one flexes the neck on the side where the horse resists; resistance of the left haunch, flexion on the left side. The inside hand, placed low and immobile, determines and maintains the bend, the outside hand supports in order to prevent the shoulders from swerving to the right or to the left.

The inside leg vibrates to solicit the displacement of the haunches, eventually supported by the whip, lightly touching the horse behind the rider's leg. The outside leg does not oppose the displacement of the haunches.

Beware of using your hands too much, thereby making the horse step back or allowing the pivoting shoulder to escape. The latter must be set by the outside hand, supported and positioned almost in the axis of the shoulder. One must also be sure to regulate the yielding of the haunches step by step, and not try to drive them round as one movement. One must then go vigorously forward and straight, yielding with the fingers.

Pirouettes executed with hands that check are prime occasions for making the horse overbend. These pirouettes can be started with a spiral at the walk, becoming ever tighter, until the pirouette is attained.

8. The Half-pass

Definition

Half-passes are two-track exercises wherein the horse moves more or less laterally and crosses his outside legs in front of his inside legs, the forehand tending to precede the hindquarters, with the head slightly turned in the direction of the movement; the nose is vertical and straight.

Formerly, equestrians executed the half-pass with a generally pronounced incurvation of the horse; present-day equitation practices it with the horse's body almost straight. The half-pass is performed at all three gaits and, at the passage, on all the tracks of the *manège*: short sides, long sides, diagonally, head and croup to wall (which many nations term travers and renvers) on circles, voltes, and demi-voltes. For the moment, we shall only discuss the half-pass at the walk.

The half-pass is the most advanced movement on the so-called two tracks which, together with the *rassemblé trot*, is the foundation of high school equitation.

The half-pass at the trot on the diagonal. Sirius, 4 years.

The half-pass at the trot on the diagonal. Tintoretto, Hanoverian, 5 years.

The Half-pass of Baucher

The Baucherist School approaches the half-pass starting with flexions and rotations pertaining to all parts of the horse's body: flexions of the neck, flexions of the ensemble of the horse, rotations of haunches and shoulders. These are first undertaken in hand, then mounted. It ignores the shoulder-in.

Even though these exercises bring to a very rigid horse some degree of suppleness, they have always seemed to me insufficient as a basis for sudden progression to a mounted half-pass in the forward movement. The key to the half-pass is, indeed, the shoulder-in, a posture that horses take spontaneously in a state of freedom so that they can displace themselves laterally from a danger, yet are still able to look at it. It is the natural reflex of a good war horse.

One will never know to what extent Baucher was completely candid, for he never once mentioned the words "shoulder-in" in his *Méthode d'équitation* although it was already in use before him; quite obviously he

The half-pass.

wanted to be considered a pure innovator. One will never know how many generations of *écuyers* were led astray on these uncertain tracks. Yet, the shoulder-in is part of Baucher!

To see through this ambiguity one must read carefully certain lines of his *Méthode* (1874, 14th edition, p. 110) which are devoted to work on two tracks.

"A horse must not execute more than one step on two tracks, then two, then three. First the rider must make use of the snaffle rein and the leg on the same side, that is, in the opposite direction in which the horse is moving. *Although the position which ensues* (!!) is contrary to the beautiful position a horse must maintain, one continues this effect with the hand until the horse no longer resists the leg. Soon thereafter, the rein on the determining side will serve to position the horse."

Baucher achieves the important feat of recommending the shoulder-in, using almost the same words and the same aids that La Guérinière used in his chapter on the shoulder-in in *School of Horsemanship*, where he wrote: "He must be made to walk forward along the wall aided by the inside rein and leg."

While never once uttering the name of the exercise and pretending to say that it is a matter of a passing mishap in the progression of the *Méthode*, Baucher, nonetheless, describes it perfectly to us.

The man Baucher designates as his most loyal disciple, General Faverot de Kerbrech (undoubtedly out of respect for the ambiguity of his master), places himself in the same impossible situation: how does one edit a coherent method, how does one prepare for the half-pass, without going through the shoulder-in as prescribed by the masters of the past?

The general gets himself out of this situation by using an artifice hardly less subtle than the one used by Baucher. In his *Dressage du Cheval de Dehors* [*Schooling of the Outdoor Horse*], he describes the "lateral effects" which are nothing else than the shoulder-in; but neither will he use the word even once. Judge for yourself: "Ask for little yieldings of the croup by using leg pressure on the same side as that employed by the rein. These lateral effects must bring about the end of the horse's nose on the same side as the semi-taut rein, and make the haunches escape on the opposite side... One makes the horse take a few steps in this slightly bent and oblique position, then straightens him out again. It is understood that the other rein and other leg of the rider must have contact with the horse during these lateral effects."

The less experienced readers perhaps find it difficult to show any interest in this historical and technical digression. They may ignore the upheavals that Baucher and his school brought to European equitation when they declared that they had started out from ideas and means completely new; yet they find themselves incapable of getting out of the impasse with respect to an important movement in high equitation: the shoulder-in.

As a result they resorted to this distortion that we have seen: execute the shoulder-in by disguising it. What is curious and not very honorable with respect to the finesse of the riders of that period – and even on to this day – is that, as far as I know, no one has ever raised this issue of equestrian cant. However, several generations of Baucherists have tried in vain to approach the half-pass without going through the shoulder-in, and went to their graves as fools!

I knew Maître Armand Charpentier, who in 1947, directed me in my first steps in the saddle. He gave me a collection of *Soirées de l'Etrier* [*Stirrup Evenings*]. He was then in his nineties, of exceptional vigor, a man of the 19th century who had known, and seen riding, many a disciple of Baucher, such as Captain de Saint-Phalle and Faverot de Kerbrech. Here is an anecdote related by Charpentier, as told to him by Monsieur de Saint-André – the "lion of the times", he added. "He returns one day from Rouen with a magnificent Warmblood named Regulus… He was a stallion and could only go in one direction, that is, he could only turn on one side and had exasperated the patience of many an *écuyer*. Monsieur de Saint-André took him to the *manège* of Baucher and said to him: 'I doubt that even you, Maître, can make him turn to the right…' Baucher gets on the horse, follows the track on the left rein, with the left curb rein, his left leg active near the girth. At the end of a few minutes he manages to bend Regulus… He then goes on the track on the right rein, and, upon his first request, Regulus turns to the right… He says: 'Actually, all I did a few minutes ago was execute a sort of shoulder-in of Monsieur La Guérinière. But while he synthesizes I will analyze and break down the difficulties in order to vanquish them one by one.' "

What did he mean by this, other than that he had just executed the shoulder-in, which he considered only a brief expediency. It is truly a pity that Baucher was not satisfied with the many contributions he made to equitation, rather than trying to appear as the one who had invented everything.

The First Elements of the Half-pass at the Walk

I usually proceed in the following manner: since my horse is laterally supple and mobile thanks to the shoulder-in, I take the track, forward and straight, with as much equilibrium and upward movement as he is capable of. I still do not dare mention the *rassembler*. I go very carefully past the first corner of the short side; I cover 4 or 5 meters on this side then turn at right angles to it; I cover a few more steps on this inside track, halt the horse who is slightly incurvated, his shoulders and head oriented in the direction of the half-pass (that is, to the right, if I were on the track on the right rein, or vice-versa). This halt, which will be followed by several more, allows me to resolve the difficulties the horse may encounter in executing the first steps of the half-pass, namely, correcting the delay or excessive movement of the haunches (haunches either dragging, or attempting to lead), the flexion of the neck, the search for lightness – all of them pertaining to losses of balance that are easier to recoup at the halt. This is "the breaking up of strength and movement". Long live Baucher with his: "I break down into segments the difficulties in order to vanquish them." This procedure is directly inspired by La Guérinière, who moves from the shoulder-in to croup to wall: "When the horse has been obedient during a lesson of the shoulder-in... After working him, for example, to the right, and after having turned him into the corner at the end of the *manège*, halt him there, croup to wall, about two feet from it... one must hold him back with the hand and gently put pressure on him with the left leg to make him take two or three lateral steps, then halt him for a while, praise him, then begin again" (La Guérinière).

Half-pass at the walk.
Spartacus, Lusitano,
5 years.

La Guérinière also breaks down difficulties by halting, re-balancing the horse, then taking off again. But with this difference: that he approaches the half-pass from croup to the wall, which is more constraining in that the horse must not advance, even though this little diagonal gives one more or less the scope to advance. Herein lies the advantage that a wall on the long side has for a horse, against which he likes to cling.

The half-pass starts out with a light flexion and a semi-shoulder-in. The head must be in the vertical position, ears placed horizontally at the same level.

The inside rein limits itself to forming and controlling the bend, the outside one limits the bend and brings the haunches forward by holding the shoulders slightly back. The outside leg moves the horse laterally by means of light touches, that is, by vibrations and not by pressure; the inside leg at the girth "blocks" the bend of the horse, but also contributes to impulsion and a more or less forward direction of the lateral displacement. An imperceptible twist of the rider's pelvis in the direction of the movement facilitates the half-pass, as it does the shoulder-in.

Half-pass at the trot. Ultra, 4 years. The outside rein is adjusted and positioned at the wither, inside leg is at the girth.

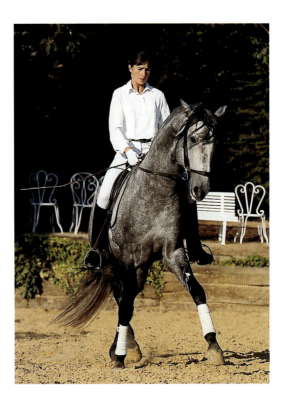

It is in connection with the execution of these two exercises that one must immediately put into practice alternate *descentes de main et de jambes*, the horse moving with the sole assistance of the pelvis and seat of the rider.

Finally, let us insist on the need to prepare correctly all the aids, for any intervention in the course of executing these exercises would have destructive results.

9. Recapitulation Model of "The Time to Learn"

Now that we have arrived at a point in our study which began simultaneously with the breaking in of three youngsters, and also served as a diary of their schooling, I believe it is of interest to recapitulate the procedures as one carried them out.

At this point, nothing is carved in stone. According to circumstances you can reverse the order of gaits and exercises. You do not have to adhere to a strict order: walk, trot, canter. What is important is to know what you are doing and why you are doing it! For obvious reasons this implies work that is structured, that is, work that follows a diagnosis that has been set down and a gymnastic program decided upon in advance. All too often one sees riders who connect the sequence of their exercises neither coherently nor with any logical objective.

A cold horse will be worked almost immediately at the trot; his walk and trot may even be interrupted by strike-offs at the canter to make him more attentive. A very supple horse may proceed easily from the shoulder-in to the half-pass at the walk then to the half-pass at the trot, which we have not yet covered. A well-balanced horse will easily canter from the walk, whereas a horse leaning heavily on his shoulders will have to be flexed at the haunches.

I have broken in and worked for six months with an Andalusian horse belonging to a friend who, without my using the slightest force, was able to execute the passage and the piaffe beautifully; he could do the pirouette and change leads. He could do all this correctly because he possessed an exceptional natural equilibrium, yet he was not capable of sustaining with regularity the three gaits and transitions. The airs came naturally to him and my work program took this into consideration: I developed simultaneously the natural gaits, without which the airs would have lost their attraction.

My horse Florido, bought when he was four, within thirteen months could change leads at every stride. However Miguelista continually missed single lead changes even after three years, then, within three months, executed them at every stride.

Thus nothing is absolute, nor is anything "writ" in advance. Each horse is an exciting but sometimes disappointing "bag of tricks"; projects that are pursued too systematically often shatter because of the different personalities of the horses. However, in high equitation, as in all other creative activities, there are permanent rules to which one must adhere. They sprinkle my remarks sufficiently so that I need not discuss them here again.

Relaxation and putting the Horse into His Equilibrium

If a young horse is hot or nervous, if he has not been worked the day before, it is always advisable to prepare him for his gymnastic lesson on the lunge for a dozen or so minutes, at the three gaits, on each rein. In addition to work on the single circle, it is good practice to use the progression of circles, interspersed with an extended straight trot on the tracks. The rider should accompany the horse, using long strides, without running.

Then, after a few minutes of work in hand on the lunge, with varied strike-offs and halts that are square and straight, the whip is placed on the horse's leg to indicate the movement and to keep the haunches in place. The horse takes a step back, calm, then goes forward, straight. His ensemble should be flexed lightly, the inside hand gently pulling his shoulder inside, into a shoulder-in position, with the right (outside) keeping the shoulders in check with the right snaffle rein, and the haunches controlled with the whip.

Now, get on the horse and, in order to control the quality of the work, amuse yourself by getting him to execute the same steps that you worked in hand. If you do this correctly, you will be surprised how easy it is.

Right away, move on at a straight walk on the track, bend the horse as you turn the corners, neck stretched and with this stretching extending into the back, with an ample and determined walk. Do two or three circuits around the *manège* on each rein, and circles at each end. Take advantage of the stability of the walk to verify your position from poll to heel. At the trot, for which the horse is forewarned by the voice, engage your seat and activate the calves by flexing your knees. Should this not suffice, touch with the whip and proceed at a rising trot, just easing the seat a little forward in the saddle rather than bumping on it. Cover the same ground that you did at the walk.

Establish a precise contact with hands kept still and low and fingers mobile so that, as soon as the horse relaxes, he also relaxes his poll and jaw, and can trot without hollowing his back or throwing back his poll. There should be some impulsion, but always legs without hands, and some contact with the corners of the mouth, but always hand without legs.

Increase the amplitude of his strides on the final circuits.

On circles, ride transitions from walk to trot, trot for three or four strides, then return to walk.

Figures and Exercises at the Walk

Proceed once more at the walk with a more shortened frame – but one that is compatible with the horse's aptitude. Go large, then turn lengthwise and crosswise into the *manège*, execute circles at the ends, then do a serpentine. At the very point where a circle is ended, at the short side, take a semi-diagonal with a slightly flexed shoulder-in; continue this lateral movement parallel to the long side until the middle of the track on the long side. Repeat these lateral movements once or twice from the middle of the short sides to the middle of the long sides. Then, at the second corner of the short side, execute a geometric volte, a prelude to the shoulder-in into which you link on the track.

Do not hesitate going back to executing circles and voltes if they have been poorly executed. In that the volte prepares the horse for the bend of the shoulder-in, when you close the volte at the beginning of the long side, proceed to the shoulder-in along the wall without necessarily going the whole length of the *manège* – 10 meters will suffice.

At the slightest contraction of the horse, without using force, begin a new volte and once more take up the shoulder-in as you arrive on the track. Extend the walk at the end of the long side, then make a demi-volte on one track which will lead you obliquely back to the long side just left, but on the other rein. When you arrive at the track, at an angle of 30 to 35 degrees, bend your horse towards the outside of the *manège* at a counter-shoulder-in. Turn two corners in this position and, after having pivoted at the second corner around the outside hind leg – in relation to the bend – go on the diagonal at the shoulder-in and straighten the horse on the track. Change rein by means of a half-pass, beginning at the middle of the short side. Why not do one on the entire diagonal? Because it is better to exercise horses for short distances when doing lateral work. Be rigorous when doing a few strides well flexed and almost parallel, rather than lax with respect to two endless tracks.

Once rein changes have been accomplished, extend the neck and the walk and go large once or twice, then continue the same series of exercises on the other rein. Note that nine out of ten horses bend, even "break" the neck more easily to the left than to the right. This brings with it considerable inconveniences such as head-in rather than shoulder-in, which results in their moving on only one track.

In the case of the half-pass from left to right, the bend is less easily accomplished and the horse has greater difficulty "seeing" where he is going on that rein than on the other. However, bending his neck to the left does not mean that he will turn better to the left than to the right. On the contrary, with a "broken" neck, that is, the neck exaggeratedly bent laterally, one will have greater difficulty making the haunches follow the imprints of the shoulders.

It should be noted that whether you are on one rein as opposed to the other, depending on whether the horse is flexing to his "soft" or "stiff" side, the "dosage" of aids will obviously differ.

I cannot emphasize too much how important it is to give frequent periods of rest at the walk, using loose reins, or at the halt. This varies, of course, with the intensity of the work, the temperature, the strength and training of the horse. Let us say that for every fifty minutes of work in the *manège*, a rest period of five to ten minutes is normal.

However, one must not use these fifty or sixty minutes doing only lateral work! I have observed this much too often. No matter how beneficial it is to the horse, two-track work is very demanding. Keep the dosage in small amounts so that, you do not find yourself one day owning an irrevocably dulled horse.

The Same Exercises at the Trot

You will now do the same exercises at the trot, with the exception of the half-pass. Let us pay attention to the strides at the walk which precede and bring about the trot. Always return to the regular halt as soon as the equilibrium has been disturbed, regardless of the gait and the exercise. Baucher called this the breaking down of force and movement. Let us say more specifically, it is re-establishing the balance that has been disturbed at a particular movement, namely, a precise halt with united limbs.

After having executed these exercises at the trot, begin a new sequence with more shortened steps around the *manège*, on inside tracks, which will test the horse's straightness away from the walls. Then do a serpentine, then a large circle on one track ending in a spiral inward then enlarged, then take up the spiral again at a shoulder-in. Continue with the spiral in this position, ending with a rotation in the form of a reversed pirouette with the normal bend; that of the shoulder-in. Enlarge the spiral, then go large. Accomplish all this at the trot, excluding, of course, the reversed pirouette.

At the walk, as at the trot on one track, ask for transitions within the gait. Shorten the steps at the walk, go large once, then extend them; do the same at the trot, also at the rising trot to also to relieve the horse's back. You can combine the half-pass with the shoulder-in at the walk. After the second corner, do six or seven strides of half-pass at the walk, straighten, then go straight on an inside track until the end; change rein and begin the same exercise once again.

Make sure that your horse is able to go from lateral work to walking on one track, straight and without the help of the wall. If all goes well, this exercise will then be done at the trot.

As always, after the second corner of the short side, execute five or six strides at the half-pass, then, without changing the bend, move your outside hand gently to the side and, vibrating your inside leg at the girth, return to the track at the shoulder-in. Always keep your horse parallel to the wall, a semi-shoulder in front of the haunches, otherwise the horse will not cross his limbs.

One can accomplish this counter-change of hand two or three times in succession. It gets the horse used to reversals of a lateral movement and prepares him for counter-changes of hand with bend changes. We will do this later at the trot when the horse can execute the half-pass more easily.

Work at the Canter

We have now reached the stage of work at the canter, but nothing prevents you from executing a little canter once or twice going large, while working at the walk or the trot. On the contrary in fact, and this is essential when working with a somewhat cold horse. On the other hand, in the case of a nervous or restless horse, nothing should be rushed. Work at a slow walk or a regular trot will calm him.

Pay great attention to the cadence of the gaits, which should never be slack or lusterless; also pay attention to excessive rushing, especially when doing lateral work, since this would allow your horse to evade crossings of the legs.

With respect to the strike-off at the canter, do a circle, then, with a light shoulder-in position, strike off the moment this position is held in check by the wall. This will prevent the horse from falling onto his outside shoulder. Strike off from the trot if the horse is not very flexible or not too advanced; if you start off from the walk, prepare for the canter by shortening the walk somewhat, so that you can obtain the flexion on the haunches and raise the forehand at the very first stride. Describe a circle, go large, then do another circle at the end of the *manège*. Lengthen the canter by stretching the horse, then end on the circle in the center of the *manège*, allowing his neck to stretch downwards, using long reins, pushing with the seat, but only intervening with hands that are quite open, now to the inside to keep the bend, now to the outside to prevent the horse from falling in.

With a good seat and quiet legs, this exercise should calm horses who bore on the hand and help them find their balance. Ride more transitions to and from canter on the circle, interspersed with just three or four strides of trot.

Take up again a canter that is regular, shorten it somewhat to make a demi-volte at the beginning of the short side, arriving at the counter-canter on the long side well before reaching the corner, so as to arrive under the most favorable conditions; the worst thing would be to arrive either facing the wall, or with the horse's head looking directly into the corner. Rather, reach the corner parallel to the wall, at first without doing a half-pass (although the half-pass at the canter is easier than at the trot).

Practice the canter in short sequences. Schooling a horse at the canter is accomplished less by cantering around than by multiplying strike-offs at the canter that are straight, be they canters on the true lead, or counter-canters.

Complete your exercises by striking off at the canter on both the true lead and the counter-canter, on straight lines and on circles, with the horse straight, using a slight shoulder-in to straighten the haunches, thus avoiding a haunch-in position, which usually provides a way for the horse to resist.

An excellent exercise consists of doing a half-pass at the walk, on the diagonal, then, if the half-pass is light and well-balanced, striking off at the canter, still doing the half-pass on the same diagonal, keeping parallel to the sides. In this manner one reaches the opposite side of the *manège* at the counter-canter.

Do not neglect to execute a few exercises of the shoulder-in at the canter on semi-diagonals and the long sides. This is less difficult than one expects if you continue to punctuate your canter correctly with the *outside leg* – seemingly contrary to the direction of the movement – *while vibrating with the inside leg* and stretching the pelvis in the direction of the movement.

Conclude with the Search for Cadence at the Trot

We are now reaching the end of our work. We have reached a moment of rest and, before leaving the *manège*, you will finish by going large two or three times on both reins, executing the most elevated trot possible. If your work was performed with tact and reflection, the horse should be at the peak of his receptiveness. It is during this phase, a few trimesters from now, that you will begin the first steps of a gentle passage, after having gone through the *rassemblé* trot. It is with this in mind that you will seek to excel, refine your movements and aids to verify and glean the fruit of your art. If the cadence of your trot is lighter and more floating than ever, regular and ready for all kinds of transitions, then be happy for you are on the Royal Way. Should the opposite be the case, check all aspects of your work.

After *the time to understand, the time to learn* is now coming to a close and *the time to do the exercises and airs* will begin.

CHAPTER THREE

The Time to Do –
The Exercises and Airs

AT AN EARLIER STAGE, beginning with the breaking in, which we called *the time to understand*, we established a veritable codification between the young horse and ourselves. Lungeing exercises, elementary work in hand, applying the first aids, while still lungeing, then helped by the *écuyer* at his first free steps around the *manège*, all contributed to the creation of a first two-way communication.

The time to learn, comprising the second period of schooling, dealt with teaching the young horse elementary movements, serving as a foundation for more elaborate exercises. Nothing further could be undertaken until our horses were able to cover perfectly straight the tracks of the *manège*, to be correctly flexed at the turning of corners, and to maintain correct bend without falling to the inside on circles and voltes.

When first ridden, it was necessary to obtain from the young horse variations within each gait so that he never fell into a monotonous routine. Then came the first, timid lateral mobilizations, which accustomed him to yield to the transverse tensions of the seat and leg, while also executing the first crossings of his limbs. Elementary – still prudent – flexions were accomplished more thoroughly when approaching the counter-shoulder-in and shoulder-in.

Movements of increasing complexity in all directions of the *manège*, from the serpentine to the spiral, permitted us to verify the quality of our work and refine the horse even further.

The half-pass, the fruit of the shoulder-in, and also rotations of the haunches, made it possible for us to mobilize the horse's body laterally. Finally, we ensured that the horse canters and counter-canters with ease both around the arena and on circles, and that his halts are calm and regular.

We have now arrived at *the time to do* and will begin exercises and airs which will enable our pupil to utilize all his resources each day a little more and a little better. It is also the time for *rassembler*...

1. Checking the Rider's Position

Let us first ensure that we control the pliability of our seat at the three gaits. After twenty or twenty-five months of active work, our own body and that of the horse must be aware of each other and have some sort of mutual understanding. This means that we regulate the walk by engaging, and more or less accentuating the actions of our lumbar vertebrae, combined with intermittent and light wrapping around of the upper parts of the legs, but without raising the heels. We must stretch the lower part of our back in a forward direction, and must never round it, for in that position, the horse can take charge.

In this position, thighs back, waist forwards, shoulders straight, we are seated more on the anterior perineum [lower front aspect of the pubis] than on the ischia [seat bones] and this is for the better, because it favors the forward movement, putting the horse in a state of optimal receptiveness to the vibrations or tappings of the calves, or even to a touch with the whip.

It is also the only posture which allows one to set the horse into *rassemblés* and engaged halts, without him moving forwards or backwards: he is placed between the tension of the rider's back and the ends of his fingers. The horse's back, progressively suppled and freed of tension, feels more comfortable, thus uniting more intimately than ever with the rider's. *Both parties must espouse this interaction in such a way that, at the walk and trot, the movement of the one absorbs that of the other without any separation.* The canter is the easiest gait for the beginner to absorb if he is passive and supple, but the most difficult one for the rider who, when executing *high school* exercises, must communicate the gait variations, with their differing equilibria and, above all, speeds, with his seat alone.

The effectiveness of the rider's back at the canter will be monitored by means of visual observation of the seat. *The rear part of the seat, which moves forward at each stride, must never be detached from the saddle by raquet-like jolts*; there must be no gripping with legs, or heels being raised.

The rider's torso, vertical and almost immobile in the dorsal [mid- and upper] section, must literally undulate in the lumbar [lower] section. One may be surprised when one becomes aware of this development, since one is dealing with a subject one had supposed settled. But we are entering a phase wherein the horse will be initiated into a *rassemblé* equilibrium, and he will never achieve this if the rider's equilibrium has not evolved similarly and in tandem with that of the horse. If this has not occurred, there will be separation and a break in communication between the two.

I bring a minor (common) example of this to the attention of onlookers in the following way. I place a rider of ordinary ability on one of my horses who has attained the *rassembler* and I have them move at the walk. The rider has the typical posture I usually detect among "amateurs": rounded back, flabby lumbar muscles, raised knees, shoulders leaning backwards – which blocks the action of the lumbar region. While walking alongside, I stress my corrections with respect to his position by means of pointing with the whip. I make his leg come down by pulling the thigh backwards, I make him sit closer to the horse's center of gravity by asking him to push his waist forwards, which moves his seat from the ischia to the anterior perineum (lower front aspect of the pubic bone). I make him hold his elbows alongside his body, hands still, reins above the withers, and have him bring his shoulder-blades closer together.

Once this has been accomplished at the walk, I bring him into an active phase, vibrating or tapping his legs, mobilizing his fingers on reins that have been pre-set: to the pupil's surprise, the horse goes progressively from a shortened walk to the start of a diagonalization, then up to the piaffe.

This is the objective to be achieved by both rider and horse during the coming months. This will occur if the recapitulation model at the end of the previous chapter continues to develop correctly and you approach the work that follows in the horse/rider equilibrium I have just described.

Try to achieve this, examining your own posture or, better still, make the transformation obvious.

2. Cadence

At this stage an additional fundamental element must occur, one that is closely linked to what preceded, namely, establishment and control of the *cadence*. Without it, *high school* equitation, like dance, will not materialize, and what is done cannot be called an art but is, rather, a simple gesticulation that is more or less acrobatic.

At this point I want to honor the man who revealed to us what rhythm and cadence give to equitation. Honor is due to the only *écuyer* who never asked me to admire the simple spectacle of a four-year-old colt, still chubby, lunged on a circle and already light: Maître Oliveira, who took such lightness for granted, and never bragged.

Every aspect of his equitation, his equestrian gestures, rested on the aim of creating and maintaining the conformity of the gaits of his horses with a musical beat one could actually hear, even in the silence of the *manège*. In recalling this, I mirror the reflection of a music lover of the 18th century who wrote that "music lacking rhythm is vague and cannot be sustained without boring one".

3. The Rassembler

We have already devoted some time to a definition of the *rassembler*, indicating its advantages, that is, its importance, whether for jumping obstacles or as the final touches in the practice of high school equitation.

We had this objective in mind at the outset of the first lessons and we never left it throughout all the exercises. It must now make its appearance as we work at the airs of high school equitation. Gymnastics and suppling work have already given the horse a superior equilibrium. We have verified the quality of our own position in determining the desired distribution of the horse's weight and his overall balance. When this stage is completed, the *rassembler* ought to be sufficient to determine the airs above the ground, the passage and the piaffe, and the shortening of the canter for the pirouettes.

4. Curb and Snaffle Bits

Until now we have worked with a simple snaffle. How and when do we decide to *go from the snaffle to the curb* and, above all, *why the curb?*

As we conceive it, *mouthpieces are instruments of communication* and not of coercion. The two bits act quite differently: the snaffle acts from front to back; the curb, with its branches or arms, has a leverage action which multiplies its effect and, through the effect of the port, acts in the upward direction.

Obviously, a horse who has been well prepared yields easily to the action of a snaffle; the complementary touch of the curb bit perfects and finalizes the position already worked at with the snaffle. This result can only be attained from a horse sensitive to a snaffle, that is, one who flexes his poll and jaw to a light action, without any head-tossing or constraint. It is then possible to ride the horse with a double bridle, but should he never take two steps leaning on the curb bit or, worse still, held in check by it.

The actions with the curb bit must be only temporary and intermittent. If one wants the horse to respect the curb bit and retain his readiness for the finishing touch with respect to the *rassembler*, it must only act as swiftly as lightning, a substitute for the snaffle, when he seeks its contact. This flashing "taking up and yielding" reinforces the respect the horse must show for the snaffle bit, the action of which he perceives in tandem with that of the curb bit, respecting it in a different way.

I hold the curb reins adjusted one centimeter longer than the snaffle reins. As soon as the horse opposes me with any force, I let go contact with the snaffle, retaining the same degree of contact on the curb bit as when the resistance occurred. Right away, this opposition yields or retreats. At the same time, I return to the previous adjustment of the snaffle, and so on, whenever a resistance or an intentional leaning on the bit occurs. This procedure makes the horse more respectful of the snaffle bit, through the power momentarily given it by the curb bit.

The absolute rule must be that *never* should the power of the curb bit be used, except momentarily, to cope with any menace that may occur. Should sensibility and common sense not suffice in convincing you of this, you should be aware that the curb bit, utilized as a means of blocking opposition, will have only two possible results: rearing and falling backwards on the part of horses with sensitive mouths, and desensitization of the mouth by cutting off circulation.

The action of the curb bit must occur predominantly on the outside of any bend of the neck.

And lastly, you should know that a horse who has reached the final stages of his schooling, who is confident and has been communicating for six or eight years with a hand that is intelligent and precise, can be led on a curb bit rein *with only one hand*. Horsemen of the past even performed the supreme test of perfect communication. For work in hand, to obtain flexions of jaw and neck, the double bridle was necessary; but once these flexions were executed and obtained, in hand, they returned to the snaffle bit to work with the novice horse, mounted.

5. Relaxation

Throughout the entire schooling of the horse, and even during his entire life, relaxation and warming up before work are essential. The method will not change greatly since, by definition, to obtain relaxation, one must always start off with the natural gaits and, during this phase of the lesson, avoid the inevitable constraints which suppling movements provoke (but which form an essential part of a thorough lesson).

However, one must not neglect the equilibrium of the horse, but should help him, with kindness, to go from a horizontal equilibrium to one that is more elevated, for which previous work has already prepared him.

If he has been worked the day before and does not have too tempestuous a temperament, lungeing is no longer an indispensable part of the system. One goes to the track at the walk, which is immediately regulated with ample and regular strides; the neck placed in its natural position.

One goes large two or three time on each rein, interspersed with a few circles, controlling the horse with the snaffle rein; the curb rein is adjusted at semi-tension. One goes from the walk to a rising trot that is well cadenced, paying particular care that the horse does not push his nose out horizontally in opposition to the hand, since this brings about the hollowing of the entire spinal column.

On the contrary, without attempting to put the horse into the ramener, one must encourage him to relax at the poll and jaw, which he cannot do if the hand is held too high, and moves. To avoid this problem, place a hand on each side of the neck, wrists still and fingers lightly mobile, then act on reins that are gentle, the action being downwards, rather than towards you or upwards. Maintaining impulsion, continue this "embracing" gesture, controlling the cadence from the seat. After going large twice, and making a few changes of rein at the trot, return to an energetic walk, doing a careful transition, which will determine the quality of the gait to come.

Go once more large at a regular and ample walk, return to the trot, then do a circle and, using your voice and your inside leg at the girth, strike off

Relaxation at an ample trot, the poll is relaxed and flexed, the jaw is supple.

at the canter with your outside leg placed somewhat back. Here, too, pay attention to the transition, maintaining regular and fluid strides.

Go large once or twice at the canter, then return to an energetic trot around the *manège*, then execute a fluid transition to an extended walk. After three minutes rest at a free walk, repeat the exercise on each rein.

This is a sort of relaxation which already encompasses a schooling of the horse, if one respects the correctness of straight lines, inflexion on curves, cadence and the energy and fluidity of transitions.

The purpose of relaxation is not to tire the horse but to warm him up before he begins to do exercises that are more intensive and demanding. To end the relaxation period, return to a careful working trot, then go on to a walk. To repeat the point made earlier: *flexion of the poll and jaw must be the result of a successful period of relaxation.*

Since the beginning of his schooling, our horse has experienced all this suppling. Now, a rider with a correct position, able to direct his aids, begins the kind of training which will give the horse a carriage with a more effortless forehand, his joints acquiring a more comfortable flexion, which will become apparent from the position of his haunches and hocks.

While one has not yet sought the complete positioning of the nose (which, of course, differs from horse to horse), one has kept the poll at the highest point of the horse. Therefore, it is already possible to execute these exercises in part, so long as the horse has a poll and a jaw that are softly flexed when this is solicited with one's fingers. The new equilibrium will materialize further through the engagement of the rider's lumbar vertebrae, together with the oscillating legs, and alternating with the vibration of the fingers. This is, indeed, an application of the famous and excellent principle of "hand without legs, legs without hand".

6. Use of the Spur

"Just as the horse must be light to the hand, likewise must he be light to the legs." A truth expressed by Baucher's most faithful disciple, General Faverot de Kerbrech, who precedes his exposition on "using the spur" in this manner. For Faverot and the whole Baucherist School, this is an indispensable element in the "preparation" of the horse if one wishes "to have absolute mastery over him, prevent any resistances, and guide him wherever one wishes and at the gait one wants", whatever the circumstances. It is a systematic and progressive exercise executed, if the hand finds no opposition, when equal pressure, first from two legs, then from two spurs, instantaneously brings about the forward motion of the horse. It is done from a halt or a walk to attain an acceleration proportionate to the pressure. It even includes those "little attacks" (but without any opposition from the hand) "which give back to the horse's strength the direction to go forward". The end result of this elaborate refinement to get the horse used to the spur is "the co-ordinated effect with the spur" which brings about relaxation of the jaw, destroys resistances, immobilizes the horse, or obliges him to maintain the cadence that he already has.

One can find this technique in Faverot's Dressage *Méthodique du Cheval de Selle*; it is certainly not debatable, either in principle or in application. It trains the horse to receive the spur as a simple stimulus as well as a means for the *rassembler*, or for immobility in place. It is the rationalized exploitation of the same reflex used more savagely by the Arab rider to halt his horse with the spur.

If, in all circumstances, the horse must yield to the motion activated by legs or spurs, is it really necessary to go through the entire Baucherist technique?

My first answer is that these means are the prerogatives of an *écuyer* who possesses the seat of a centaur and the hand of a Swiss watchmaker. Should these assets be lacking, you risk bringing about an example of the most incredible stubborn defenses.

I might add that one should distinguish between sensitive and energetic horses and those who are cold and languid: to put a cold and languid horse to the spur will only highlight his very weakness. If one owns a horse with an acceptable dynamism, the aids we have already mentioned do not exclude the light pinching of the spur as espoused by La Guérinière and those soft attacks of the Baucherist school, which suffice, being already quite delicate in themselves. The main principle is not to grip with one's legs; rather one must always be sure of employing legs that do no more than tap at regular intervals; not putting constant pressure on the flanks, but ceasing their action the instant it has been performed.

When this action proves to be insufficient, one must then make little lance-like taps with the spur, which also assumes a very controlled leg; the wrists advance simultaneously. This is an exceptional action, but it has some danger in that it could open up the seat slightly, as though it were going to envelope the horse; nonetheless, this action is, indeed, very useful and can easily re-establish the forward movement.

I have never used spurs with rowels or, more precisely, every time I came upon them used despairingly on despairing horses, who were cold or languid, I immediately denounced their use, disgusted by what they provoked, for example, the interruption of cadence or the beginning of defenses by the horse.

One sometimes observes riders – even international champions – who compete in the arena, trying to diagonalize their horses by using brutal action with their rowelled spurs, and sees their horses refusing to leave the ground when they try to execute the piaffe in front of the jury. This convinces me that Xenophon was right when, 2,400 years earlier he wrote: "When a horse acts through constraint, he does poorly, just like a dancer who is taught by means of lashes of the whip or goads."

Here is a final recommendation with respect to the use of the heel and the spur: never put strong pressure on the stirrup irons with your feet. Because they attached to the horse's back through the stirrup leathers, which are fixed to the saddle, the horse can feel every single movement. Putting strong and useless pressure on the stirrups only adds to the bumps your seat receives, which in turn effect your feet and legs, making them move with a frenzy, and rendering them incapable of making the lightest touch with the spur.

7. Contact and the Natural Flexion to the Left

"One must always feel the effect of both reins in the bridle-hand [hand of curb] (the left hand is the bridle-hand). It is much more difficult to bend a horse to the right because most horses are naturally more rigid on that side than on the left. Thus when one pulls the rein to the right to bend the horse to the right, *one gets the feeling that the outside rein is in the left hand*." (La Guérinière, *School of Horsemanship* – 1733, Chapter 7; On the bridle-hand and its effects.)

One can only have high school equitation when this fundamental difficulty has been taken care of – that is, the horse is definitely straight. If this principle is not respected, we have one factor, namely, the usual failure.

The horse moving on the right rein bends his neck and his head naturally to the left. He carries his shoulders on the same side and thus can no longer be parallel to the wall of the *manège*, which is the foundation stone of straightness in forward movement.

On the left rein, he retains the same deviation. Riders, unaware of this, are satisfied because, on this rein, the horse is bent on the correct side.

This phenomenon is common with mammalian quadrupeds. Observe the dog advancing towards us. He is always slightly oblique with respect to his axis as he walks.

The functional predominance of one of the horse's sides, which some people attribute to the slight bend of the mane or to the position of the fetus "in utero", is thus a natural position, but it is a damaging hindrance to the equilibrium and regularity of movement in the mounted horse.

This natural tendency to throw the head and neck to the left is associated with a spontaneous disinclination on the horse's part to accept a voluntary and free contact with the right rein. If not corrected, this crookedness will be to blame for the horse's lack of balance in general – his irregularities with respect to diagonal airs and lead changes from left to right, and defenses that will soon become obvious, more often than not, as a refusal to turn or bend to the right.

Exercises to bend the ensemble of the horse, from the circle to the shoulder-in to the right, are indispensable. But they are insufficient if the rider *does not pay constant attention not only to a flexion that is correct on the right as well as on the left, but to contact, to tension – signifying communication – as alive and attentive to the right as to left.*

When one seeks contact on the right, the reflex action of the horse is to accentuate this "contraction-flexion" on the left in his attempt to avoid the right rein.

The usefulness of these flexion exercises on the right is easily understood by trainers when they work on the right rein and feel its rigidity, however, when they work on the left rein, where the flexion is spontaneous, they are satisfied.

But this flexion to the left, on the left rein, is without interest if the horse defends himself against contact with the outside rein – that one the right. Under these conditions, the basic role of the outside rein cannot be assured when on the left rein, even with a good bend to the left.

Therefore, one must be totally attentive in communicating with the right corner of the horse's lips when one works on the left rein, as well as while working on the right rein, when one feels difficulties flexing to the right.

To neglect this will bring about serious problems when one begins to refine the gaits and work on the *rassemblés* airs, for the horse will try to avoid this constraining equilibrium, which places all his flexed resources [joints, muscles, etc.] totally at the disposal of the rider.

If the horse has not been worked efficiently on the right rein, that is, if he is not bent and obedient with the same contact on each rein, he will turn his head and neck to the outside and his haunches towards the inside. On the left rein, he will turn his shoulders to the inside and his haunches to the outside. This is evident when one seeks the piaffe and the passage.

In this case, when on the right rein, I bend the horse's ensemble to the right by maintaining a definite contact on the right rein, making sure that "the feeling of the outside rein stays in the left hand" (La Guérinière).

On the left rein, I do not bend him to the left, but stay with the same inflexion that exists on the right rein, that is, with a slight counter-shoulder-in. This position is identical on each rein and its purpose is to correct this constant tendency on the part of the horse to make his shoulders flee to the left and his haunches to the right.

This is how I correct the piaffes and the passages when the cadence gets lost because of the impossibility of channeling and diagonalizing them when the horse refuses contact with the right diagonal aid.

It is the same at the *rassemblé* canter, which I work at the shoulder-in to the right, on the right rein, and at the counter-canter to the right, with the bend one has at the counter-shoulder-in, on the left rein.

8. The Rassemblé Walk

We now begin the *rassemblé* walk, or school walk. It is obtained through starting out at the school trot and not by shortening the ordinary walk. The walk does not possess the necessary impulsion to allow changing from an ordinary walk to a school walk, for one would fall right away into a compression, bringing about the extinction of the gait.

The school walk must maintain the specific qualities of the school trot, that is, the still and raised position of the neck and strides that are elevated and regular, thus shorter than at the ordinary walk. As is the case with the school trot, the back must be raised and the neck flexed; so, too, the hind legs, otherwise they would advance under the mass in an exaggerated manner.

The horse must move at a four-four equal time as soon as he goes from the diagonals of the school trot to the school walk. One attains the best preparation for the *rassemblé* walk when one goes frequently from the *rassemblé* trot to a regular walk.

One shortens the strides by engaging the loins so that the horse continues to go forward, then one takes up again with a half-halt. The main thing is not to take a step with any weight on the hand and to maintain the engagement of the haunches. One must therefore send the forehand forward, then raise or, rather, maintain it, through half-halts with the outside rein, until a light equilibrium has been attained.

One must then go from this *rassemblé* walk to an extended walk, maintaining the regularity of the strides, then return to the *rassemblé* walk. At first, return to the school trot frequently to prepare short sequences of the school walk.

After having introduced the horse to the school walk on straight lines, one should move at the same gait on to curves, then on to the shoulder-in and the half-pass.

The usefulness of the school walk lies mostly in the fact that it is a preparatory, rather than a gait for itself. It is neither a gait for war, nor is it a parade gait [a parade gait is a very precise, perfect halt from a trot or a canter].

To put a horse at the school walk is to bend the bow before letting the arrow fly. It is from the school walk that one begins the pirouette, the rein-back and striking off at the *rassemblé* canter; it is this gait that will generate diagonalization in place, which will become the piaffe. We will discuss in due course how astute shortening of the four-beat school walk, performed with impulsion and lightness, progressively produces the two-beat diagonalization.

9. The Rassemblé Halt

During the previous session, you undertook the introduction of halts – immobility, regardless of the carriage of the young horse, thus obtaining the regular halt, that is, straight, with limbs united on the same line. We will now begin the *rassemblé* halt or the school halt.

The care we took in working in hand and riding our horse straight, and at the shoulder-in, gave us control of the inside hind leg at the halt. What does this mean? Observe a group of riders around you as they work in the *manège* or the arena. Observe them when they halt, or, in the form of a game, ask them to halt either from the walk or the trot, and notice the position of their horse's haunches and the hind legs. Whether they are novices or not, three-quarters of them will immobilize themselves with the haunches inside, the inside hind leg thrust out. *This is the position a mounted horse, whose equilibrium is not adjusted to the seat of his rider, adopts instinctively*; it is the natural stance a horse takes when he wants to escape the control of aids, be they lacking or vague. It is always by placing this inside hind leg to the side that the stubborn horse will seek support to prepare his defense – to rear, for example. With this distorted balance it will be impossible for the rider, not only to move off again straight, but to rein back or go from a halt to a trot, or a cadenced canter.

In seeking to teach the school halt, the preparatory work invested in the suppling exercises will immediately bear fruit and enlighten you with respect to matters that were previously unclear.

We are now at the school walk, straight in the shoulders and haunches, and we are going to ask for a halt. With the stride that precedes it, we engage our lumbar vertebrae a little more. In the equilibrium of the *rassemblé* walk, the horse is very sensitive to our aids pertaining to position, and we vibrate the thighs-legs ensemble. Elbows are placed alongside the body above the top of the pelvic bone; the inside hand, immobile at the level of the withers, assures the straightness of the neck; the outside hand or, better still, the steadied fingers, will give a half-halt.

The half-halt emerges from the pelvis; the outside elbow, linked to the hip, carries itself at the moment that the rider's inside buttock engages to set the inside haunch of the horse.

The inside hand, set, creates an anchoring point which, when immobilizing the snaffle bit in the mouth, gives effect to its action. Immobile and low, it prevents the horse from butting upwards with the nose. The outside hand, its action sustained, maintains the poll at its highest point. Between the action of the two reins and the yielding of the hand, the horse re-establishes balance and self-carriage.

The halt is asked for and attained in lightness, the hands are lowered and advance one centimeter, the rider maintaining his position, which is very *rassemblé*. The horse is halted with limbs united, his hind legs slightly in front of the vertical, neck raised, poll flexed, mouth relaxed. In this posture, he can depart quite well from a halt to the *rassemblé* trot, to the canter, the piaffe, or the rein-back. All his resources [joints, muscles, etc.] are stretched and in position.

You will not achieve a perfect halt right away. It is important that the horse is quietly immobilized at each request for the halt; also *if the halt is irregular, do not correct him in place*. First, because you will not succeed, second, because you will annoy him and make him move once the halt has been requested. Should you fail, or if the halt is imperfect, go forwards and ask again. The halts must be maintained for three or four seconds, otherwise, once halted, the horse will want to move off again.

These principles are the same for halts from the trot or the canter. All that has been said about the use of the hand and reins concerns the snaffle, but it is not a bad idea to have a light contact with the curb rein on the outer side of the horse's bend.

10. Outside Rein, Inside Rein

Our equitation has become more and more precise and rigorous. We have seen the complexity of the *rassemblé* halt and the influences, sometimes in isolation and sometimes in association, that outside and inside reins can exert. Let us develop a little further *"the why and the how" of the effects that inside and outside reins can exert*.

The horse is placed perfectly straight, that is, he is walking with his axis rigorously parallel to the wall. His neck is straight, thanks to the control of the inside rein held by an immobile hand at the level of the withers. The outside rein, more supportive, prevents the horse from "falling into the interior", especially into corners which were prepared for by the vibrating of the fingers of the inside hand. The horse could interpret this as an indication to execute a volte, whereas the corner is only a quarter of a volte: *in contact, the outside rein eliminates all ambiguities*.

I repeat that the inside hand intervenes only to indicate, by vibrating the fingers, with wrists immobile, any turns or direction changes. But it also has another role of equal importance: to forestall any negative effects that might be induced by this very formidable outside rein, called correctly "the rein of the *écuyer*" – undoubtedly because a novice rider always clutches his interior rein, while his outside rein is more or less abandoned.

Most of the actions of the hands must be done with the outside rein perfectly coordinated with the inside rein. I cite the most common of these: on the left rein, your horse bends his neck easily to the left and so risks leaving the track; you support precisely with the outside rein to avoid that happening. If your inside rein does not observe scrupulously its job as just described, then any intentional inversion of bend towards the outside becomes virtually impossible and the simple and indispensable support of the outside rein will, in fact, invert the bend to the outside, making you lose control of straightness and direction. For example, the horse is on the left rein. He will bend his neck to the right through the action of the right rein, not limited by the left rein, and, "breaking" at the base of the neck, he will fall on to the left shoulder, leave the track and enter the middle of the *manège*. Since perfect co-ordination between the inside rein and the outside rein is lacking, you have just succumbed to the perverse effect of that very indispensable outside rein.

You should know that, on a circle at the trot or the canter, centrifugal force will add to the loss of the bend and will make you terminate your circumference, either by veering into the center or going off at a tangent.

It is only now that I tackle this important problem, because we are entering on this very delicate path which is *rassemblée* equitation; it is also assumed that we no longer have any difficulty with the precision of our aids and our seat. If this is not so, then recommending actions as precise as these – which take a long time to attain – was premature. On the other hand, those who do not fulfill these conditions rigorously, have no hope of getting past what I call this formidable wall of the *rassembler*.

Every quest for equilibrium, for the improvement of cadence by the support of the forehand through flexion of the hindquarters, each rassemblé halt, each transition, will require *the precise execution of a half-halt with the outside rein, which must be performed coherently by means of the immobility of the inside hand.*

11. The Rein-back

"One method to get him to put himself on his haunches to adjust his hind legs, to assure the position of his head and make him light to the hand." (La Guérinière.)

I have always turned away from teaching the rein-back to riders who have not yet reached a serious equestrian level and to horses who have not attained a minimum of the *rassembler*. Another perverted aspect of contemporary instruction pertaining to this exercise is the use of the leg during the rein-back. As we shall soon see, it is the result of a decadence which reproduces but deforms without any understanding the excellent prescriptions of those *écuyers* of past times. To rein back, one must create an equilibrium that is favorable to transferring the movement backwards. No one can rein back a horse who has halted with a hind leg set back, or has misaligned shoulders.

The prerequisite for the rein-back is the *rassemblé* halt, as we have just studied it. One could then rein back almost without taking the time to halt, directly from the *rassemblé* walk.

To have the horse rein back at the beginning of his schooling, one can disengage the back of one's seat by bringing the torso forward and hollowing the lumbar vertebrae, legs quiet.

Since the rein-back is done with diagonal pairs of legs, it is logical that it should be solicited likewise, that is, by closing the fingers first of one hand then of the other, which the horse will quickly understand by backing each time a diagonal is requested.

Preparing the horse for straightness is a basic requirement, since the neck serves as a rudder and when, for example, flexed towards the inside of the *manège*, it will deviate towards the interior. Because of this natural tendency for the neck to be bent towards the left, it often happens that, when the horse is on the left rein, he throws his haunches towards the left when going backwards. To avoid this, one must place a slight bend on the right by placing the right rein at the withers and initiating the request for rein-back with the left rein.

If the horse places his haunches too far to the right, one slackens the right rein by adjusting the left one more. The leg must barely be allowed to intervene to correct the deviation in the rein-back, for it would only risk confusion when using the aid for a forward movement; however, the seat can contribute by putting weight on, and pushing the buttock on the side opposite the deviation.

If there is a deviation of haunches to the left, the reins must act as indicated, weight of the left buttock towards the right, together with a slight twist of the pelvis, also to the right. This is exactly the opposite of the movement made with the seat when one wants to halt the horse who is at a slight shoulder-in, with the inside hind leg engaged.

After the rein-back, and without a halt, go forwards, preferably at the trot or the canter. The ideal is the opposite of the rein-back movement, done by a deep engagement of the lumbar vertebrae, together with envelopment of the seat, rather than by a jab with the spurs.

A final word to explain why this howler – the use of the leg in a rein-back – is prevalent in modern-day schooling. A rein-back must, of course, start off from a halt slightly on the haunches. For that reason, in order to achieve engagement at the halt, the *écuyers* of the Enlightenment recommended that one animate the horse prior to "releasing him delicately from the thickest part of his calves". However, when dealing with the rein-back, they point out right away that one must "maintain descending legs". From this point emanates the confusion on the part of modern-day teachers who, unable to halt their horses *rassemblés*, come upon blockages at the rein-back, and try to get out of this by kicking.

12. Pirouettes

The Reversed Pirouette

When we reached the stage of *the time to learn* we had prepared our horse to yield laterally to the seat and the leg alone by rotations of the horse's haunches around his shoulders, with the bend typical of the shoulder-in. We did not require the kind of bend, which is more difficult, that enables the neck and the head to see the arrival of the haunches. This is now the exercise to accomplish it: the reversed pirouette.

This pirouette goes back to Baucher; it did not feature with La Guérinière, and German equitation, which was of French tradition – at least up to the first third of the 20th century – still ignores it. We know the reasons for this: it is believed that this pirouette, that is, with the haunches going around the shoulders, provokes a stretching of the horse, namely, a hollowing of the muscles of the loins, and that it throws the horse back on to his shoulders.

This may be true if one begins the reversed pirouettes too soon, that is, before the horse has attained a semblance of his equilibrium and the *mise en main*. It is obvious that forcing the rotation of the haunches with a hollow horse, neck and poll rigid, more or less planted on his limbs, will only make him stubborn. We have seen likewise what happens when the rein-back is introduced too soon; but it would also be ill-fated were the ordinary pirouette begun with a hollow horse.

Asking for the reversed pirouette once a united equilibrium is established will not throw the horse on to his haunches; rather, it will give an additional sensitivity to the mobilization of the haunches. It is when executing the half-pass that one will reap the first fruits of success, that is, when one deals with the displacements of the haunches on the more difficult side, usually from left to right, where the horse hesitates in displacing his hindquarters or even throws them to the left, thereby blocking the movement. If one has previously worked at making the hindquarters yield by rotation at the more natural bend of the shoulder-in, it will be much easier to approach the reversed pirouette, which is essentially the same exercise but which deals *with the bend when the horse sees his haunches coming towards him* and, consequently, to obtain their displacement with the half-pass.

The reversed pirouette is asked for in the center of the *manège* by halting the horse on an inside track, preferably parallel to one of the long or short sides.

When executing a reversed pirouette, the outside foreleg, in relation to the bend, must not fall out but, rather, mark the step in place and serve as a pivot around which the haunches describe a complete circle. Starting from a flexed and *rassemblé* halt (and after having adjusted his reins, the outside rein supporting to avoid the falling out of the shoulders), the rider slides his outside leg backwards, closing it or tapping lightly behind the girth. Should the horse not understand the vibration of the leg, a few touches with the whip can complete the action. As soon as the horse yields by moving one or two steps, the rider stops the action of the outside leg, then the support of the rein on the same side; the horse maintains his position but relaxes when the movement is interrupted. The rider takes up again the rotation in the same manner, then stops it with a *descente de main et de jambes*. This breaking up of the pirouette into segments reassures the horse and gives him the time to assimilate all the signals. It also allows one to halt him at will at the very last step, which is essential.

Ordinary pirouette.

Once the pirouette, broken up into sections, has been executed, make the horse go forward, reins long, go large, then repeat the same exercise on the other rein.

If the reversed pirouette is requested with legs that push too hard and hands that check, stubborn behavior can arise. The notion *"hand without legs, legs without hand"* must predominate in this exercise, but one abandons it immediately thereafter and has the horse go forward when one sees the slightest sign of him overbending.

Reversed pirouette.

The Ordinary Pirouette

This has a variety of advantages, the most obvious being the mobilization of both sides of the horse's shoulders, but it is also the indispensable step to preparing the pirouettes at the canter.

I find its execution more difficult than the reversed pirouette, undoubtedly because it takes less action from the horse to throw his haunches around his shoulders, rather than the reverse. Likewise, while the legs predominate in the rotation of the haunches, it is the hands and the seat which must carry along the rotation of the shoulders; however, if the action goes beyond a simple signal, it could result in becoming a permanent risk to the rein-back.

With an ordinary pirouette, the horse's shoulders must make a complete rotation around the inside hind leg (in relation to the horse's bend) which is always oriented in the direction of the movement. At first, one places oneself along the wall, which dissuades the horse from throwing his haunches towards the outside. The presence of the wall limits us to making demi-pirouettes which, at first, will suffice. *As is the case with the reversed pirouettes, one must begin the ordinary pirouettes by breaking them into parts.* One asks for one step of the pirouette, one halts, one seeks lightness, one takes up one or two more steps, one re-establishes once again the equilibrium, and one lets the horse complete his demi-pirouette almost without any aid. One must approach ordinary pirouettes at least a little of the *rassembler*, that is, with poll and neck flexed, hind legs united and engaged. Whereas, with respect to a reversed pirouette, one must take off from a complete halt, with the ordinary pirouette it is not a bad idea to start out from a half-halt, or, in the spirit of La Guérinière, from "an almost halt", wherein the horse marks a slowed-down, almost diagonalized step, in place, which will assure him a great deal of mobility.

At first, one must not seek the demi-pirouette in place but, rather, advance lightly, stimulating the horse with the inside leg. Advance with the hind legs describing a semi-circle of 1 or 2 meters, which helps the horse to understand the exercise and avoids any loss of equilibrium which would bring about his falling to the side and overbending.

The aids for the demi-pirouette are a light signal with the inside hand to determine the correct bend, then a placing of both hands towards the inside without force or tension: the outside rein is placed on the base of the neck. At the same time, turn the pelvis and the shoulders slightly in the direction of the movement, while activating the outside leg with strong touches to avoid any swerving to the outside: the inside leg maintains the movement of the inside hind leg.

When this exercise is executed with ease along the wall, go at a walk to the center line, slow the horse down until he is almost moving in place, then (as always, breaking up the movement with periods at the halt), ask for a complete pirouette. Tension on the reins should be even less than before, since the horse no longer has the wall behind him and could over-bend more easily. More pronounced signals with the outside leg will avoid any sideways swerving.

It can be useful to ask for a pirouette when performing a half-pass at the walk on the diagonal of the *manège*; for it is then facilitated by the lateral movement and the bend it entails.

One executes a half-pass. At X one goes into a complete pirouette and continues with the half-pass to the opposite track. After executing pirouettes on straight lines, one must maintain good impulsion, moving forwards and straight. One straightens the horse by pushing with the outside leg, making sure that the horse does not fall on to his inside shoulder. Finally, whether the pirouettes are reversed or ordinary, *executing* them is very demanding and one must not repeat them more than once or twice.

13. The Half-pass

During the phase of *the time to learn*, we have already introduced our horse to the half-pass at the walk on short sections of the diagonals. The exercises of the shoulder-in developed his lateral mobility at the three gaits, the ordinary pirouettes made him sensitive to the displacement of his shoulders, more or less accentuated, indicated by the hand, and the reversed pirouettes made him aware of the displacement of the haunches, indicated by the leg.

Forewarning

The horse must be forewarned that he is to begin the half-pass by undergoing a little preparation which will become a true codified signal. Not only will this preparation place him in the required equilibrium, it will also make him understand that, a few steps farther on, he will have to begin the half-pass. The rider who asks his partner to take the position of the half-pass and, at the same time, to execute it, will only have steps that are hesitant and irregular.

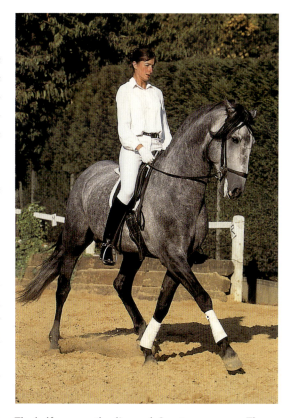

The half-pass on the diagonal, Spartacus, 5 years. The extreme sensitivity of this horse forbids, at this stage, a contact any stronger than that seen in the outside rein.

So far as I am concerned, what I call "securing the half-pass" is the decisive moment for this exercise, which will determine its success or failure.

How can one forewarn the horse? By always being aware of his astonishing ability to perceive things and by getting him used to clear and logical signals. Exploit this goodwill by always preparing ahead of your requests. As an example, I use the horse who is being taught lead changes. If he rushes, it is because we have pushed him too quickly in preparing him with our aids, and, when we ask for a lead change, he will be ahead of the game. Under these circumstances, it is therefore a matter of exploiting what was an unfortunate excess of goodwill.

If one gets the horse used to a sustained lead-in to the action of the aids, without immediately modifying his equilibrium, then one or two steps prior to the start of the half-pass will serve to make him ready and, instead of encountering inertia, the rider will experience immediate complicity in the execution of the movement. This preparation may be only a vibration with the fingers of the inside hand and of the outside leg, which does not yet change the horse's position, but indicates to him that he must get ready.

Carriage Corrections during the Half-pass

Taking into account what has preceded, it is logical that one must avoid resorting to carriage corrections during the half-pass; should difficulties occur, ride the horse straight and forward out of the movement, then try again.

Of course, this is not always possible during a test. There are also the almost constant corrections that have to be made with respect to haunches and shoulders when doing the half-pass on circles [circle haunches-in], when the lateral distance between shoulders and haunches must be maintained.

With respect to the deterioration of the position, corrections must be anticipated. In other words, as soon as the sensitivity of the rider tells him that the haunches or the shoulders are going to drag, lag behind, precipitate, or be ahead, he must act.

If the haunches lag behind, or the shoulders are ahead, then the outside rein slows down the shoulders by moving more or less to the side, the outside leg reinforces the action and touches with the whip are given on the outside.

If the haunches are ahead, or the shoulders lag behind, then the inside rein opens, the outside rein acts at the base of the neck in the direction of the movement, and the inside leg acts at the girth.

The inside hand must always return to the withers. Its essential role is to preserve the bend and *to prevent it from inverting when the outer rein acts* together with the inside leg at the girth – which holds the bend and can also contribute to an increase in the forward impulsion, should this become insufficient.

The Constant Angle

When doing the half-pass, "the horse displaces simultaneously his shoulders and his haunches on the same side", says General Decarpentry. However one should add that the novice should avoid making aid corrections that are too strong or repetitious, which could be translated as either too early or too late for the shoulders and the haunches to act. The horse must displace himself *maintaining rigorously the same obliqueness*, forelegs and hind legs having the same cadence. This re-enforces further the importance of the horse's position and equilibrium before he has carried out the first step of the half-pass. Having taken care to forewarn the horse, the actual aids must then be applied harmoniously; one must avoid breaking them up into too many segments.

At the outset, it was necessary to proceed with a succession of actions which had the aim of mobilizing almost successively each of the horse's parts: the inside rein, which indicates the direction of the bend; the outside rein, which limits it and eventually holds back the shoulders; the outside leg, which moves the horse laterally, while the inside leg, at the girth, holds the bend and adds impulsion.

Now that our pupil is familiar with this exercise, we no longer have to break the succession of aids into fragments. The horse has been "forewarned" that he must execute a half-pass and, literally, "put in situation" to receive the aid for the stride which will precede the first lateral step. This is what I call "the monobloc aid" of the body.

Before leaving the track to execute the half-pass as a single movement, I rotate my torso slightly in the direction required, while, simultaneously, my fingers give the bend of the neck in the same direction. My inside leg vibrates at the girth to prevent the horse from going prematurely into the lateral movement.

The inside rein fixes the bend of the neck, then, with the outside rein, I act to slow down the shoulders and keep them parallel to the two long sides of the arena, while the outside leg determines the half-pass.

It is then that my inside leg, which holds the horse's inflexion, also helps to control the lateral movement, assisted by the outside rein.

With the following strides I take the horse, already "molded" in his bend, onto the diagonal. I have left the track at an angle of 35 degrees in relation to it, with an harmonious inflexion of the ensemble; I must continue maintaining this angle along the entire course, avoiding problems that could retard or advance the movement of the horse's forehand or hindquarters.

The Bend at the Half-pass

The inflexion of the ensemble of the horse must be the same from the poll to the insert of the tail, which rather strangely limits the bend of the neck when one realizes how limited is the possibility of lateral vertebral flexion.

The horse must look where he is going. Any excessive action of the inside rein increases the bend of the neck until it "breaks", causing a stopping action of the lateral displacement and a loss of impulsion! In order to move laterally, why must one always place the shoulders in front of the haunches, regardless of the bend? Because, if the axis of the horse remained parallel to the tracks or – even worse – if the haunches passed in front of the shoulders, the crossing of the outside lateral legs in front of inside laterals would be impossible, and the horse would hit his inside legs against his outside legs.

How is it possible that, without turning around to see the haunches/shoulders alignment one can be sure that all is in order? It suffices to verify that the outside ear of the horse, placed in front of the inside knee of the rider, forms an imaginary line, parallel to the two sides between which one displaces oneself. This is a little personal and quite beneficial trick, which can be done without turning the head, to control the correction of the horse's obliquity. This helps the novice, and could be useful to many an experienced *écuyer*!

If the horse displaces himself laterally when, for example, moving on a diagonal, without any consideration for the *rassembler*, he can be held straight simply by placing his shoulders a little more in front of his haunches, which will allow him to cross his limbs. Should he displace himself on curved lines (a demi-volte, or a circle), that is, when his forelegs and his hind legs describe two concentric circles, a flexion is necessary to correct this.

The Difficulties of the Half-pass

Some horses have greater difficulty than others in executing lateral movements. This may be a consequence of their conformation, or because of contractions. It is absolutely useless forcing such horses to do the movements. One must know what one can preserve and what one must concede.

If we began the half-pass as recommended in *the time to learn*, by breaking up the movement into sections, this will be a guarantee against any struggle. If the shoulder-in is now being executed correctly, the only new difficulties that can possibly arise are lack of impulsion because of resistance, inertia, or loss or excess of the bend. If the horse does not become active again through re-enforcement of the aids, one must not hesitate to interrupt the lateral movement and take off right away, straight and forward. If the problem relates to maintaining the bend of the neck in the correct direction, one had better *yield temporarily with this bend* and allow it to invert itself as in a shoulder-in, *but one must not yield when it comes to keeping the horse parallel between the two long sides.*

Finally, look for any occasion to use a descente de main et de jambes on both tracks, which is where the rider always tends to clutch at the reins and grip at the horse's flanks.

Cadence

Obviously, it is at the walk that the young horse will be in the most advantageous situation to understand what is expected of him in this rather special position. This is how we taught it to him. And it is to the walk that one must return each time one runs into any difficulty.

Should the horse become distressed when executing the half-pass (two-track movement) at the trot, one must stop him, relax him, and take up the half-pass once more at the point where it was interrupted, but at the walk; then return to the half-pass at the trot or canter.

Contrary to what one might imagine, as soon as the canter is reasonably cadenced, the half-pass at this gait on a straight line is easier to do than the half-pass at the trot.

It is of primary importance that the cadence of the *rassemblé* walk, trot, or canter – gaits that require the practice of exercises on two tracks – remain unaltered, regardless of the transitions executed on either one or two tracks. Any modification of cadence, any precipitation or slowing-down, are signs of the loss of the *rassembler*, the equilibrium, or the impulsion.

It is at the shoulder-in that yielding of hand and legs can be practiced most beneficially in order to contribute to the lightness and the brilliance of the gait.

A horse who is flexed and moving on two tracks, maintains his *rassembler* with a *descente de main* more easily than when he is moving straight and on one track.

The Position of the Rider at the Half-pass

I am not trying to contradict anyone with respect to a precept which recommends that one place one's bodyweight on the side of the movement;

my disagreement lies in the fact that the novice has erroneously and systematically misinterpreted this recommendation. While basically in agreement with this precept, I believe it should be formulated differently. One must hold oneself perfectly straight, keep one's vertebral column aligned with that of the horse, and imagine the movement of the pelvis and the seat that you will make if seated on a stool placed on a smooth floor. Holding your arms crossed, you must move it sideways without the help of your hands. It is the mobilization of your outside buttock, moving in the direction of the movement, that will make the stool slide: the right buttock which pushes the stool towards the left. This movement must not provoke a see-sawing effect towards the outside by the rider; rather, he must keep his shoulders parallel to those of the horse and look into the direction of the movement.

The Different Exercises at the Half-pass

These can be practiced on more or less long straight lines, on curved lines, and on a combination of both. Most of them can be executed at the three gaits and at the passage. *One must not abuse exercises on two tracks, be they the shoulder-in or the half-pass.* While they are excellent from the point of view of gymnastics, if well executed, they also constitute an important expenditure of energy since they involve the horse in taking up positions which are exceptional in terms of his natural state. They are thus constraining and tiring. Any abuse, either doing them for a long period, or with forced demands, could bring with it the progressive extinction of the horse's spontaneity.

When dealing with a young horse, not very *rassemblé* and working on two tracks, if a loss of impulsion occurs, one must go to the rising trot for a few strides, rising on the leg on the side of the half-pass. If the horse has been well worked with respect to transitions at the trot on one track, seated or rising, he will soon re-activate his half-pass at the trot.

The Demi-volte

Starting from the middle of the short side, executing a half-pass, is the second phase of this exercise, following the one we already practiced when we began his schooling.

At the end of the demi-volte, the inside rein and the leg on the same side, at the girth, maintain the bend; the outside leg, behind the girth, with the support of the outside rein, determines the lateral movement. On arrival at the wall, one eases the inside rein and adjusts the outside rein to straighten the horse.

The Half-pass Executed on the Full Diagonal of the Arena

Moving from one long side to the other, lacking reference marks, is started two horse's lengths after the corner. Aside from the points of departure and arrival, this is the same exercise as the preceding one.

The Half-pass, Head to Wall

Called the "travers" by the Germans, this was not practiced by La Guérinière or discussed by the Germanic School, under the impression that he preferred the deviation at the straight walk. One could apply the same reasoning to all exercises done on two tracks and obtained by force with hand and spurs. Actually, whether the wall of the *manège* is in front of the head or in front of the croup as the horse does the half-pass, or whether the horse executes the half-pass on the center line, where there is no wall at all, all these reservations are rather childish. Ultimately, there are just two options, of which only one should be done: either the horse moves lightly and obediently, controlled by the aids, or he is forced and, regardless of his position with respect to the walls of the *manège*, he will always act correctly in the first instance, and poorly in the second.

That said, it should be understood that the presence of the wall at the horse's shoulder is a moral as well as a physical barrier which helps him flex and one must be careful of the tendency of the haunches to come in too much.

The Half-pass on the Volte with Croup in

One goes from the half-pass, horse's head to the wall (travers position) to a half-pass on a volte, tangentially to the track. The horse executes the half-pass, head towards the outside; his forelegs describe another smaller, concentric circle. This exercise combines well with an ordinary pirouette, when the horse screws round upon his hind leg/pivot without raising it.

The Half-pass, Croup to Wall

This is the "renvers" for the Germans. The horse does the half-pass from the center of the short side, moving to the long side. A horse's length before arriving at the long side, one slows down the shoulders with the outside rein, inside hand and leg maintain the bend of the horse, which is the same when at the half-pass croup to wall.

The half-pass on the Volte with Croup out

One goes from the half-pass, croup to wall, to a half-pass on the volte that is tangential to the track. The horse's head is turned to the inside. His hind legs describe a large circle and his forelegs a smaller concentric circle. This

Exercises at the half-pass.

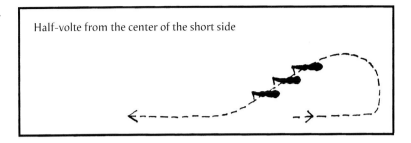

Half-volte from the center of the short side

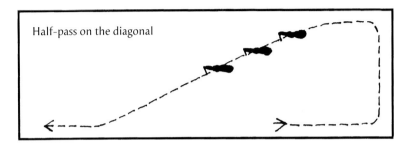

Half-pass on the diagonal

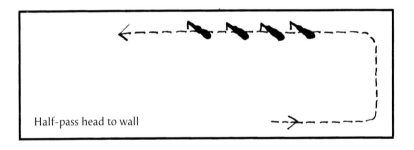

Half-pass head to wall

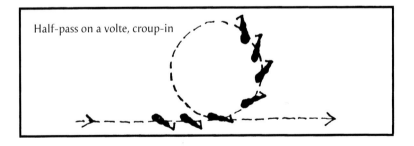

Half-pass on a volte, croup-in

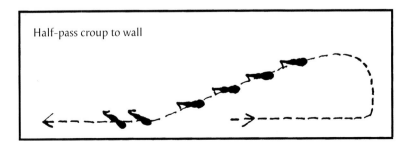

Half-pass croup to wall

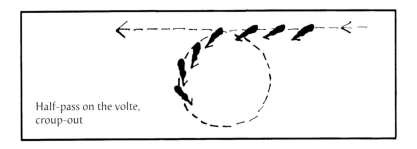

Half-pass on the volte,
croup-out

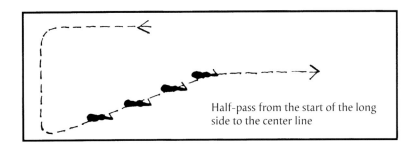

Half-pass from the start of the long
side to the center line

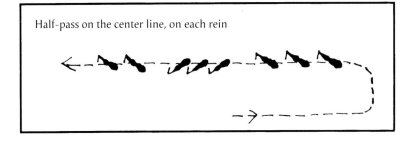

Half-pass on the center line, on each rein

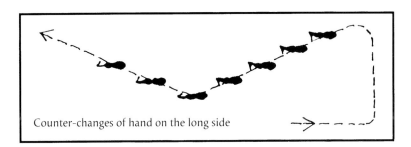

Counter-changes of hand on the long side

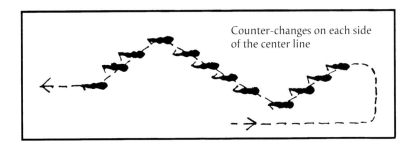

Counter-changes on each side
of the center line

is a difficult exercise, similar to the half-pass on the volte, croup-in, which assumes a horse who is considerably advanced, going on two tracks, whose equilibrium is similar to that of a horse doing a reversed pirouette.

The Half-pass from the Start of the Long side to the Center Line

Straighten the horse on the center line and walk straight. The chief objective of this half-pass lies in the difficulty of straightening the horse on the center line without a supporting wall.

The Half-pass on the Center Line

Moving from one end of the *manège* to the other, on each rein. When the horse has been properly suppled, one can invert his bend completely at every two or three strides; this is an alternative to lateral work, from left to right and right to left, having a most brilliant effect when the horse is perfectly *rassemblé* and cadenced.

The Counter-changes of Hand on Two Tracks on a Long Side

One does the half-pass from the beginning of the long side in to the center line; upon arrival on this line, and without any change of gait or cadence, one inverts the bend and the movement to return to the long side, still doing the half-pass.

The counter-changes at the canter require a lead change on the center line. One can also, without changing the lead, return to the long side at a shoulder-in.

At a walk or a trot, the inversion of the bend is done with the hand acting on the neck simultaneously with the outside leg, which, before becoming the inside leg, inverts the flexion of the ribs. The other leg, now the outside one, is placed behind the girth.

This is translated by the following aids: a stride before the line where the change of hand occurs, the hand which is still the outside one inverts the bend, and the leg on the same side moves the haunches to the other side before returning to the girth. Together with these hand and leg effects, the hand which was the inside one advances to allow the appearance of the new bend, while the leg on the same side, controlling the inversion of the haunches, is placed behind the girth.

Counter-changes on Each Side of the Center Line

Following the length of the *manège*, after one has taken the center line, one executes three steps of the half-pass to the left, then six to the right, six to the left, then three to the right, to find again the center line and advance straight along it.

The Half-pass without Advancing

The horse displaces himself laterally without advancing even a centimeter. This can be executed to educate a horse, or a rider who controls the mechanism of his aids for the half-pass poorly. Of course, the horse must be placed quite obliquely in relation to the sides of the *manège* between which he displaces himself.

In that a harmonious and easy inflexion is indispensable to executing the three gaits, one must not hesitate to return to the bend of the shoulder-in on a straight line and on circles as soon as the horse becomes rigid when doing the half-pass.

One cannot ever insist too much on the important contribution of the shoulder-in and the half-pass to the rassembler of the horse. "The practical use of lateral gaits is so essential that one can judge the schooling of a horse by the degree of their perfection." (Gustav Steinbrecht, *The Gymnasium of the Horse* – 1885).

14. The Range of the Three Gaits

During the period of *the time to learn*, we studied the three gaits in their more elementary form, because at that stage the young horse had not yet been baptized into the channel of his aids. At that time he ignored the regular cadences and the rigorously precise distances covered.

He was only familiar with the simple variations of transitions of gaits which allowed him to go from an ample walk, reins long and neck stretched, to a more shortened walk, his neck slightly supported, and from an energetic rising trot on straight lines to a slightly more elevated sitting trot, allowing him to turn corners or go on circles of 12 meters calmly and without swerving to the side.

At the canter, which he started from a trot on the circle, he lengthened his horizontal equilibrium on straight lines, that is, placing some weight on the shoulders, then for better support, one put him on large circles.

Some preliminary transitions within gaits were sought, more to break the routine of unformed cadences than to create a precise range of gait variations, which were still a distant goal.

As we saw when we studied the halt – which, at first, was simply a position of relaxed immobility, but is now a rigorous position, straight, limbs united, hind legs engaged, neck raised, poll flexed – the walk, trot, and canter must from now on be worked with the same demands for precision in the range that is appropriate to them.

The few years we have spent giving daily gymnastic exercises to our pupil, to supple him and develop his muscles in order to establish a constant communication with him, allowing us to be heard or to understand his reactions, have, indeed, created a condition of receptivity and permeability.

The Walk

As always, we would quite willingly have placed ourselves on the side of M. de la Guérinière who, with his usual clarity and precision, states that there are two kinds of walks, "the walk in the countryside and the school walk". Alas, article 403 of the regulations of the F.E.I. (and taken over by the French Federation), decreed that there were four walks: the *rassemblé* walk, the medium walk, the extended walk, and the free walk. There is nothing incorrect with this enumeration and we consider ourselves lucky that they held to that number, for nothing prevented them from coming up with four more or forty more intermediary walks. Indeed, if one examines the spectrum of steps of a horse from the maximum of an extended walk up to the *rassemblé* walk, the possibilities of classification become mind-boggling. Add in the variety of breeds and varying ways in which the joints articulate from one horse to another, and we have been given the notion of infinity.

"The school walk is different from the one used in the countryside in that the action of the former is more sustained, shorter and slower and more *rassemblé*... When the horse is obedient at this lesson and one wants to turn him into a hacking horse, take him on a long and straight line and give him a walk that is extended and lengthened." (La Guérinière. *School of Horsemanship* – 1733).

But, it is said, one must be part of one's century, that is, if you want to be active on these perilous arenas, one must not forget the medium walk and the free walk. Let us add, and never return to this, that the same holds true for the multiplication of trots and canters.

Now allow me to talk about the gait that has perhaps the most harmonious range of all, from the "*rassembler*" to the "extended" and let you hold to the medium, the mid-medium or the intermediary range you have chosen...

The walk is the most indispensable gait for teaching the aids, the movements, and the exercises. The rapid gaits always bring about a greater nervous tension, and cadences that are more delicate to sustain. At the walk, the horse is calm, his attention readily available, his receptivity outstanding. But we have gone beyond this stage and no longer use the free walk or the medium walk, except during periods of relaxation or rest.

Now that you work at your school exercises, whether at the walk, trot, or canter, there is only one correct tempo, whether it is at the walk, trot, or canter, and that is the school (or *rassemblé*) walk, trot, and canter. Of course, I do not exclude the intermediary gaits, including the indispensable extension to maintain stretching, as well as maintaining the horse's attention without the use of words. Likewise, when you work on two tracks, it is the school gaits, that is the *rassemblé*, that you use.

We achieved the *rassemblé* walk by means of gymnastic exercises which freed the movements, but also with frequent transitions from the working trot to the *rassemblé* trot, and to the walk. At first we practiced transitions at the elementary gaits, reins quite long, so that they emerge from a step that is alert and energetic, avoiding irregular strides. Little by little, thanks to the game of "taking up and giving" the horse understood the nature of a calm, regular and ample walk. Since his trot has become more sustained and *rassemblé*, the moment has arrived for him to do the transitions from the *rassemblé* trot to the *rassemblé* walk.

This is where the quality of the rider's position operates at a maximum because, in order to go from the trot to the walk without losing the *rassemblé* equilibrium, or going against the hand, the horse must be attentive, as though for a halt, to the deep engagement of the rider's seat and the vibrating action of thighs/legs, alternating with half-halts on the outside rein – the inside hand always immobile. However, should the horse respond to this action by leaning on the hand, repeat the half-halt, keeping the inside hand still, thereby avoiding a false bend of the neck and maintaining its position. All this must be repeated until the transition is light.

While respecting the slogan "hand without legs, legs without hand" when involved in these actions, it is, nonetheless, fundamental to bring the action of hand and legs very close together. Keeping the inside hand immobile is just as important.

At the *rassemblé* walk, the horse moves, with markedly raised legs, making energetic steps with his hind legs. At all times must he be able to go into extended and regular strides, stretching his neck, yet maintaining contact; he should then be able to take up as easily once more his *rassemblé* walk.

When the *rassemblé* walk attains a better level, the rider begins to feel an outstanding sense of release. The strike-off straight and light at any gait becomes a reality; the pirouette at the walk, and also at the canter, from a halt, becomes possible. It is also with this equilibrium that the piaffe can be broached, when a shortened step transforms this gait at four beats into a gait that is strictly diagonalized. It is the air of the piaffe as described by G. Steinbrecht.

The Trot

The trot, like the walk, is officially classified into four categories: the *rassemblé* trot, the working trot, the medium trot, and the extended trot. The F.E.I. definition of the *rassemblé* trot does not raise too many problems. "The horse executes strides that are shorter than with the other trots, but he is lighter and more mobile." This is rather a poor definition when attempting to be precise, but it does resemble the so-called *rassemblé* trot practiced today, which no longer entails the light augmentation of the moment of suspension, the raising of the play of limbs and their light and elastic placing on the ground, which characterize and define the real *rassemblé* trot.

The working trot is defined by the F.E.I. rules as "an intermediary gait between the *rassemblé* trot and the medium trot wherein a horse not yet trained and ready to execute the *rassemblés* movements, can still present himself with a good equilibrium and in hand". Then follow some useful sophistries such as "equal and elastic strides", "active haunches", "impulsion emanating from the hindquarters", "strides as regular as possible", etc.

The only precise rule of concern relates to the medium trot: "head somewhat more in front of the vertical than at the *rassemblé* trot and the working trot" (which appears to assume that the horse working at medium trot is not yet schooled); "head and neck slightly lowered". The extended trot: "maintaining the same cadence, lengthens its strides to the maximum, thanks to a very strong impulsion from the hindquarters. The rider allows the horse to lower and stretch his neck without seeking a point of support on the bit." I might add that if he takes off as he should, from a trot that is truly *rassemblé*, I do not believe that he has to lengthen his neck by much, but will remain slightly on his haunches.

My statements contain no polemics, but I find it difficult to tackle the range of gaits while ignoring the official international position concerning them, for it is upon their rulings that we are judged in competition. Furthermore, reading their rules carefully produces no clear understanding of them: "each gait is determined in relation to the others" – but none is defined with precision.

A careful observation of the best riders in competitive dressage reveals the weak difference between their medium trot and their extended trot and the *non-existence* of the *rassemblé* trot, confused with the working trot. This does not seem to bother the judges too much, but it is there that the real explanation lies pertaining to the general weakness of the piaffes and the passages.

Let us return to the trot of our pupil. In the earlier phase of his breaking in, we were satisfied with a rather rigorous rising trot merely to maintain the regularity and straightness of strides. We went on to the sitting trot on circles, careful that our weight and its impact would not bring about any alteration to the horse's back through locking. If this happened, we returned to the energetic rising trot, then back to the sitting trot as soon as the gait found once more its impulsion and cadence.

In resolving basic problems, we gradually tackled voltes that were a little tighter, then proceeded to gymnastics for exercises on two tracks at the trot in all the combinations already studied, with the shoulder-in and the counter-shoulder-in, combined with the half-pass.

Then we sought the cadenced trot at the shoulder-in, with halts and strike-offs from a halt, still executing the shoulder-in; counter-changes of hand on two tracks, first with the half-pass towards the inside of the *manège*, returning parallel to the track with a shoulder-in (thus the bend unchanged), then a counter-change of hand with a change of the bend. Then followed transitions from the trot to the rein-back practically without time to halt between the two, with an immediate return to the trot, etc.

The Working Trot

All this kinetic movement practiced out of respect for the characteristics of lightness has placed our horses in a position which allowed us to go from an ample and regular sitting trot (one of these intermediary trots which one can call a medium trot or working trot) to the *rassemblé* trot, elevated and supple.

The Rassemblé Trot

One must *never* confuse the *rassemblé* trot with the abominable trot often executed instead of the *rassemblé* trot (or the passage). This "*passagé*" trot is just the appearance of a failed attempt at a passage forced between hand and legs. It is characterized by a kind of diagonalization, with weight on the hand and a false floating of four legs.

The Medium Trot

Once the medium trot has been obtained, the balance of this gait variation, which produces upon demand cadenced limb movements of equal amplitude, makes transitions to it from the *rassemblé* trot possible, because the limb movements are the result of flexion of the joints.

We broach transitions from the *rassemblé* trot to the medium trot preferably by starting with a shoulder-in on a diagonal or with a half-pass from a corner to an inside track, executed at a *rassemblé* trot. The engagement of the hind legs, and the *rassembler* which the exercise on two tracks produces, gives a most vigorous extension when one straightens the horse on a straight line, because of the stretching (as of a bow string or spring) of the hind legs and the extension of the forelegs.

The Extended Trot

This is how extensions of the trot begin. We will return to them when we come to *the time to perfect.*

Here we are attempting to go through the range of trots because we now control the elastic stretching as well as the relaxation of the horse's resources (his joints, muscles, etc.) which produce cadence and rhythm. It is these transitions which form the "dancing horse" by means of the refinement of aid contacts which allow receptivity, impulsion, and obedience.

"The horse-partner" is a state wherein the horse responds immediately to all the demands of his *écuyer,* readily surrendering his combining his equilibrium and movement to the rider's will. It is when the school trot has been successfully achieved that we will broach the true passage and enrich the piaffe, which we will see when we come to *the time to perfect.*

The Canter

A range of four canters is officially set down, with the exception of the counter-canter or the false canter. They are the *rassemblé* canter, the working canter, the medium canter, and the extended canter.

The Rassemblé Canter

This is characterized by a shortening of the strides and not by a decrease in impulsion. The strides gain in elevation what they lose in amplitude. Lightness increases in accordance with engagement of the hindquarters and as the horse's frame becomes rounder with the *mise en main.*

The Working Canter

This is described by the F.E.I. as "intermediary between the *rassemblé* canter and the medium canter" (itself described as intermediary between the working canter and the extended canter!)

Let us state more explicitly that it is the first refinement of the natural canter obtained in the *manège* through frequent strike-offs, first from the trot, then from the walk, with a return to the striking-off gaits, on circles first, tightened then enlarged, individually and as spirals, then the counter-canter, first on straight lines, then on circles.

In a word, the working canter is developed through all the exercises which work all the principal joints of the hindquarters, improving the elasticity and strength of the horse, as well as his receptivity.

The Medium Canter

I would prefer to say that it is the natural canter, which forms the basis in this search for impulsion and regularity. It is responsible for the straight positioning of shoulders and haunches, contributing satisfactorily to the even distribution of weight; yet, even if the load is still greater on the shoulders, this is necessary to allow the neck to preserve a certain amount of freedom. This is, after all, the regularization of the outdoor canter.

The Extended Canter

This is the maximum development of the strides at the canter without any change in rhythm, lightness, and the *mise en main*. The quality of this canter is a direct function of the quality of the *rassemblé* canter which it precedes.

I will add to this enumeration of the canter the slowed-down canter, or the canter in place. Far from being a fantasy gait, it precedes unquestionably the real pirouettes at the canter. It is obtained by increasing the *rassembler* with a superior impulsion accompanied by a reduction of stride length, alternating with light half-halts and a yielding hand. We will return to this.

We have seen how the canter, while more comfortable, less disturbing and more easily sustained by novices than the trot, was yet the most delicate gait to practice in a framework requiring gait variations and manège figures. We will get to that.

Centrifugal force, a consequence of the speed of this gait can, on curves and in corners, cause significant displacements such as the hooking up of legs and hands, which contradict the intentions and signals given by a rider whose seat is not perfect.

A horse's interest in striking off at the canter in an enclosed area or a small circumference and, above all, with a more engaged equilibrium, is infinitely diminished, thus less than when striking off on a long straight path in the forest!

Almost all riders, even, and especially, the most advanced ones, have been shaped by this atrocious concept of compressing their legs against the horse's flanks; it is virtually impossible to have a nice cadence in this position, since it is the lumbar region of the rider who, by means of a real forward undulation, must enrich and modulate the rhythmic impulsion while keeping the legs quiet.

Our pupil is now at the medium canter, cadenced and regular. He can easily depart from the diagonals of the *manège* at a counter-canter; he can do the half-pass and can execute the shoulder-in at the canter with ease.

One must now take him on to the *rassemblé* canter, passing through the intermediary stages, which must not be done too quickly.

Horses, like riders, must take the time to acquire a natural equilibrium as we have just discussed, otherwise they fall back into the trot or into a hurried gait. The exercises at the canter must also be brief at the start, until the horse is capable of carrying himself in his new equilibrium.

One takes off at a slow step which already possesses the straightness, the slight elevation, and the common resonance between rider and horse.

After a few good strides and the use of precise and light aids, one returns to the walk, which one makes more pronouncedly *rassembler* in order to strike off once more, which makes the horse more sensitive to the signals of the aids. One multiplies these strike-offs and halts, attempting each time to refine one's aids, and simply respecting the slogan "hand without legs, legs without hand". One canters large with a cadence that is better than that of the working canter, taking special care never to decrease the energy of the strides by seeking a shorter canter. As elsewhere, here, too, one momentarily sacrifices the exercise to impulsion.

At both ends of the *manège*, one executes circles from 20 to 12 meters with a continuous zeal, which is a test that reveals the temperament and level of the horse. The classical play of the joints of the hindquarters, the harmonious flexion of the ensemble on the curve, the horse's acceptance of the signals on the bit, are all indications that we are on the right path. Doing voltes from 10 to 6 meters in the corner is another difficulty to overcome and from which we can also receive information with respect to the development of the *rassemblé* canter.

After completing these curved figures, one will develop the amplitude of the canter by vigorously extending it, as one does to return to the medium or natural canter. That is to say, by tolerating a return to the horizontal of the entire vertebral column. With an equilibrium that is more on his shoulders, one will place the horse on a large circle, reins long, without bringing him in hand. Only the seat and light lateral indications with the wrists keep him on the circle. Transitions from the shortened canter, supported by the aids, to the horizontal canter controlled by the circle, will maintain the purity of his actions and allow, after this effort, the relaxation of his back.

When these first exercises have sufficiently improved the suppleness and propulsive strength of the canter, it is time to transfer, very progressively, the weight back to the hindquarters.

Even if I repeat myself, I do so to attract your attention when I discuss the timescale involved in seeking the *rassembler* at the canter. Lest you forget, its development, described in a few pages, takes two or three years to accomplish.

Any thoughtless forcing always leaves serious traces behind at the walk and trot, which are indelible in the horse's mind, and are sometimes even accompanied by physical injury when these excesses occur at the canter.

One seeks the lowering of the hindquarters and the raising of the forehand. These are not attained through solicitations from the reins; rather, they are the result of flexion of the hind legs.

All the exercises at the walk and trot contribute to the development of the horse's receptivity, and it is thanks to them that our horse is already in good shape; thus he will not react to our first requests at the canter by resisting the aids, holding his hind legs rigidly, and opposing the hand. With this in mind, we will connect, at the canter, a series of figures which the horse already knows at the walk and trot – and which we have even practiced at the canter in brief sequences.

We begin by verifying the straightness of the working canter on one track by bringing, if necessary, the shoulders in front of the haunches with the outside rein towards the inside; this occurs on the straight as on curves. In the corners, as on curves, one heeds the action of the inside leg at the girth while one's lumbar vertebrae, supported by the outside leg, give the rhythm to the canter.

The Crooked Canter

At the slightest awkwardness, at the slightest attempt to force a shortening of the canter, the horse will throw his inside hind leg or his haunches to the side, especially to the right. This is how he reacts to escape the *rassembler* imposed upon him without any preparation.

Should this occur, the shoulder-in on the same side will be of no help; on the contrary, it would accentuate the tendency of the haunches to bend to the inside. The first thing to do is to interrupt any attempt at seeking the *rassembler* by pushing the horse vigorously straight forward and lengthening on the outside rein with the outside leg, but without letting go either with the inside leg or the inside rein. This will straighten the horse easily.

The second reaction will be to return to the circle, where the rider will find it easier to take up his horse again and put him onto the aids. Now that the gait and the distribution of the equilibrium is re-established, it will be necessary to return to the straight line, maintaining the same rhythm as on the circle and at *manège* corners, which are quarters of a circle.

It is on the right rein that the horse tends to become more crooked at the canter. However, should a right shoulder-in worsen the situation, a left shoulder-in at the canter (flexing the horse to the left), will be an excellent corrective exercise.

Finally, at the counter-canter to the right, the wall can prevent the horse from throwing his haunches to the right. Go often from the canter to the right to the counter-canter on the same rein, then do a left shoulder-in at the canter. When the horse counter-canters straight without rushing, turn to the center line of the *manège* without changing rein. One leaves the track at A. At the counter-canter to the right, the horse will need the support of the left rein which, at the same time, prevents him from bending too much to the right. One moves the left leg back less than one does at the canter on the correct lead, and occasionally it may be necessary to move the right leg back a little (this is the only instance when the inside leg goes back a few centimeters).

Premature Lead Changes

I have not yet said anything about lead changes although many riders, having obtained or, rather, unleashed one involuntarily, do not wait long enough to solicit them.

I, myself, have made this kind of mistake during my first schooling program and thus want to prevent you from making the same mistakes.

Everything I have said about the usual tendency of deviating the haunches and the means of avoiding this, or how to straighten them again, will make you see the trap: the aids for straightening are very similar to those for lead changes. I also wish you much joy if you have made the mistake of attempting a few lead changes before having obtained the start of a *very straight rassemblé* canter.

Now that the canter is correct on the track, along the walls, on circles and voltes, one must go to the inside tracks, turning to the center line or a few meters from the wall in order to control the quality of the turn without the support of the angles of the *manège*, and also to achieve straightness without the support of the wall. Starting from circles at the canter, describe spirals by reducing the circles to voltes of 5 to 6 meters in diameter, then enlarge them to return to the original circle.

From large circles, and in the interior of these circles, execute the figure of eight at the canter. Still within the large circle, change rein, describing the figure S, maintaining the constant rhythm of the canter.

From circles begun with the shoulder-in at the canter, to prepare the bend, continue initially to haunches-in at the canter, then finally to the croup-out position, which is an element that prepares for pirouettes at the canter.

At the far ends of the tracks, beyond the first corner of the short side, do demi-voltes that become tighter and tighter to return to the track, executing the half-pass with the horse parallel to the long side. Hold the horse's shoulders back with the outside rein just a stride before they arrive at the track, and follow this with some strides at the canter, croup to the wall.

Return to the counter-canter, slowing it down with slight half-halts with the outside rein, in the direction of the inside hind leg, while giving it rhythm with the cadenced actions of the outside haunch. [Here, outside and inside relate to the bend.]

Straighten this canter by lengthening it with a deep engagement of the lumbar vertebrae, maintaining a light *mise en main*.

Go to the center line at a canter. Halt, rein back, then strike off again at the canter, straight, from the rein-back.

The varied combinations of these exercises, mixed with transitions, are numerous; well executed, they sharpen the horse's finesse and put him in a state which will allow him to absorb single lead changes and demi-pirouettes, which we will study very soon.

15. Diagonalization

It is perhaps appropriate to remind oneself that diagonalization [diagonal mobilization] of the limbs of a horse is the simultaneous movement of the foreleg on one side with the hind leg on the other. The trot is a diagonal movement; the piaffe and the passage are also airs characterized by diagonalization of the limbs, with the piaffe being executed in place, while advancement with elevation and the moment of suspension are evident at the passage.

Work in hand. Diagonalization at the piaffe without support of leg bandages. The interesting point here is that one can see the use of the whip on the outside of an off-hind leg to prevent it from escaping to the outside.

We already prepared this diagonal mobilization of legs quite some time ago. First, when doing the work in hand during the period we named *the time to understand*, we taught the horse to walk straight, to execute voltes, shoulder-in and rein-back, to go from halt to trot and back to halt, and, finally, we introduced a light diagonalization, which is the prelude to the piaffe.

All the exercises carried out in hand were simple, yet delicate, and we pursued them all, mounted, throughout the horse's schooling, usually after a brief relaxing period at the lunge, before beginning work in the saddle. However after about a year of training, we returned to these exercises only when circumstances justified it.

At the end of two or three years of the horse's schooling, I sometimes return to these short exercises of the *rassembler*, in hand, even if only to obtain a diagonalization that is more elevated, with a more pronounced moment of suspension.

The Rassembler of the Walk and Trot, Touchstone of the Piaffe and the Passage

With mounted exercises, which we have studied since *the time to understand*, during *the time to learn*, and now with *the time to do*, we have worked at suppling exercises of all types in order to arrive at an easy mobilization of the joints.

We have developed the longitudinal and lateral flexions of the ensemble of the horse. Without provoking a locking (or contraction of) any one of these parts, it is now possible for us to shorten and elevate the three gaits, after having extended them.

The quality of these results is expressed by the *mise en main*, which General Decarpentry defined as "an example of the perfect adjustment of forces in motion".

The *mise en main* constitutes a state of lightness and lack of tension which are evident in the *rassemblé* movements as well as the extended ones. In *the time to do the exercises*, we prepared the *rassemblés* walk and trot which, one also calls the school walk and school trot.

With the diagonal mobilizations that we obtain without difficulty, the equilibrium of our horses developed towards the *rassembler*, for it is true that diagonalization and *rassembler* cannot be disassociated if one wants to achieve the piaffe and the passage.

Observation of hundreds of dressage riders from many parts of the world, who have practiced for quite a while, reveals or confirms that the piaffe is the result of the *rassemblé* walk, the progressive shortening of

At the stage when the young horse goes from mobilization in place to diagonalization. Everton, 4 years.

which (while preserving straightness and lightness), brings about the first mobilizations of the horse's limbs in place.

The same holds true when one tries to develop the trot, a diagonal movement, towards the passage: the *rassemblé* trot is the obligatory phase preparatory to a supple and brilliant passage.

I insist on this point because too many dressage rider believe that by simply pushing and holding back, in tempo, they will create this diagonalization of which they dream. This is not possible, even with very talented horses.

To convince oneself of this, one should attend one of the Andalusian "ferias" where one can find the total range of Spain's horses. Because of their conformation and suppleness, they are much more capable of executing the airs above the ground than are the horses from the North. You will, however, witness very little in the way of regular and rhythmic diagonalizations but, rather, disorderly and annoying gestures – in other words, movements that are rushed, without elasticity, executing little, meaningless hops. These are the results of primitive pressure exerted on the metal in the horse's mouth and by spurs on his flanks.

Almost all riders involved in European competition are no longer familiar with the *rassemblés* walk and trot. They tackle the piaffe and the passage directly, with such a strong tension on the bit – this, their horses can tolerate only when executing extended movements, but it makes *rassemblés* movements impossible. The results are piaffes that are practically glued to the ground, and the passage becoming merely a "*passagé*" trot.

During their initial stages, the piaffe and the passage must be worked on independently from each other; the former, through a progressive shortening of strides at the *rassemblé* walk, the latter, starting out with the *rassemblé* trot.

Both are set in motion by "half-halts whereby the hand holds on to the horse only a little longer but without halting him completely… One can repeat this often without breaking the stride of the horse and, since it is with this aid that one brings back and supports the forehand, one thus obliges the horse to lower the haunches, which is what one actually solicited." Marvelous La Guérinière!

I taught the piaffe and the passage to many horses of different breeds. All of them required three or four years to attain the beginning of a calm and regular flexion in all their joints and musculature which brings about their mobilization.

The Means

It all began with the first regular halts from the walk and the trot, obtained with lightness, perfectly straight, forelegs and hind legs united and square. Then followed transitions from the walk to the rein back without any intermediary halts, returning to moving forward, always without any temporary immobilization, first at the walk then quickly at the trot. Then came the "halts", which had become more *rassemblés*, that is, the hind legs came to a halt squarely and engaged. In this position they were ready to relax and disengage in the exact proportion to their initial engagement, making strike-offs at the trot progressively more elevated.

At this level it became possible to obtain one or two steps of a diagonal mobilization in place with a transition of the trot. This was all the easier – or less difficult – since my partner responded clearly to this request: from the halt he went into the trot, which was a self-imposed action and the exploitation of the movement in place – a feature noticeable with mounted horses who see their neighbors take off while they are still somewhat restrained.

But take heed. In no way should you seek to repeat this slight diagonalization for more than one or two steps, but rather go off right away into a trot that is the shortest possible. Neither must you try to execute right away actual elevation and a moment of suspension with this diagonalization, for this would only provoke dissociation of the limbs. Rather, it is necessary that everything is carried out naturally for the horse and that his whole being becomes supple and muscular in order to achieve the real piaffe, as we will see it subsequently.

Another way towards diagonalization in place occurs at the transition

from the working trot and the school trot to the halt, followed immediately by moving forward with the same rhythm and without the horse becoming totally immobilized. This is the half-halt of La Guérinière which I consider "an almost halt", for La Guérinière describes it as "an action one executes by holding back the bridle hand close to one (which does not mean holding on to the rein), nails brought slightly up *without completely halting the horse* but only holding back and supporting the forehand".

To be successful, the half-halt must produce an action upwards and not backwards. When the horse has been prepared as has been described, this request to slow down, but stopping short of a halt, alternating with a slight solicitation of the legs, together with a diagonalized cadence, produces a true beat of the trot in place. There, too, one must not be tempted to repeat this gesture, but, rather, one must immediately engage the seat and, progressively encircling him with both legs, carry the horse forward with the cadence of the school trot, which was the one used before the half-halt.

An exercise complementary to all the others, which G. Steinbrecht utilizes to create the first strides of the passage, is what he calls the "piaffé walk". I use it to prepare diagonalization. Steinbrecht obviously starts out with a well-suppled horse, whose walk is already *rassemblé*. He puts him at the walk in a semi shoulder-in, where he holds him with halts and

At the stage when the horse goes from diagonalization to the piaffe. Nymphéa, Lusitano mare, 5 years.

165

half-halts which follow each other in quick succession and stimulate engagement of the hindquarters "with semi-stretched reins held by a light hand exerting brief resumptions", and "with a frequent repetition of short and animated actions of hand and legs", until the first strides of suspension take place.

I proceed in the same manner at the strike-off but, above all, I try to shorten the strides of the walk progressively while inciting the horse to engage his hindquarters in animated fashion along the length of the *manège*. I make sure that I maintain the impulsion of the strides at the walk, making them shorter and shorter, while scrupulously dividing the actions of hand without legs and legs without hand. Without fail, the steps diagonalize as they become shorter; I then yield with the hand and go forward at a free walk. I resume then these movements once or twice.

These different approaches of diagonalization in place take up the first two or three years of the horse's schooling. In hand, one can start them already in the first years without any risk – that is, if the rider is alert and experienced. One continues them, mounted, with transitions from the rein-back to the trot, then from the *rassembler* halt to the trot.

I repeat that all these exercises must be executed with a perfect straightness; the horse's reaction is always to avoid the *rassembler* by throwing his haunches towards the inside. One must prevent this by a slight degree of shoulder-in. During the period of "hand without legs" *the horse tends to go backwards if the descente de jambes is not completed with the engagement and tension of the rider's lumbar vertebrae going forwards.*

When linked together progressively and wisely, these modest means allow one to succeed at the *rassembler* and the piaffe without interrupting the continuity of the work.

The Diagonalized Pirouette

The diagonalized pirouette is an interesting example of the result one obtains when approaching the first diagonalization at the early stages of schooling, for it is true that teaching something to a very young horse over a lengthy period can be less traumatizing and better assimilated than teaching it piecemeal when he is more mature.

We have seen that, if one wanted to prevent the inside hind leg from falling out or becoming stuck in place when doing an ordinary pirouette, it was necessary to approach it with a slowed-down step almost in place.

I have also indicated elsewhere the considerable difficulty one can have in attaining a pirouette at the piaffe when the horse is 7 or 8 years old (which is usually when this happens), for this is a complex air. Since it takes two or three years to develop the piaffe, the horse in question was by then 10 years old, and trying to teach him the pirouette at the piaffe caused terrible misunderstandings each time, resulting in contractions.

With my recent horses, namely those who began their schooling at the time of writing this work, I linked the teaching of the ordinary demi-pirouettes, then the complete pirouettes, to a light diagonalization; this allowed me to have horses who, at the age of six or seven, were able to execute pirouettes at the piaffe on each rein without discomfort or concern.

This goes to show that the teaching of these movements or doing these exercises – usually considered difficult – can be accepted psychologically earlier without causing any blockages or traumas. To achieve this, one must merely suggest and give indications rather than impose and use force.

I know how much time it takes to put a young horse to the canter when one imposes the aids and uses force. I am also aware of the difficulties that arise in getting the horse to execute the shoulder-in or the half-pass when force is used, by constraining him with the inside spur and the traction of the reins. I am even aware of the problems that the young horse encounters when he is mounted for the first time and the rider pulls on the inside rein to bend him on the circle...

With gentle aids that guide rather than constrain, we obtain these exercises with a relaxed horse ten months after his breaking in.

The same applies to diagonalization, the base for the *rassembler*, prelude to the piaffe. One must awaken the horse, encouraging him by the most natural means possible and above all, *by the perfection of the seat.*

16. The School Trot, the Doux Passage, and the "Passagé" Trot

We have studied the trot in many of its variations as we did with the other gaits, and we will return to this once more.

I believe that everyone has by now understood that this bias of mine, namely, progressing chronologically, does, indeed, correspond to the actual unfolding of the horse's schooling and justifies the long-range planning of these successive phases, which lead to an equilibrium that becomes more and more refined.

Furthermore, these stages mirror the evolution of the actual schooling begun simultaneously with the first chapters of this work. The progress made by our pupils justifies these frequent returns to each gait, exercise or air, which are only really established after three or four years.

The same holds true for the trot, which we have already tackled on a number of occasions and which we have tried to make more and more *rassemblé*. Indeed, we have now arrived at the *rassemblé* trot, which can be defined as the most shortened, most measured and cadenced trot, a succession of regular gestures, *écoutés* and sustained, wherein the stride gains vertically what it loses horizontally. [The term *écouté* – "heard" was common with the former *écuyers*, denoting the form of trot described here, the idea being that regular, measured and cadenced beat could be identified by its sound.]

The Rassemblé Trot, or the School Trot

Although it is a precursor to the passage, this is different from the passage, in that it does not entail the moment of suspension wherein the horse *seems* to be supported for a moment on each diagonal.

As Maître Oliveira has described it, the school trot is the touchstone of the schooling of the saddle horse which, when this gait is perfected, comes close to being the most complex air of equestrian art, even including those airs of the canter. It is the obligatory phase before tackling the passage and the piaffe.

However, the form of trot, in which slowing-down the actual speed provokes an acceleration in the frequency of steps, has no relationship with the school trot – it is, rather, a gait that is short and rushed and renders the horse, who is compressed between hand and legs, insensitive.

If the true school trot brings out the perfect formation of the horse, it can also bring out his slightest defects pertaining to symmetry in a most pitiful way.

It is first prepared at a medium trot and a working trot, straight and flexed, on circles and voltes. Any veering of the haunches, or resistance of a hind leg on a spiral at the trot, are signs of contraction, that is, of insufficient preparation. In that this gait rests on the sophistication of diagonalization, the slightest contraction of a limb will transform it into a limp.

It is by returning to working on circles, spirals, the shoulder-in at the walk, then at the trot, and at the half-pass, that one will obtain better action and engagement of the defaulting hind leg.

Rassemblés halts from the trot, followed by three steps of a rein-back, immediately linked to a strike-off at the trot, perfectly in hand, straight and light, indicate the equal functioning of the hind legs and the sensitivity of the horse to light aids.

An improvement of the school trot can be verified when it becomes part of a light half-halt and maintains itself by imperceptible means, including the *descente de main et de jambes*. Alternate caresses of the horse's sides by the rider's legs, a deeper engagement of the seat and modulation with fingers are immediately translated into an improvement of the *tride* of the gait [a term that has been more or less lost, signifying the brilliance of a gait]. It develops and perfects itself through transitions from the *rassemblé* trot to a more extended trot and through transitions from the halt and the walk to the trot, and vice versa.

The *rassemblé* trot must not be a lusterless gait with skimpy steps but, rather, it must always be animated and cadenced, even if it is just performed for a few strides. Before the rhythm weakens, one must intensify the impulsion and redeploy the animation, allowing it to unfold into more extended strides.

These variations alert and invigorate the horse, who understands that he has to express his animation now more vertically, now more horizontally, but always with vigor and an excellent tempo. They improve receptivity, contact with the hand, and obedience to the aids. This is where one understands the tremendous value of the trot as a teaching gait, as compared to the walk, the slowness of which is not very favorable for releasing impulsion. The same holds true for the canter, the stability of which one really masters at the end of the horse's schooling, when his equilibrium and speed are his own and are no longer factors of instability.

Departures from the walk and from *rassemblés* halts to the school trot, with frequent transitions and alternate aids of retention and propulsion, allow one to obtain the best action from the hind legs.

In doing these delicate movements, I repeat once more the importance of the immobility of the inside hand, held still at the level of the withers, which is an inviolate point of reference *for the half-halts* given with the outside rein. The inside hand assures that the head-neck bend is preserved, despite the half-halts made when closing the fingers in an upward direction with the outside rein.

However, the true school trot is gradually disappearing. It is seldom seen in the competition arenas where it is nevertheless prescribed under the name of the *rassemblé* trot. One sees all kinds of compressed trots, totally lacking suppleness and grace, and sometimes a trot which the judges may consider *rassemblé*, but in which the amplitude and equilibrium are much closer to the working trot.

The Doux Passage

This charming term [*doux* means "gentle"] defines the first phase of the passage which a horse executes with tact and rhythm. It takes its place here since it can only be obtained after having developed and perfected the *rassemblé* trot. Before the first strides of the passage have been developed in their majestic amplitude, cadenced with elevation, with optimal relaxation at each diagonal, a more or less lengthy period of transition (of at least several months), will be necessary in which the horse can find again, in his new cadence, a stable equilibrium which he achieved at the school trot.

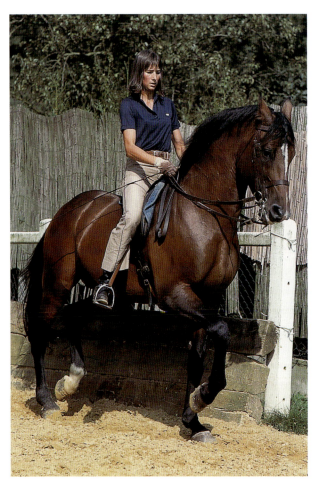

The beginnings of the passage. Tintoretto, 5 years.

The aids which favor the development of the *doux* passage are clearly more rhythmical and are closer in succession than those of the school trot. They will always more or less surprise the horse and provoke some changes in his behavior. This should not worry one, but one should simply reduce unreasonable demands and obtain initially just two or three strides that are slightly suspended.

The first requests to go from the *rassemblé* trot to the doux passage requires the horse to be perfectly parallel to the wall or even with a slight shoulder-in, for the reaction against the *rassembler* is always for the horse to veer his haunches to the inside and the shoulders to the outside.

The rider must link himself even more closely to the movement of his horse through a supple seat. His thighs must be pulled down, knees firmly on the saddle, with lower legs free. *The legs alternately have contact with the horse's flanks when the foreleg on the same side strikes the ground*: right leg when the right foreleg touches the ground, left leg when the left one touches it.

At this stage, after doing a half-halt, the action of the hand must limit itself to preserving the regular cadence of the trot and the flexion of the poll and jaw: in other words, lightness. It must check any precipitate forward movement which the alternate stroking with the legs can provoke; above all, one must not tolerate the slightest weight in the hand.

If this necessary action of the hand is accompanied by a diagonalized stride, it is of prime importance that this is immediately interrupted and a light *rassemblé* trot picked up again. Any tolerance of force against the hand will result in an open and hollow *doux* passage and this will then turn into the "*passagé*" trot. In any case, as soon as the horse indicates a slight response to our aids, we return to a light *rassemblé* trot, so that, from the start, he distinguishes clearly requests for a trot and those for the passage.

As a general rule, I never ask for more than twice, three or four strides on each rein per lesson; I then stop and return with precision to the trot, in order to avoid any compression.

In *the time to perfect the airs* we will return to the passage in greater detail when, in a few more months, our horse will execute the transitions from the *rassemblé* trot to the *doux* passage with ease.

The "Passagé" Trot

One often sees horses involved in competition, even at a high level, execute a totally perverted form of the *rassemblé* trot: This is the "*passagé*" trot with a "false hovering". In general, they do a passage of the same poor quality, with diagonalized steps, a hollow back, dragging hind legs and a tendency to force the hand. The gestures of the forelegs are open because of lack of flexion and the whole movement is rigid.

This deviation of the trot results from a myriad of errors in conception, technique, and also the choice of the type of horse.

In high school equitation, horses with long limbs, whose weight is on their shoulders have been used, thus confusing the low action of the Thoroughbred with the elastic amplitude of steps necessary. The poorly conceived dressage tests gave competitors the erroneous idea of developing exaggerated and premature extensions of the trot without having worked the horses first, or at least simultaneously, in the direction of the *rassemblé* trot.

Finally, the absence of sanctions on the part of the jury against any compression of aids, and the general absence of lightness, result in this evident alteration of the nature of the passage and the *rassemblé* trot.

It is obvious that a horse who has been pushed against the hand by hard legs and thrown onto his shoulders during his entire early schooling, without having known a moment of cadence that is light and shortened, reacts to the trainer's aids when the passage is requested, by becoming totally unbalanced. He understandably confuses the signals for the extended trot on the shoulders with those of the passage, from which emerges the unbalanced gestures with the forelegs and the dragging hindquarters pulled forward by the shoulders.

In conclusion, it is obvious that *the school trot is, indeed, the touchstone of all the rassemblés airs* and that one must never take the risk of stretching a horse excessively so long as one does not have the means of shortening him back to his previous length [making him *rassembler*].

Even a basically wise but inexperienced trainer, who tries to obtain the first strides of the passage, sometimes finds his pupil responding to a simple request for the medium trot with a few steps slightly "*passagés*". In this case, the "*passagé* trot" occurred because of involuntary movements of the rider's legs, which alternately hit the horse's flanks at the moment when the hand acted upon the mouth. The horse confused these aids with those his rider had given him earlier, more or less adroitly, applied to bring about the passage. This incident is not a tragedy if one quickly eliminates the causes of this misunderstanding: in general terms, imprecise and poorly coordinated movements of legs and hand by the rider, which cause the good horse confusion for which he is not responsible, and for which he must not be punished.

If this happens, right away advance your wrists and go into a dynamic trot with a lightening action of seat and legs, avoiding inopportune movements. The "hand without legs, legs without hand" motto, with considerable space between these signals, will re-establish the cadence of the required trot.

17. Single Lead Changes

Our horse has easily worked through the range of canters. At the first request, he is capable of developing amplitude of the gait by extending vigorously, as well as returning gently to the medium canter. At the counter-canter he maintains a cadence identical to that of the true canter, he executes serpentines, circles, and voltes easily, without veering. He is straight on straight lines; he executes the half-pass with ease. Conditions are now in place to enable one to begin the study of lead changes.

The obliquity of the bodies of quadruped mammals in relation to the axis of their walk is natural. It is especially noticeable in the locomotion of the horse at the canter, even at liberty. At this gait, he tends naturally to become crooked. The see-sawing motion of the canter is done diagonally from back to fore and fore to back; it is felt through the seat of the rider, whose weight and shifts of weight increase further the tendency for the horse's haunches to veer inwards.

As we have seen, striking off at the canter requires the outside leg to be placed slightly behind the girth, but this must not aggravate the throwing out of the haunches. This is avoided by putting weight on the inside buttock and unleashing the departure with the inside leg. The supporting outside rein limits any excessive inside bend.

I insist on the straightness of strike-offs at the canter because the aids for lead changes are similar to those of successive canter strike-offs, on the correct lead and counter-lead. In both cases, one must limit as much as possible the obliquity in which the horse always finds himself at the canter.

The Mechanism of the Canter

While well analyzed at the end of the 19th century, thanks to the cinema, this mechanism is still imperfectly known. It is a succession of leaps composed of three beats.

Canter to the right

— first beat: the left hind leg touches ground;

— second beat: right hind leg and left foreleg;

— third beat: right foreleg.

The moment of suspension occurs between the third touching of the ground (right foreleg) and the first of the next stride (left hind leg). Based on these elements, some writers established a technique to capture the lead change in accordance with a well-timed moment in this lightning succession of movements.

On paper these recommendations cannot help the pupil. Even if he knows the mechanism of the canter by heart, it is impossible at this level for him to calculate when to give the aid to change in the few tenths of a second which separate the start of the first beat and the end of the third one, in order to enable the horse to change at the second beat of the following stride!

Actually, these writers describe the aids for lead changes, analyzed from effects to causes, after years of observational groping which are difficult to avoid. Nevertheless, it is not very useful to students start out on this path. It is more appropriate to hold to a progressive education based, on the one hand, on suppling and the preparation of the horse's equilibrium, and, on the other hand, on the refinement and sensitivity of the rider's seat, which will determine when he can feel the right moment to ask for the inversion of the two bipeds [laterals].

Preliminaries for Lead Changes

To envisage lead changes, one must first control the canter To control it is not simply to be able to accelerate it, to slow it down or to halt it, *it is to determine the energetic and regular cadence of each stride* while having regard for the figures being ridden.

Because of apprehension, changes often provoke acceleration or the holding back of the cadence, both detrimental to the following change. This is why one must master the regularity of the gait at all times. This control is prepared little by little, using the means we have generally studied. To disregard this could have severe consequences. A skilled rider can obtain changes from a 4-year-old horse. However, he will only astonish the novices until they see him stumble over difficulties which he, himself, provoked and which will make him lose a great deal of time in obtaining straight and flowing sequential changes.

Furthermore, if demands are made too early, certain problems will occur, such as difficulties with the counter-canter or the shoulder-in at the canter which is sometimes so useful; the reason for this is that the aids for this exercise is almost the same as those for lead changes. The inexperienced horse will not fail to be confused.

Thus reversals occur more or less in line with premature solicitations. When this happens, there is a tendency for the horse to become crooked, alternately oscillating the shoulders and haunches, rather than flexing the required hind leg – a reaction that will considerably complicate attempts at successive lead changes.

Another result of this reversal is when the horse learns to change the lead with the foreleg but continues to canter with the same hind leg. This is the disunited canter, which can become habitual.

Lead change, right to left, on the diagonal. Fandango, of pure Spanish breed.

Preparatory Exercises

We have now accomplished our preliminary work at the canter. Here are the first preparatory exercise-tests for lead changes.

One moves forward straight on the track at the walk and strikes off at a canter, alternating between a canter on the correct lead and a counter-canter every 4 to 10 strides, the frequency being decided upon in both a pre-determined and a random manner. One does the same on circles. The strike-offs must be immediate and flowing, *the horse kept straight and light*. If he leans on the hand, execute a half-halt with the outside rein to stop this, lighten him, then strike off again. Continue with this until he retains his lightness. Cross the *manège* diagonally at the canter, stop at X, and strike off again on the other lead.

One then continues with strike-offs from a halt, transitions from the canter to a halt, striking off again from halt. With this exercise, the aids for the halt must simultaneously modify the horse's lateral balance – that is, his obliquity must be modified, so that he is ready to strike off on the other lead. For example: I am at the right canter, inside rein at the withers, which assures a slight bend to the right, outside rein holding in check and supporting the forehand; my inside leg is at the girth, my outside leg is slightly farther back.

I halt to strike off again to the left: my inside hand (the right one) now becomes the outside hand and effects a half-halt, upwards, while my outside hand (the left one), which now becomes the inside one (in relation to the new left bend), becomes immobile at the level of the withers. Simultaneously, I turn my torso slightly from right to left, placing my left leg at the girth, the right one a little farther behind.

With this same movement I obtained a *rassemblé* halt from the horse, while simultaneously I gave him the position for the strike-off on the other lead.

One must continue this work of halts and strike-offs from a halt, in both a pre-determined and a random fashion, but on circles far from any support of a wall.

What is important when doing these movements – that is, movements on smaller circles, that become more precise, is the overall sensitivity of the horse to the aids for the halt and the strike-off. Verification is evident when one feels the lightness of the horse, his relaxed and attentive immobility, and, especially, *the total absence of head-tossing at the moment of the halt and the strike-off*. This is of paramount importance. We have seen the similarity between lead changes in the air and halts/strike-offs. One should be aware that the same actions the horse makes when he is resisting the contact in a halt or a strike-off, he will do with lead changes in the air, which will result in disunity provoked by the jolts which the horse gives to the rider's hand when he resists. Should this occur, cease lead changes immediately.

When preparing for lead changes, stop doing changes through intermediary strides at the trot between two canters. If these are done in this context, any changes in the air will be almost impossible thereafter.

Preparing the Flexion of the Neck

An excellent preparation towards relaxing the neck with lead changes in view is the exercise relating to neck flexions. I noted the excellence of this preparation as done by Madame Otto Crépin – for me, the world's best competition rider of the 1980s and 90s, I have applied it to my own horses with immediate good results.

This is how it goes:

Preparation is first at the halt, then at the walk because at this gait – the most stable – the horse learns best and one can get him into the habit of flexing his neck and head laterally at about 35 degrees. One sees to it that he neither twists nor lowers them by soliciting with the inside rein with finesse, while compensating with the support of the outside rein.

First phase of the exercise
At the left canter, for example, one works first at a working canter with a good cadence and slight shoulder-fore position, that is, the left shoulder is in front of the left haunch.

One then goes large, once, with the neck bent to the left, while keeping the horse's body straight and parallel to the wall. To do this, one keeps the left leg on the girth, the right one slightly farther back to prevent any veering of the haunches to the right. One plays delicately within these four points (inside rein and outside rein, inside leg and outside leg) to maintain cadence and bend.

Second phase
Continuing on the left rein, one straightens the horse's neck *slowly and progressively*, inverts the bend towards the outside, "bantering" or playing a little with the outside rein, controlled by the inside rein; the inside leg is at the girth, outside leg somewhat behind it to maintain the horse's body straight and parallel to the wall.

After one or two circuits of the *manège* with this counter-bend, having turned the second corner of the short side, one goes diagonally, *keeping the neck bent to the right and the horse's body parallel to the long sides*, as when yielding to a single leg.

Third phase
In this manner, one reaches the end of the diagonal and goes onto the opposite long side at a counter-canter to the left, with the neck bend to the right. One goes large, once, the horse's body always parallel to the wall.

Fourth phase

One lengthens the horse's neck progressively and then bends it to the left while still at the counter-canter to the left, respecting the correct bend of the neck and the straightness of the body. One takes the diagonal, on which one straightens, then lengthens the horse at a medium canter.

One continues this exercise in like manner, at a canter to the right. It is clear that this exercise is different from the shoulder-in and the counter-shoulder-in wherein one asks for an inflexion of the ensemble of the horse. It is an adjunct which will allow us to broach the preparatory phase of the lead change – which is a slight inversion of the bend of the neck – without unleashing any concern or the contractions which usually result from this, especially from left to right.

It would be good to repeat these exercises especially when one is at the counter-bend, cantering always parallel to the track but 1.5 meters from it. When we execute the lead changes, we will see the advantage we can get from this.

Where Should Lead Changes Take Place?

Some *écuyers* believe that they should take place at the extremity of the diagonal as the horse turns into the first corner. I, myself, do not use this method because I have noticed that the horse who finds himself arriving at the corner at the counter-canter will contract somewhat, always more so than on the track.

Others recommend the tangential point of two circles. I do not practice this at the beginning, in that it risks giving a crooked lead change by reversal. Usually, I ask for my first lead changes in the middle of the long side, going from a true canter to a counter-canter. My horses are already perfectly familiar with the counter-canter and, with the wall to the outside, have no tendency to throw out their haunches. Nothing stops one from also trying to go from the counter-canter to the true canter. I avoid changing in the proximity of corners for so long as the horse does not change lead on the circle.

Execution of the Lead Change after Preparing the Neck Flexion

For example, let us take the case of the lead change from left to right, usually the more delicate because of the difficulty of bending to the right.

On the left rein, at the canter, one places the bend first to the left, then to the right.

After having passed the second corner of the short side on the left lead, with the counter-bend to the right, body parallel to the wall, one does a few strides of half-pass to the left, then, having the bend of the neck already to the right, one gives the aids for the change from left to right. If the horse has been prepared with a reasonably good impulsion and equilibrium, he will be in the best position for a successful lead change from left to right, returning to the track from which he departed after the corner.

Contrary to what may be a concern, if the horse is perfectly controlled by the aids, this preparation will cause neither deviation nor wavering. I was able to witness this with the horses of Madame Otto Crépin, her novice horses, as well as her Grand Prix horses, executing counter-changes of hand when worked in this manner on the center line.

What Cadence must be Used When Asking for a Lead Change?

Every horse has his own canter, more ample for one, shorter for another, more or less see-sawing. One must ask for the first changes when the horse has his most natural canter, but in its most accentuated and regular form. The changes often provoke precipitation; one must then immediately re-establish the cadence by half-halts with the outside rein until the regular, measured canter returns. It sometimes happens that the horse, sensing the forthcoming request to change, will canter with short strides. One must then put him into an energetic movement before asking again.

A return to repeated transitions from the *rassemblé* trot to the canter and from the walk to the canter is indispensable as soon as the horse loses this cadence.

The haunches should not be too overburdened, which occurs when either the horse's neck or his gait becomes shortened, which provokes a delay in the lead change of the hind legs. It is better to stretch out the canter during the first changes. Very flexible horses will throw out their haunches on one side or the other upon each request. It then follows that successive lead changes and changes at every stride become impossible; for them to succeed one must limit the incurvation and, to that end, the use of one's outside leg, channeling the horse astutely with the aids.

Great self-control is needed with some horses who are surprised by the first lead changes, which puts them into a sorry state. This is the only exercise which cannot be achieved progressively and by slow degrees – as is the case with the passage, for example. The result is sometimes great nervousness; one must know when to return to the walk with long reins, or even adjourn the exercise.

I have taught lead changes at every stride to more than thirty horses; one of them, Miguelista, constantly became disunited at single lead changes even after three years of schooling; then, within four months, he went from correct isolated lead changes to successive lead changes and lead changes at every stride...

What are the Aids for Lead Changes?

As stated earlier, I think it is an illusion that a rider who is attempting his first lead changes should try to time his aids correctly by instantaneous, logical analysis, through breaking down of the components of the steps. I believe, however, that it is possible for him to seize quickly the moment of suspension when they must act.

The aids are those of the striking-off at the canter from a halt, applied with much more tact, since the horse is already cantering and his balance is far more vulnerable. Furthermore, when one considers the differences in temperament and sensitivity of each horse, the dosage of aids cannot be determined in advance. However, the person who schools his horse for many years will know his general reactions and will take them into consideration.

Let us, for example, take the lead change from left to right. One gently straightens the bend of the neck to the right. One inverts the movement of the seat and the lumbar vertebrae, which first act from right to left, then from left to right and, *at the same time*, one brings the right leg to the girth and the left one behind it.

The role of the right leg is to hold around it the new inside; that of the left leg, acting vigorously behind the girth, is to unleash the lead change.

This is a theoretical plan, which must sometimes be acted out completely.

Simultaneously with the left leg action on the side which unleashes the lead change, execute a more or less accentuated half-halt with the left rein, which has now become the outside rein. If the horse is insensitive to the leg, tap lightly with the whip behind the outside leg (never on the croup), and give an accentuated aid with the seat to accompany that of the legs, etc.

It is important to return constantly to canter strides that are animated and straight, for the practice of lead changes greatly disturbs the canter. One must therefore space these out and make frequent pauses, and also change the area where they are requested in case of repeated failures or disunity. Whether out of anger, or on the basis of failed attempts, avoid absolutely obtaining lead changes by force.

We have several months before us in which to render single lead changes easy and regular. We will soon approach successive lead changes and changes at every stride.

18. The Quarter and Demi-pirouette at the Canter

Why do I not speak right away of the pirouette at the canter? Because to prepare for this air it is important to split it up into its many components.

Here, as elsewhere (but more so in this case), it is fundamentally important to break up the difficulties into their multiple elements in order to make them understood and resolve them one by one.

How is the movement of the pirouette at the canter formed? With pirouettes at the walk, with the correct bend and a cadence that is almost diagonalized; with strike-offs at the canter from a halt, light, straight, and elevated; with a half-pass at the canter and croup-in on circles, first from the *rassemblé* canter then slowed down to a stride in place.

We have already studied some of the movements, and we will soon come across others which are indispensable before one can execute the complete pirouette at the canter. Soon we will soon begin the quarter and demi-pirouettes.

The Demi-volte, Haunch-in

This will be the first element in the make-up of the pirouette at the canter. When one arrives at the canter at the end of a long side, one gives the horse a reduced bend of the shoulder-in, one leaves the track laterally, executing the half-pass, describing a demi-volte of 6 meters in diameter. One turns the horse's shoulders towards the inside until his body is parallel to the long side to which one returns, and continues doing the half-pass.

The aids that allow this conversion from a forward and straight movement to a circular movement towards the interior of the *manège*, still going laterally, up to the track from which one set out, are principally an encircling with the outside lateral aids, which not only encompass the horse's body to prevent it from swerving to the outside (like an elastic wall), but, in fact, return it towards the long side of the *manège*.

As always, the inside rein must assure the preservation of the bend and the inside leg, the movement and engagement of the inside hind leg.

Of course, the rider must not allow himself to go with the centrifugal force which pushes him towards the exterior; rather, he must compensate for this by turning his shoulders towards the inside, pulling them backwards in order to remain as close as possible to the center of gravity, and pushing on his inside ischium [seat bone].

Furthermore, one must heed the tendency of some very flexible horses to begin crossing and throwing their haunches into the inside, placing them almost in front of their shoulders. This makes them actually check themselves and remain in place. To prevent this tendency, one reduces the bend with the outside rein, even eliminating it very briefly or inverting it, and *one picks up again the movement of the inside hind leg with one's leg on the same side, eventually supported (if necessary) by the whip.*

The Volte, Haunch-in

This is a half-pass executed with the head towards the outside of the circle, haunch-in. It is begun first at a walk (and, at the outset, in brief sequences at canter), then worked at in the trot.

This exercise is indispensable because it puts the horse into a true pirouette situation: the forelegs describe a larger circle than the hind legs, resulting in two different cadences – that is, the impacts upon the ground differ between the forelegs and the hind legs. A rectification of the obliquity must be given to the horse's shoulders at almost each stride, by bringing the hand in the direction of the movement, in order to maintain a constant position in relation to the circle.

Since it is also difficult to describe a well-defined geometrical circumference, at the outset I trace one on the ground to serve as a guide. One starts from a circle of 15 meters in diameter, which one decreases progressively.

The Quarter Pirouette

Week after week, one will reduce the distance between the corner and the area where one turns the horse towards the interior, which will give us imperceptibly a quarter of a pirouette. One must understand that this exercise is one of those which disturbs and physically exerts the horse most. One asks an enormous expenditure of energy from a creature whose equilibrium is still very unstable, especially with regard to lateral movements in place!

Therefore it is very important to break the difficulties up into elements and to stretch them out time-wise.

If mentioning my own experience does not annoy too much, I will say that it has made me understand how much violence a horse can keep within himself, and to what extent progressive calm can open up his attention and make him listen to us.

To execute those changes, which are the beginnings of the pirouette, one must realize *the necessity of having reins almost loose*, and not imagine that one can grab the forehand with one's whole arms in order to turn the horse. One must be satisfied with pivoting one's torso and waist in the direction of the movement, wrists slightly to the inside; the outside rein at the base of the neck acting in the same direction, but without pulling; the outside leg slightly back, holding and bringing the haunches towards the inside, with one's inside leg continuing to give cadence to the inside hind leg and impulsion to the ensemble.

The seat must never slide from one side to the other; on the other hand, torsion towards the inside to set back the inside shoulder and bring forward the outside shoulder will put weight on the inside haunch and contribute to keeping it in place.

However, one must not try right away to keep the inside hind leg in its footprint. One can allow it to describe a small quarter of a circle, which one will decrease progressively, but one must often return to this quarter circle each time the horse stands tightly in place, or swerves.

Let us now examine the best exercises to train the horse to execute these quarter pirouettes, which will put him into the natural equilibrium for the full pirouette. First exercise him to slow down his strides at the canter or verify his ability to suspend one or two strides at a pace that is "*écoutée*" [shortened, measured]. This can be obtained when he is at the *rassemblé* canter and the rider sits deep and close to the horse's back, thus alleviating his forehand to the maximum. Half-halts, in an upward direction, linked to the action of the hip and outside leg, ask for a decrease in the amplitude of the strides.

To accomplish this gymnastic form of movement, it is sometimes preferable to put the horse into a counter-canter for the first slowing-downs, the wall limiting the tendency of the horse to veer to the side on the lead he is cantering on.

If one does not want these slowing downs towards the canter in place to provoke the extinction of a brilliant canter, it is essential that they are followed by frequently riding the horse vigorously forward, doing so always for the same reason: *the horse is vibrant only if he always expects a dynamic transition.*

Another exercise, which will animate the haunches on two tracks for a pirouette at the canter, consists in leaving the end of the long side on a demi-volte, then returning parallel to it, executing the half-pass, holding back the shoulders upon arrival at the long side to position the haunches, while continuing with the half-pass to the end of the *manège*.

Let us now observe the exercises which will help the further development of the horse's equilibrium and the position of the rider/horse partnership, as they imperceptibly move towards the pirouette or, rather, towards fractions of the pirouette.

At the beginning of the long side, execute the half-pass at the walk, head to wall (travers position), with an angle less than 35 degrees. Pay attention to the incurvation, make sure that you have the minimum of a light *rassemblé* and, in this position, strike off at the canter, head to wall, for four or five strides.

Halt, verify lightness, and strike off once more. Repeat several times from a very calm walk, keeping the horse in the position of the half-pass, head to wall (travers position), until strike-offs and halts are executed easily and flowingly.

Go into a canter at the first corner of the *manège*. Now, have care – the shoulders must execute a quarter of a circle at the canter and the haunches must canter in place! The aids for the ordinary half-pass at the canter are no longer appropriate. When the horse's head reaches the bisection of the angle of the corner, the inside leg, at the girth, holds the haunches at the canter in place, while the outside leg continues to give the rhythm of the canter from left to right (if one is on the right rein).

According to circumstances, the two hands, moving from left to right, contribute to the increase or decrease of the cadence when the shoulders turn. The inside rein, opened more positively, turns the shoulders faster, the outside rein, on the contrary, moderates the movement of the shoulders, which can throw themselves too far to the inside.

If one does not make the gross errors of pushing the horse's head into the wall or allowing the haunches to pass in front of the shoulders, this is an excellent strategy to prepare for the pirouette. The horse finds it quite natural to move away from the corner by turning his shoulders towards the right. One must then halt him, still in the position of the half-pass at 30 degrees from the wall, caress him, move straight, and start again on the other rein.

For a brief moment, the exercise of the pirouette compels the horse to bear his whole weight on one hind leg. When, to this, are added the usual contractions a horse exhibits when beginning a difficult movement (and should inconsiderate force be used), one runs the risk of injuring the pivoting hind leg or discouraging the horse. One must thus content oneself with a little at each lesson and, when the horse has understood what is expected of him, one will be surprised how easily he will pass through the two corners of the *manège* in quarter pirouettes.

Another procedure in preparing the pirouette at the canter consists of asking for the pirouette at the walk. For this procedure to succeed, the horse must execute ordinary pirouettes at an impeccable *rassemblé* walk, and he must be united when striking off at the canter from a halt.

One begins with two or three steps of the pirouette at the walk then, by means of voice and balanced application of the aids, one unleashes the canter while stressing the equilibrium resulting from the pirouette at walk.

Should the horse execute only two strides of the pirouette at the canter, one should be satisfied, caress him, ride him forward, and start over just once or twice more on each rein.

The purpose of this procedure is that, by striking off from a walk almost in place, the risks of becoming unbalanced are less severe than when one suddenly transforms the canter, straight, or even from two tracks, into a pirouette at the canter.

The Demi-pirouette at the Canter

One can begin teaching this before the horse executes the quarter pirouette easily; the reason one can do so is that, before executing the desired exercise completely, there are individual elements and a "plotting out" that one can teach the horse.

As soon as he begins to understand the haunches-in on demi-voltes that have become smaller and smaller, one can prepare him for the demi-pirouette by means of a strategy that is somewhat different, but which utilizes, nevertheless, one that has already been applied.

At a canter, one takes an inside track parallel to the wall and 5 meters from the long side, on the lead situated to the side of the wall. One covers this track at a canter that is energetic, but very rounded, [that is *rassemblé*] and cadenced.

When one arrives, perpendicularly, 2 meters from the short side, one halts and immediately links on to a demi-pirouette at the walk, turned

Demi-pirouettes at the canter with Fandango, 11 years and Spartacus, 6 years.

towards the corner the horse finds facing him. The training he has received allows him to easily make a half-turn in place. As soon as he is parallel to the long side, one strikes off once more at a very straight canter, on the lead which is to the inside of the *manège*. When, on each rein, the horse has understood what is expected of him, one must cover the same distance without interrupting the canter.

The importance of this strategy is that, facing the corner, the horse pirouettes of his own accord without the assistance of the hand – which yields. The horse then executes his own demi-pirouette at the canter.

It is beneficial to utilize every one of these exercises which we have just described. Some horses will profit from certain exercises, and have difficulties with others. It will be profitable to go from one to the other until one finds the one that is the most helpful for the individual horse.

Here, then, is a serious preparatory program for the quarter pirouettes and the demi-pirouettes. When they are achieved, we will tackle the complete pirouette.

BELOW LEFT The demi-pirouette at the canter, to the left. Nymphéa.

BELOW RIGHT The demi-pirouette at the canter, to the right. Nymphéa.

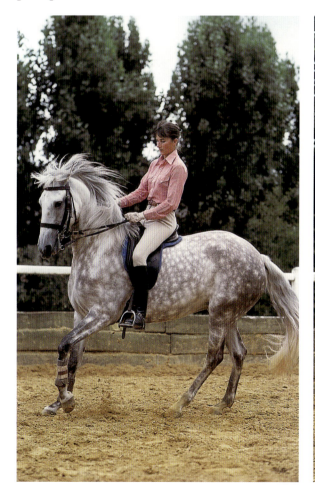

And this is how *the time to execute the exercises and airs* ends. As was done at the end of *the time to learn*, we now give you an outline of a recapitulation model at this stage: then we will broach the last phase, *the time to perfect*.

19. Recapitulation Model of "The Time to Do"

When we started this study three years ago, working with the three young horses aged 3 and 4, we covered the period of *the time to understand*, which included the breaking in, work in hand, and the initial contacts with the horse, mounted.

Then came the *time to learn*, when our pupils were initiated into simple movements on one track, then on two tracks, also to basic suppling exercises and to the transitions of the regular gaits.

Then came *the time to do the exercises and airs*, composed of bringing together movements already taught, a phase that General Faverot de Kerbrech wisely called "*l'assembler*" – "assembling" or "gathering together".

To allow you to discover the level of your knowledge and the schooling of your horse, we give at the end of each period a repeat model, recapping upon what had been previously taught, to prepare you for tackling the next phase. Here, then, is the recapitulation of *the time to do the exercises and the airs* which our three horses, now 7 and 8 years old, were able to execute.

Unless the horse has missed a day of work – which never occurs more than three times a year – and unless I intend working him in hand, I do not lunge any horses at this age, but get on them right away.

Relaxation

Relaxation and warming up simultaneously, on both reins, take up several minutes at an ample and regular walk going large around the track, without seeking the slightest *mise en main* but, rather, a horizontal lengthening of the entire spine, including the neck, with a well-opened angle. The horse must not be held yet must be perfectly controlled by the aids to remain straight and parallel to the sides, rounding the corners correctly, and walking with energetic and regular strides. One then covers the same area at the rising trot, always in this horizontal equilibrium and heeding the dynamism and regularity of the gait.

I add here a precise comment with respect to the position of the horse's poll and, in correlation, his back and lower jaw: in order that the horse has a carrying equilibrium, although we allow him to be on his shoulders, *it is necessary that his poll and lower jaw flex slightly and that his back is raised*. In a word, it can be open but not hollow – which happens when he inverts his poll and his nose is horizontal.

To accomplish the required outline, place your hands low on each side of the horse's shoulders, fingers acting *alternatively downwards* as soon as the horse leans on the hand or tries to use force. Use a light contact, but do not abandon it.

This relaxation period is helpful if accomplished on long straight tracks, thus, if possible, on outside tracks and for a dozen minutes. There is nothing to prevent a few strides at a free and regular canter on each rein and in the same position.

Work In Hand

Before beginning the exercises mounted, it is beneficial to work in hand and ask for a light *rassembler* with contact, at a halt, a rein-back, and a walk more and more shortened, until it can be transformed into a piaffe by diagonalization. Caress and reward the horse.

At the Walk

Some schools, mainly the Germanic ones, do not work on two tracks at the walk out of fear of losing impulsion. If there is no compression caused by simultaneous actions of hand and legs, impulsion never gets lost. The walk is the gait that is the most propitious for teaching movements, rather than for any brilliant demonstration.

It is never a bad idea to begin moving straight, at a walk, on the track, to put the horse in hand by means of the *rassembler* and to perfect all this by a volte at the start of one of the long sides, followed by a shoulder-in along the same side. Then, straighten the horse at the end of the long side and do a demi-volte, which puts us back into a counter-shoulder-in. In like manner, go to the end of the long side up to the first corner of the short side (doing a reversed pirouette with the bend of a shoulder-in), along the short side to the second corner, from which, with a third of a reversed pirouette, take the whole diagonal at the shoulder-in until reaching the opposite end, where one straightens the horse.

Execute the half-pass at the walk on a either a part of or the whole diagonal: upon arriving at the opposite track, hold the shoulders to place the croup to the wall and continue with the half-pass (renvers position) up to the end of the track and include the corners where, this time, you will execute a quarter of a reversed pirouette with the bend of the half-pass (the horse looking in the direction in which he is moving).

Starting with a volte, do the half-pass head to the wall (travers position). Pass through the corners with a quarter of an ordinary pirouette (the shoulders turn around the haunches, while, with the croup to the wall, the haunches pivot around shoulders). Return to the track at the walk. Halt. Rein back three steps straight, go off again forwards and straight, extend the walk and describe a serpentine at the walk.

Do not think that you are held to a ritual or a rigid order: walk, trot, canter. On the contrary, do not hesitate to mix the exercises together at the three gaits in a way that will always hold the horse's attention and avoid any drowsiness – which can affect both rider and horse when a slow and regular gait is prolonged. Change gaits often and, within these gaits, do some transitions. To make my exposé clear, I hold myself to a progression which in no way obligates you.

Do not forget to turn across the *manège* to inside tracks and profit by executing some ordinary and reversed pirouettes there.

From a walk that becomes shorter and shorter until it becomes diagonalized in place, ask for some steps at the piaffe on each rein. Then go forwards energetically, now at a walk, now at a trot. Emphasize your rest period by going at a free walk, but straight, then ride more transitions to the shortened form.

At the Trot

You can replicate the basic outline and the figures already accomplished at the walk. It is when going from the trot that is slightly *rassemblé* that you will work at the *rassemblé* walk itself.

Be attentive and rigorous regarding the straightness on one track and the correction of the bend when going laterally.

Constantly verify that the horse's shoulders do not squeeze against the wall, which would put your horse crooked. Actually, he will always tend to shape himself into a "croissant" when you put him into the *rassembler*; never accept this deviation and take him up once more from the straight halt. Correct any excessive flexion through impulsion; place the outside rein and the wrists towards the inside.

At this level, you must note the cadence and rhythm of the horse. It is at the trot that correct cadence and rhythm will first appear, earlier than at the walk and much earlier than at the canter. Take off at the working trot. Go on to the school trot, make it as *rassemblé* as you can on a circle. Leave this circle and, with several half-halts, activate alternately your legs to bring about a few strides of the *doux* passage. Return energetically to the medium trot, slightly extended, even if you have to go into a rising trot to do so.

On each rein, do serpentines and spirals, verifying the flexion on loops and circles; be sure that there is no veering. From the shoulder-in at the trot, ask for halts, with engagement of the inside hind leg.

Rein back three of four times and take off again at the *rassemblé* trot without any transitional strides. Work at some extensions of the trot in the following manner: do a circle at a very cadenced working trot and, after reaching the point of the circle situated on the diagonal of the *manège*, leave it and lengthen the trot on this diagonal, first at the rising trot then, progressively, at the sitting trot.

We will subsequently return to the study of the extended and lengthened trot when our horses will be more *rassemblés* in *the time to perfect* section.

At the Canter

Strike off at a medium canter around the *manège*, with a mixture of circles 12 to 20 meters in diameter. Then go into a working canter on voltes of 6 meters at any point of the track. Pause for a few minutes, then take up the working canter again and go into a half-pass on the diagonal, with the horse parallel to the long sides. Remaining at the counter-canter, do a circle in counter-canter at one end of the *manège* go on another circle in true canter, tangential to the first one, which will give you a figure of eight.

Execute a few energetic steps at the piaffe to put the horse on his haunches. From this piaffe, go off into a slow canter, *descente de main*, and let the canter unfold. If the horse throws his haunches to the inside, go off once more from the piaffe into a very slow counter-canter.

After another pause, return to the track at a *rassemblé* canter. At the end of the long side do a very tight demi-volte, haunches-in, which you continue with, returning to the long side executing the half-pass, croup to wall (renvers position). Straighten the horse before reaching the first corner, then return at a canter on the true lead, on the diagonal; after having turned the second corner, straighten the horse again.

Ride a half-pass at a walk, head to wall (travers position), on the long side then, 10 meters from the first corner, go into canter, still in this position. You are then ideally positioned to pass through the corner in a quarter-pirouette. Then return to the walk, head to wall; take up the canter once more and, in the same manner, turn through the second corner. Interrupt this work often and caress a great deal.

From the short side, at a walk, turn into the middle, lengthwise, 4 meters from the long side, keeping your horse very parallel to the track. Strike off at a canter, on the lead towards the long side then, a meter before reaching the opposite short side, do a demi-pirouette at the corner and take up again, on the other rein, the path you have just traveled.

After pausing again, take up the working canter, change lead at X on the diagonal, then go from a canter to a counter-canter, from a counter-canter to a canter on the track. Terminate the session with a trot as *rassemblé* and as light as possible, from which, now on a straight line, now on a circle, you ask for a few strides of the *doux* passage, immediately followed by the *rassemblé* trot, without the horse ever going into any strides of the "*passagé*" trot.

The one before last phase or our schooling now ends; with the next chapter we will begin the one which never ends: *the time to perfect*.

CHAPTER FOUR

The Time to Perfect

WHEN, IN THE PRELIMINARIES of this work, we wanted to define our philosophy, we presented our conception of what this equestrian art ought to be, and discussed the instruments of this art and its most elevated objective: the *rassembler*.

Those who had the patience to follow this study step by step will have certainly noticed from the very first lesson in hand, then mounted, that we gave ourselves a permanent goal: to achieve each day an enhancement of the horse's balance through the gymnastics of suppling and muscular development.

All our exercises had, and continue to have, as their aim an improved functioning of the joints in both the straight, forward movements and the movements on two tracks, with a progressive and improved flexion of the haunches and hocks, brought forward and engaged.

Without ever using force, we succeeded in getting the horse to freely elevate each gait, to obtain a regular and elastic rhythm, a self-induced tonicity, these qualities being available at all times, in order that we can begin, under optimal conditions, the exercises that will lay the foundations for the school airs.

What precisely characterizes the phase we are now covering in *the time to perfect*, is the acquisition of the *rassembler*, already partially obtained, which allows for the creation of a new equilibrium at the three gaits and its utilization or, rather, its development, to approach the extensions of the walk, trot, and canter.

1. Balancing the Gaits between Their Elevation and Their Extension

I am always astonished to see upper level riders of high school equitation on horses afflicted with horizontal or inverted necks, who, at a fast trot, push these horses on to their shoulders, against the hand, with additional force from legs and spurs. This kind of training of young horses, whose trot one would wish to develop, simply results in putting them more and more "on the nose", as the English say with humor.

Ten or fifteen minutes of this sort of work daily will result in horses moving rigidly, making caricatures of themselves in whatever faults they had within them.

I tried – in vain of course – to understand the reason for these exercises of imbalance which offend against nature. I asked myself by what magic would these poor creatures one day rediscover their triumphant neck and their diligent haunches! A few glances around the arenas proved to me that these horses' necks would never be raised, nor could they raise them themselves...ever. Lengthening and extension are not prepared by pushing horses against the hand, nose in the sawdust. These movements can only be attained through progressive flexing of the horse's resources, that is his joints, muscles, etc., which, in order to be utilized correctly, must first be stretched or, if you prefer, put at one's disposal.

To push a horse with a horizontal equilibrium in an attempt to achieve lengthening, is simply putting onto the forelegs an excess of weight which never corresponds to their carrying capacity, but actually reduces it.

So long as the hindquarters, constituted with powerful joints and muscles, are not first accustomed to being flexed and, after any extension of the gait, to taking on again the excess weight transferred when the forehand is discharged of it, "extensions" are simply a horse falling constantly on his shoulders; a loss of balance towards the forehand, never recaptured.

Only by maintaining the balanced position and redistributing the weight onto the hindquarters will any catlike extensions be possible at the trot and the canter.

The Rassemblé Walk and the Extended Walk

Because characteristics of the walk are its relative slowness and its regularity, it is the most propitious gait for any communication between rider and horse. It does not engender any nervousness, rather, it reduces tension. During *the time to learn* it was at the walk that we explained to our horse the elements of movements, and their techniques. Further, we sought the walk's regularity rather than its shortening; it was a gait of transition and a gait at which to relax.

Now, we have to make sure that our exercises at the walk are executed *rassemblés*. The horse will now take strides that are elevated, concise, and regulated, and able to go into a canter or a piaffe at any time. However, the little tonicity that the horse develops at the walk makes control of any activity in the hindquarters somewhat difficult; thus the rider's seat must engage deeply and alternate legs must vibrate with the precise action of the fingers, thereby making the horse shorten and raise his step, by regulating it. An excellent way of attaining the walk "raised and *écouté*" is the repeated transition from the *rassemblé* trot to a measured and cadenced walk. This latter action profits both from the impulsion emerging from the *rassemblé* trot and from the flexion of the joints, which is indispensable to the school trot.

The importance of the *rassemblé* walk becomes evident in movements on two tracks; it is also the best way of attaining ordinary and reversed pirouettes and, of course, the piaffe. It is evident that a horse, open [unbalanced] and on his shoulders, will have great difficulty executing a shoulder-in or a half-pass.

The progressive shortening and elevation of the walk, combined with an increase in impulsion, are brought about at the first diagonalized steps in place.

Extension of the *rassemblé* walk must begin with the impulsion of the hind legs, facilitated by the engagement they had acquired with the *rassemblés* strides. The hands – the forearms united with the pelvis – advance, all the while maintaining contact with the horse's mouth, yet allowing the indispensable lengthening of the neck. If the horse retains a link with the hand and has an ample and energetic walk, it is easy to return to the *rassemblé* walk.

The Rassemblé Trot and the Extended Trot

When we studied the trot and analyzed its range, we sketched out its lengthening towards an extension, because it was not possible to envisage it any further as long as the flexion of the haunches at the *rassemblé* trot did not suffice to develop their extension.

We have now examined more particularly the role of the school trot and its transitions in obtaining animated and extended strides and preserving the dynamism of the horse; getting him to intensify the amplitude of his lengthened strides, starting with the stretching of his resources [his joints, muscles, etc.].

Orphée, pure Lusitano,
7 years. His balance and
carriage require
perfecting.

We can now exploit to its maximum the gymnastic fund that has been stored up, and work at lengthening the trot. Starting off from the *rassemblé* trot, there are several ways of passing into the extended trot.

Starting out from a circle into a slight shoulder-in at the trot, one takes a tangent while straightening the incurvation of the horse with the outside rein. Similarly, touching the horse with the whip or the leg, one forewarns him to prepare for the transition. One induces it with an accentuated bracing of the lumbar vertebrae forwards, thighs pulled back, legs vibrating, outside hand supportive, inside hand immobile.

The outside hand prevents an excessive transfer onto the shoulders, as well as any action of weight going downwards; the inside hand limits the opening of the lower neck/head angle.

Starting out with a semi-diagonal at a shoulder-in from the middle of the short side, one acts as above, upon reaching the long side.

Starting with three or four strides of the half-pass at the beginning of the long side, one unleashes a lengthening in the same way; one straightens out on an inside track, straight and parallel to the long side and one lengthens the stride.

These three ways of obtaining a lengthening and extension of the trot, have a common denominator in addition to the *rassembler*: they benefit from the strengthened and flexed hind legs in lateral movements.

Correct lengthening assumes that the diagonal pairs of forelegs and hind legs step strictly in parallel unity, without a false over-extension of the former.

Extended strides: Nymphéa, a pure Lusitano mare, 8 years.

Fandango, pure Spanish breed, 8 years.

What should the position of the neck be when the trot is extended? The ruling of the F.E.I. stipulates: "The rider allows the horse, while remaining in hand, to lower and lengthen his neck without seeking a contact point on the bit to avoid an elevated gait."

This conception can be defended only when it is a matter of an extension executed with a horse more or less on his shoulders and not in hand. It is questionable when the horse achieves the total flexion of his joints; he can then maintain the position and elevation of his neck just as well as in a transition from the piaffe to a passage or to a trot.

It is true, however, that, even at the highest level, one sees few horses responding to this definition of the *rassembler*.

Finally, just as the *rassemblé* walk prepares the horse for the piaffe, so the *rassemblé* trot is the only way of obtaining a true passage.

The Rassemblé Canter and the Extended Canter

So far as the means are concerned, the same holds true for the canter as for the trot, since the transitions are not possible unless one masters perfectly the lightness of the forehand and the engagement of the hindquarters at the *rassemblé* canter.

On the other hand, the actual mechanism of the canter necessitates that, during the extension, while remaining in hand, the horse extends his neck and his head. One must pay attention to the risk of a possible disunity when lengthening at canter, which comes from ill-timed contacts on the part of the rider's hand or leg which the horse, as he goes forward, can receive on the corner of his lips or his flank.

The Simultaneous Development of the Two Equilibria

From these reflections, there emerges the fact that the rational gymnastic development of a horse towards an ideal equilibrium takes place continually in two directions that are apparently opposed. There is the development of the forward propulsive force in a natural, horizontal equilibrium which, at the start, weighs more on the forehand. This alternates with the effects of the impulsive aids, which engage the hind legs, encouraging them to advance and bear more weight, thus assisting in the raising of the forehand, and there are the support aids – halts and half-halts – which contribute to the placing of more weight on the haunches.

These two series of actions can only be consistent and beneficial if they are based on this lengthy gymnastic process which we have abundantly described. What is important to remember from this whole lengthy schooling period is that *we must never lengthen the steps more than we are*

Spartacus, pure Lusitano, 6 years. To understand the elevated position of their necks, one must be familiar with the very arched necks of Iberian horses. Furthermore, when a horse is *rassemblé*, he is able to retain in the other gaits, without difficulty, a position almost equivalent to that which he attains for the passage or the piaffe.

capable of shortening them and we must never elevate more than we can straighten out [lengthen].

It is by constantly offsetting these two directions with each other that the feeling of lightness in the hand and to the seat can result, and from which results the sensitivity that will produce easy transfer from one equilibrium to the other, thus maintain the scales of the balance equally. Does this mean that, of these two forms of equilibrium (that is, elevation and lengthening), one corresponds to the *rassembler*, the other to its opposite? Absolutely not. Brought to his highest level, the *rassemblé* horse can maintain himself perfectly in balance in his most spectacular extensions.

2. Exercises at the Shoulder-in

Halts and Strike-offs at the Shoulder-in

At the phase of gymnastics which we have reached, we must execute the shoulder-in easily at the three gaits – certainly at the walk and trot. Beneficial work consists of requesting, first from a walk, then from a trot, halts in the position and equilibrium of the shoulder-in, followed by strike-offs without ever leaving this position. To obtain them, the exercise must be executed in cadence and lightness.

With a correct position of both rider and horse, do a half-halt with the outside rein – inside hand and rein immobile – with a deep engagement of the rider's seat, from the inside to the outside, inside leg at the girth, outside leg slightly back to maintain the bend of the ensemble. Well executed, this gives a *rassemblé* halt with the inside hind leg placed in front of the outside one, haunches flexed and neck raised.

The strike-offs must be made from a halt to the walk and trot, instigated by the outside leg, the inside leg remaining at the girth to assure, together with the outside rein, the direction of the movement.

These exercises are tests revealing the quality achieved from one's work and help greatly in perfecting the *rassemblé* equilibrium.

Shoulder-in, right, at the trot. Spartacus.

The Shoulder-in on the Center Line

An exercise which tests the absolute mastery of the horse's equilibrium at the shoulder-in is its execution on an inside track, far from the walls of the *manège* – for example, on the center line.

This is first executed at the walk, then at the trot. When one reaches the middle of the short side on the left rein, one leaves it at the beginning of a demi-volte, maintaining the inflexion, but soon transforming it to a shoulder-in, moving from one end of the center line to the other. Arriving at the end, that is, in the middle of the other short side, one returns to the track on the same rein, goes beyond the corner, changes rein on the diagonal, and does likewise on the right rein.

The difficulty that makes this exercise important is that there is no wall either in front or behind the horse which can control any tendency to swerve forwards or backwards. The slightest deviation from the track between A and C would reveal poor control of the shoulder-in.

The Shoulder-in on the Circle

One begins with a circle on a single track. When the horse is correctly bent on the track of the circle, is light and has a regular cadence, whether at the walk or the trot, one puts him into a shoulder-in.

The inside leg is at the girth, "holding" the horse; the inside rein, which already sets the bend on the circle, stretches towards the inside, while the outside rein is placed at the base of the neck, without the hand going beyond it. The outside leg, behind the girth, controls and prevents any swerving of the haunches, which is the main concern on a circle. One is at a shoulder-in on the circle.

The difficulty of this exercise is to describe two concentric circles, one with the shoulders, the other with the haunches, which move at different cadences: the slower movements of the shoulders are on the small circle, the more ample movements are on the large circle. Thus the need to slow down the movements of the one, and accelerate those of the other.

The action of the outside rein towards the exterior contributes to slowing the shoulders down – that is, bringing the shoulders now towards the outside, now towards the center. At a shoulder-in on a circle, as on straight lines, the inside leg has a directional role; the outside leg has an impulsive role when it vibrates, and becomes restraining when it limits the spilling over of the haunches.

The laterally flexed position of the rider's loins is an essential contribution to the movement.

The Shoulder-in at the Canter

During the time to learn, we taught the young horse the shoulder-in at the canter on semi-diagonals. It will not take much for him to execute it on the track and on the circle. On circles, the outside rein – held towards the outside to prevent the shoulders from falling into the circle – and the leg on the same side giving impulsion, play an essential role. The inside leg, at the girth, holds the bend, which is set by the inside hand.

When one begins the half-pass at the canter, in whatever position across the *manège* – diagonals, head to wall or croup to wall (travers or renvers position), a demi-volte, etc. – it is paramount that keeps a check on the flexion of the horse, which is so delicate to maintain. If this flexion is lost, without interrupting the canter, return from the failed half-pass to the bend of the shoulder-in and then take up the half-pass again. Doing this on a large circle in the center of the *manège*, alternating between the shoulder-in and the half-pass at the canter, one supporting the other, has a radical effect.

We will end comment on the shoulder-in by insisting that, at a certain level of schooling, it must no longer be utilized except when the need arises.

Normally, at the end of many years, it must not be part of the systematic program, but employed only to correct a special difficulty, or simply to maintain a faltering flexibility.

3. Counter-changes of Hand [Rein] on Two Tracks

Usefulness and Definition

These exercises give the horse the final touch of lateral mobility when working on two tracks, making him attentive to inverting his equilibrium at all times at the very first time of asking.

"The counter-change of hand is composed of two lines. The first is the beginning of a wide change of hand and, when the horse has reached the center of the *manège*, rather than continuing on the same rein, he must taking two or three steps straight forward, then, after having positioned his head in the other direction, one takes him back on a diagonal to arrive on the line of the wall which one just left..." (La Guérinière, *School of Horsemanship* – 1733).

Counter-changes of hand are changes of rein or direction alternately repeated at the half-pass, moving lengthwise on the *manège*. They can be executed at a walk, trot, or canter. They are executed after the second corner of the short side, up to the opposite long side, returning to the long side from which one set out, or, again, after the second corner to the center line and back, and from the middle of the short side, or from the center line of the *manège*.

With each change of hand, the incurvation of the forehand and the bend of the neck are first oriented in their new direction. The difficulty of these exercises increases in proportion to the number of half-passes done

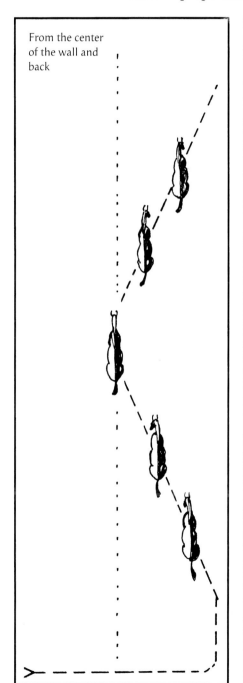

From the center of the wall and back

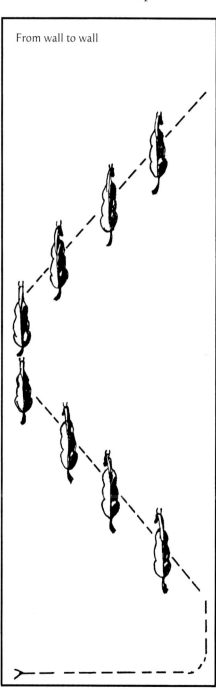

From wall to wall

Counter-changes of hand on two tracks.

covering the same distance, since to be able to multiply them, one must advance less, risking a loss in impulsion which this brings about. At first, it is easier to do them from wall to wall so that one can align oneself with the walls, thus taking off straight and parallel, forming the bend, then straightening out at the other wall before inverting the position once more.

Counter-changes of hand

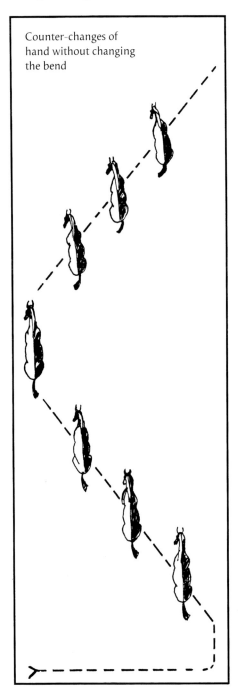

Counter-changes of hand without changing the bend

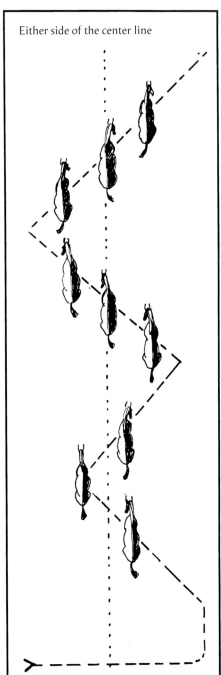

Either side of the center line

Counter-changes at the Walk

"In lateral work, the effort of the limbs crossing in front of each other can be totally exploited only at the walk, because the moment of suspension at the trot makes it possible for the horse to avoid this effort." (Decarpentry, *Academic Equitation* – 1949.)

In opposition to Germanic equitation, which seldom practices work on two tracks at the walk, General Decarpentry underscores the positive aspect. I must add once again that little can be done with a horse without first giving him the time to understand. It is therefore important to teach counter-changes at the walk, since the calmness and footfall of this gait allow the horse time to adjust his steps in accord with the inversion of his bend, a delicate process, but one which can easily upset the balance acquired in the simple half-pass.

To the novice *écuyers*, whose attention I seek, I should add that the slowness of the walk brings the same advantages as trot, while limiting risks.

For our horses, already refined to the aids in the preceding lessons, the first counter-changes are not a major feat if one takes the time to break down the different phases of the exercises very methodically.

We do the half-pass correctly on the diagonal line and we straighten at will when we reach the opposite track. Neither do we have any difficulty doing the half-pass on the diagonal and straightening on the center line, this time without the support of the wall. We do six steps at the half-pass on the diagonal line, then straighten out on an inside line, and, if necessary, in order to succeed, walk straight for several steps (La Guérinière). When straightness, that is, the parallelism to the long sides, is re-established, one inverts the position of the horse and begins the counter-change of hand towards the side from which one set out, and upon which one straightens once more before inverting the bend once again.

The half-pass. Fandango.

This very methodical process has the advantage of being controllable at all times and allows one to break down into segments both our own aids and the movements of the horse.

Once counter-changes have been easily mastered in this manner, we can go on to the counter-changes on each side of the center line.

After doing a few straight steps on the center line, one goes into three strides of the half-pass. At the third stride, one inverts the bend and does the half-pass for six more strides, one then inverts again the bend and the direction at the sixth stride, and so on, to terminate three steps from the center line, straighten, and walk straight.

The counter-changes of hand will reveal the serious consequences when, at the half-pass, the haunches go sideways, that is, in front of the shoulders, and are late in acting. Indeed, if the haunches are in front of the shoulders at the moment of the counter-change, they will be late at the departure in the new direction; if they drag at the counter-change, they will find themselves in front of the shoulders, once the bend is inverted, and thus will block mobility.

Counter-changes at the Trot

The diagonalization which characterizes the trot allows lateral movement only if the hind leg, situated on the side opposite to the direction of movement, is in support at the moment when the half-pass is requested. For example, a change of hand from right to left requires the support of the left diagonal, that is, the left foreleg and the right hind leg on the ground.

As is the case with lead changes, the precise analysis of the locomotion at the moment the aids intervene has always seemed to me to be risky. The rider who approaches counter-changes at the trot must have a long experience of simple half-passes, which have developed in him a sensitivity of the seat and its utilization.

If he keeps the exercise to a rigorous breaking down into segments and a strict co-ordination of his aids, it will, fortunately, be no additional use to him to take stock of the mechanism of locomotion at the moment of the counter-change: he will feel it quickly. An excellent preparation for a counter-change with a change in the bend is the counter-change maintaining the bend. This is easier for horses and riders because they avoid that which is most delicate: the change of the incurvation.

For example, this exercise can be done on the diagonal with four strides at the shoulder-in, simply keeping the shoulders in front of the haunches and returning to the track at the half-pass. When the horse has assimilated the reversal in direction by keeping his body relatively parallel to the walls, he will find it easy, at a second attempt, to add the change of bend.

The following is a playing with the aids for a counter-change from right to left: one arrives at the half-pass to the right with the inside hand (the right one) maintaining the bend; the outside hand limits the advance of the

The half-pass at trot.
Orphée.

BELOW, LEFT AND RIGHT
The half-pass at trot.
Nymphéa.

shoulders; the inside leg is at the girth, the outside one is somewhat back controlling the haunches. On the line of the change of direction, the left hand, which becomes the inside one, inverts the bend; the right hand slows down the shoulders; the left leg, which was somewhat behind the girth, returns to the girth, the right one goes back slightly and gets hold of the haunches, sending them to the left.

It is very important that, at this moment, the action of the hands precedes those of the legs, which then re-position the haunches to the outside of the shoulders. A simultaneous hand-legs reaction does not allow the complete inversion of the flexion of the ensemble.

When one must execute a precise number of strides, one begins to invert the aids at the one penultimate stride.

Counter-changes at the Canter

If the canter is uninterrupted, counter-changes require a lead change at each counter-change of direction.

The preparation for counter-changes begins with easy serpentines at the canter without a lead change, with alternate loops at the true canter and the counter-canter. One then goes into a serpentine with lead changes at each loop. The half-pass on different diagonals must be regular and flowing, the haunches of the horse must be mobile; finally, single lead changes must be done easily without any deviation of the haunches.

When all these pre-conditions are brought together, one begins the half-pass at the canter after the second corner of the short side, one does eight strides of the half-pass maintaining a constant angle, one then halts the horse parallel to the walls, inverts the bend, strikes off from a halt to a canter towards the wall on the side from which one has recently departed. Arriving back at the track, one halts parallel, one inverts the bend, and one is off again towards the center line.

One executes the same exercise on each rein. When the principle of the counter-change is understood by the horse, one requests it again in the same manner, but with a lead change at the first stride of the new half-pass. One must heed that the horse canters very symmetrically on each rein, displacing himself laterally with an identical angle and for the same number of strides.

One then asks for the counter-change on both sides of the center line. One turns onto the center line then, after one stride straight, one takes four strides at the half-pass to the right of the center line, changes lead, executes eight strides at the half-pass to the left, does a lead change, eight strides to the right, and so on, ending with four strides which brings us back to the center line.

The usual difficulties of this exercise are often the deviation of the haunches, contraction at the lead change, and loss of cadence. This is when one appreciates the use of the inside leg, acting at the girth, when one executes changes of direction. This inside leg maintains around itself the flexion of the new concave side, activates the hind leg which has now become an inside leg, and impels the horse into the *new half-pass*. The outside leg, somewhat behind the girth, maintains the position of the haunches.

Asking for a lead change must be done when the horse finds his straight position before he is bent in the other direction for a new half-pass.

Let us conclude this chapter with what La Guérinière has to say with respect to this topic: "All these different strategies of changes of hand, counter-changes of hand [rein, direction changes], and shoulder reversals are done to prevent the horses from becoming dulled by routine: this is the mistake those make who work more from memory than with hand and leg."

4. Successive Lead Changes and Lead Changes at Every Stride

We have already studied single lead changes at the canter; until now we have executed them without seeking to bring them into quick succession with each other. On the contrary, every time we noticed, for example, that a demand to straighten the shoulders by the outside rein provoked a non-sought-for change, we interrupted them for a few days, taking on the canter on the correct lead or the counter-canter.

Day after day, as our work progressed, we acted in a way intended to avoid any confusion in the mind of our pupil, knowing from experience that we will profit from this.

Successive Lead Changes

If a horse has been perfectly honed to executing single lead changes, in theory he should have no difficulty doing successive lead changes. However, to link the aids properly, one must be aware of the difficulties one will face and understand the causes. A single change can provoke two kinds of compromising reactions:

— through the actions of the aids, the horse can traverse [go crooked] when throwing his haunches outwards;

— he modifies his cadence, either by rushing after the lead change or withholding when he senses the aids for the lead change coming.

Any of the above is proof that these successive lead changes are premature.

Lead changes, even those at every stride, which flabbergast the public, are far from being the most delicate exercise of high school equitation. Many riders succeed in executing them although they are incapable of obtaining a *rassemblé* trot, light pirouettes, or, even less, the passage or the pirouette.

This is so because these airs require the real *rassembler*, which is not indispensable to successive lead changes.

It is necessary to have at one's disposal a sufficiently long, straight line to have the time to straighten before each change; it is better to avoid these changes too close to corners.

At first, one does not fix the number of strides before the lead change. One waits for the re-establishment of the cadence and straightness after the first one, be it the fifth or the sixth stride, and one asks for the next one. One reduces the interval, always being much more attentive to a good equilibrium than to the precise number of intermediary strides. The seat discerns the state of the equilibrium, thus, the horse's receptivity to the requested lead change.

General Decarpentry states that a horse's preparedness for successive lead changes can be related to the frequency and ease with which he can go from canter to walk while maintaining his equilibrium and lightness. Thus, if the horse goes readily into the walk after five strides at the canter, he can change lead at every sixth stride.

To me, this is already true at single lead changes, which I request only when the horse is capable of halting from the canter with the correct equilibrium and in hand, then right away striking off again from a halt, on the other lead, with the same regularity, maintaining a slight and consistent bend.

Lead changes on a circle are part of the refinement of the horse's sensitivity to the aids. As one approaches lead changes, the canter must be more and more straight and *rassemblé*. If one allows the haunches to veer either to the right or to the left at successive lead changes, it will be impossible to execute changes at every stride later.

Lead Changes at Every Stride

Until the beginning of the 19th century, lead changes at every stride did not form part of the objectives of classical equitation. It is, however, evident that the *écuyers* of that period did not ignore them and that the so-called discovery of Baucher is merely an institutionalization of a response that every experienced rider could obtain, sometimes without even having requested it. I have observed simple *guardiens* of bulls – or, rather, the horses of these "*campinos*" – execute changes at every stride simply to re-balance at the canter between tufts of gorse.

Some people believed that changes at every stride transformed the nature of the canter; this is not wrong. However, what applies to changes at every stride also applies to the Spanish walk or the piaffe backwards; if these gestures are straight and light, they cannot be contested. A few decades ago, lead changes at every stride (like trot extensions) were accepted by the Vienna School, but they have been mentioned in their official programs only since the 1920s.

When a horse executes changes at three and four strides impeccably, one can pass on to a change at every stride in the middle of the long side. The requirements are an equilibrium and a tempo that are perfectly regular, and a relaxed carriage at the horse's center of gravity.

In general, I ask for the first lead change from the canter on the correct lead to the counter-canter, then counter-canter to true canter. The inversion of the aids must be done without bending over; the rider's legs must be free from tension and synchronized with the inversion of the bend by the action of the fingers – the latter without any movement of the arms, which remain alongside the body. At the moment of the lead change, Maître Oliveira asked us to fix our sight on the upper part of the *manège* wall facing us, to avoid falling on our nose at each change.

At the slightest problem, one returns to the walk, then to single lead changes and to suppling exercises at the canter. If impulsion should decrease somewhat, one goes forward into an energetic canter. Once the horse can do two successive one-time changes that are easy and correct, one goes to three, then four successive changes and so on, as long as they remain regular, up to and including a return to the walk.

5. L'effet D'ensemble – the Co-ordinated Effect

Origins

This is an expression used by Baucher to define a mode of action of the aids which has the purpose of soliciting simultaneously the force of the hindquarters and that of forehand, in order to establish between the two the most propitious harmony.

Thus it is neither a gait nor an air, but a combination of aids to attain lightness by a perfect accord of the seat and legs on the one part, and the hand, on the other.

Baucher states that "as long as the general suppling of the horse is not perfect, the co-ordinated effects will only be sketchy" (*Méthode d'équitation*). For the equestrian masters of the 19th century, this method was destined to perfect the equilibrium of horses who were already quite advanced in their schooling, or to control horses who were inopportune or premature in their movements.

His disciple, General Faverot de Kerbrech, considers this "a co-ordinated effect with the spur" and gives this instrument a leading role, which Baucher does not, since he never once talks about spurs in the chapter devoted to the co-ordinated effect. Faverot sees this as "the absolutely sure method to prevent defenses and disorders" (*Dressage Méthodique du Ccheval de Selle* – Faverot de Kerbrech). Captain Beudant (*Dressage du Cheval de Selle*) takes up again this same idea. Gerhardt (*Manuel d'équitation*), another disciple of Baucher, who remained faithful to the ideas of his master, brings together in the same chapter the co-ordinated effect and the *descente de main* without any intervention by the spur.

Is this co-ordinated effect an innovation, a technical contribution to equitation? As a matter of fact, as is the case with a certain number of other Baucherizations, the merit of Baucher lies more in a detailed and precise formulation of an equestrian method than in a true invention. Without forcing the text, one can, for example, find in La Guérinière the same principle, which puts the horse in the most favorable situations to respond to our requests by bringing together the divergent forces. Re-read the chapter in *School of Horsemanship* "On the half-halt" and you will be convinced.

Colonel Podhajsky, the former director of the Vienna School, which considers itself the heir of La Guérinière, defines the aids of the *rassembler* in movement and at the halt, in a way that is very similar, although much more severe, than does Baucher when he describes the co-ordinated effect.

I thus come back to the definition given by Faverot, an unwavering disciple of Baucher, who, in three pages, gives quite a different slant from the one given by the master. Faverot mentions use of the cavesson as an aid in hand, energetic pressure, vigorous jabs with the spurs, taps with the whip, etc. Our own modest experience shows that a horse who responds to the co-ordinated effect as defined by Baucher, that is, who is already perfectly suppled, in no way needs such an arsenal! At this stage, the horse's defenses against the aids have long disappeared, and the co-ordinated effect has no other raison d'être than to perfect the equilibrium.

This co-ordinated effect, an action that is more or less simultaneously an aid of retention and an aid of propulsion – is it not in contradiction to the principle of "hand without legs, legs without hand"?

The wording of Baucher may be ambiguous to the new convert. The introduction to that chapter is as follows: "Soliciting within the correct limits the forces of the hindquarters and the forehand, one establishes their exact opposition or the harmony of forces." That this expression "exact opposition" shocks you is not astonishing – I was shocked in my time. I thought it perhaps an impropriety of expression or negligence of style. It took me more or less ten years to read instead "exact harmony", so true is it that *the two forces cease acting simultaneously and in a contrary sense before the "opposition" makes itself felt*. One should make clear that, at the time, the term "*opposition*" was defined in *Littré* as "to put face to face", "*vis-à-vis*", whereas today the *Robert* talks of "antagonism" and "discord".

May I be forgiven for digressing, but this matter underscores the difficulty of reading and interpreting the classical authors correctly and makes laughable certain quarrels among superficial interpreters.

Application of the Co-ordinated Effect

It can be used as a calming effect during a movement, or when there is mobility at halt, or fidgeting in place, or even to quell a diagonalization not requested. *Either* way, it can only be envisaged at an advanced phase of schooling and considered as a way of re-establishing or perfecting the *rassembler*.

Any attempt at the co-ordinated effect on a sensitive horse without much schooling will bring about defenses in proportion to its efficacy.

A horse who has been worked progressively when seeking transference of weight in one direction or the other, by a disassociation of the actions of hand and leg, will accept without surprise their acting together, when this is introduced progressively over many years of exercises. Displacements of weight, which are the consequence, allow one to bring together, more or less, the lower extremities of the horse, affecting the flexion of joints and the equilibrium, by reducing the horse's base of support.

The execution of the co-ordinated effect starts out with an engagement – a progressive envelopment of the total seat, received gently by the fingers of the hand, wrists still. It terminates with the complete immobilization of the envelopment of seat – thighs – legs, with a simultaneous and immobile closing of fingers and legs.

For example, this is the way one must act to interrupt an unsolicited diagonalization by a nervous horse who cannot hold a regular halt and confuses it with the piaffe. Likewise, can one interrupt the piaffe of a novice horse for whom a simple *descente de main et de jambes* does not suffice.

It is also with a light co-ordinated effect, applied immediately when one halts a horse, that one can perfect regularity or, again with the co-ordinated effect, more or less focused, that one regulates the cadence of a school trot or a slowed-down canter.

To obtain *rassemblés* halts, or to correct any loss of equilibrium, one can effectively terminate the envelopment of seat - thighs - legs with a delicate application of the spur just touching the hair; but a sensitive use of the seat and unusual precision are necessary, otherwise this magical envelopment can become harmful at the slightest involuntary movement.

A co-ordinated effect is applied during just one moment of a stride; if it solicits a halt, it ceases immediately the halt is obtained. If its purpose is to improve the *rassembler*, or the cadence of a trot or canter, it cannot be prolonged beyond a stride without troubling the horse, unless one takes it up again a little farther on. I am fully aware of the difficulty of expressing in a few lines an explanation which requires an observed demonstration, then to be practiced with a well-schooled horse. Alas, that is how it goes with refined and delicate equitation where, as it evolves, any explanation goes beyond the limits of words.

Rassemblés Halts and Strike-offs at the Three Gaits

In *the time to learn* we studied the simple, regular halt, then the *rassemblé* halt from a walk. It is now necessary that our halts, regardless of the gait or the air from which they are requested, are executed with a perfect mise en main. One's idea of the halt should now no longer be that of a halt as rest, or a simple, regular immobilization, but a halt in which all the forces of the horse are concentrated and ready to be utilized. This is the *rassemblé* halt of which La Guérinière says "they are to re-assemble the forces of the horse, to assure him his mouth, head, and haunches, and to make him light to the hand"; a halt that can be solicited at any moment and from which any gait and air can be obtained.

As we have seen, the co-ordinated effect will be indispensable each time the *rassemblé* equilibrium has escaped from us at halts or strike-offs.

The Halt from the Rassemblé Trot

The entire body of the rider contributes: the engagement of the back and the envelopment with the legs, done simultaneously with half-halts with the outside rein, while the inside hand maintains contact with the concave side to avoid an inversion of the bend. The half-halt must never be prolonged. If failure ensues or the horse resists, one must move the horse forward and ask once more for the half-halt without any prolonged tension on the reins.

The Strike-off from a Halt to the Rassemblé Trot

This must happen directly from a halt, completely straight and without any intermediary step. Preparation for the piaffe facilitates the first diagonalized stride of the trot almost in place, with engagement of the hindquarters. Assuring the quality of the departure at the trot is also rooted in the unchanging maintenance of the *rassembler*, when neither the neck nor the head is modified in their carriage to the slightest degree.

For the strike-off to succeed, it is necessary to have action that is simultaneous, precise and light on the part of both legs, linked to the engagement of the lumbar vertebrae, which will push the pelvis forward. The forearms, united with the pelvis, also advance somewhat, which suffices to free a part of the impulsion contained in the *rassemblé* halt.

If the horse still tries to escape or weigh on the hand at the strike-off, a half-halt with the outside rein will re-establish the complete *rassemblé* halt.

The Halt from the Rassemblé Canter

The aids are practically the same as those for the halt from the trot, that is, containing the impulsion by a play with the rein and the straightening of the torso. The inside rein remains unchangeable, setting the head and neck, while the outside hand executes one or several half-halts with the rein on the same side.

These half-halts, which the Germanic authors call "parades" (from the Spanish *parada*, meaning to retain, hold), and which emerge from a very engaged back, bring about the bending of the haunches, thus their lowering, and the elevation of the forehand.

It is with a well-applied half-halt, when the strides of the canter have become as short and as light as possible, and with an easing of the legs, that an outstanding *rassemblé* halt from the canter is realized. To avoid a backwards movement with the subtle equilibrium of the halt, one must maintain the tension of the loins and the light envelopment of the legs at the girth.

The Strike-off from the Halt to the Rassemblé Canter

This must be executed from the immobility of a *rassemblé* halt. At the level of sensitivity which characterizes this halt, the aids for the strike-off must be applied with finesse, for it is no longer a case of striking off with the single, isolated action of the outside leg.

Without exerting the slightest amount of force – with the sensitive actions of fingers – the hand must keep the horse straight on both shoulders and haunches, hind legs flexed; the hand must also feel simultaneously

213

the sensitivity of the poll and the flexion of the lower jaw. Both legs vibrate; the outside leg a few centimeters behind the girth, the inside leg with a slight forward rotation at the girth, which unleashes the canter.

At this stage of the *rassembler*, when the equilibrium is still vulnerable, the amount of force must be at a minimum. A strong action by the outside leg would only throw the haunches inwards, or, on the other hand, the horse could go off on the outside leg.

Should any difficulty arise, and if the horse traverses [steps crooked], straighten him at the *rassemblé* walk, halt with a light bend of the shoulder-in, then strike off once more, but with a reduced intensity of aids. Monitor his position constantly.

6. The Piaffe

Definition of the Piaffe

The piaffe is a diagonalization of the horse's limbs, in place, with an accentuated elevation of the diagonal in suspension, at a slowed-down and regular beat.

The form of the piaffe requires that the toe of the limb being supported is raised more than at the passage, and that the flexion of the haunches is more pronounced.

The piaffe is the most perfect expression of the equestrian equilibrium: compared to it, all the other airs are easily learned. Very few horses are capable of executing the piaffe well and only a few have reached the ability of clearly raising each diagonal from the ground.

The ability to piaffe is as much part of a horse's physiology as his temperamental nature. It also depends upon his physical predisposition at the *rassembler*, which we have already defined, with gaits naturally showing suspension and energy, allied to a temperament that is animated and vigorous.

To understand the piaffe, one must know what it corresponds to when a horse in his natural state moves into it spontaneously. It usually occurs when the horse is in a situation of crisis and in an acute state of excitement, involving an aggressive impulsion, and is also associated with playful or sexual activity.

It is a prelude to an immediate and rapid movement, for which the horse prepares himself by this static mobilization with all the fibers of his body.

Putting the body into a such a state before an intense release, can be seen when a feline gets ready to pounce. Observe a modest cat playing with a ball, or a tiger stalking his prey: all the muscles play in their sheaths without displacing themselves. The runner on the starting line is already mobile, yet still in place. It is the state of high tension for an instantaneous release.

A number of riders who have observed this in horses made angry by brutal treatment, thought they had the key to diagonalization: spurs and the big stick – everything they believed that would frighten a horse. Alas, what brought about these beautiful and rhythmic movements of the horse when they were inspired by passion, degenerated into disordered and formless behavior under blows.

Actually, there are proportionally fewer *écuyers* capable of making horses execute the piaffe correctly, than there are horses talented enough to execute this brilliant air.

Conceptions of the Piaffe

One usually reads – I myself have written this some twenty years ago – that the piaffe belongs to the passage, or even to the trot in place.

Indeed, if one holds on to the idea of rhythmic invariability, it is when starting out with the gradual shortening of the walk in great animation that the horse goes most regularly and easily and without hiatus from this gait to diagonalization. Steinbrecht qualifies this movement as the *piaffé* walk. He requests it "with the hindquarters well engaged and short elastic strides... by progressively intensifying the aids". (Steinbrecht, *The Gymnasium of the Horse* – 1885).

The School of Versailles began the piaffe at the pillars, balancing the haunches back and forth, and reducing progressively the lateral displacement, up to the mobilization of the hind legs in place. They then combined this work with the *rassemblé* trot to end up with the passage.

Baucher and his disciples replaced the formidable fixed point of the pillars by the hand of the rider, in hand, while, with the whip in the other hand, they activated the hind legs. By means of these alternate actions, they made the horse diagonalize in place. A procedure very similar is still used by the Vienna School.

General Decarpentry, as explained in *Piaffe and Passage*, prepared the piaffe with two exercises involving direct transitions between halt and trot. In one exercise, the emphasis was on a progressive reduction in the time spent at halt. In the other, from a very straight, steady, *rassemblé* halt, he would "jump" the horse into the trot, halting after just three or four strides.

So far as Maître Oliveira is concerned, his choice depended on the temperament of the horse he was schooling. To the question asked by aspiring *écuyers*: "Must one begin with the passage or the piaffe?" he answered: "With a horse energetic and gifted to execute diagonalization, begin with the passage; with a horse energetic but less gifted to diagonalize, begin with the piaffe; with a horse who is languid, begin also with the piaffe."

After having taught the passage and the piaffe to several scores of horses, I have come to the conclusion that one should prepare both airs together, in that there is a greater difference between the piaffe and the passage than between the trot and the passage. I bring them together through the transition from one to the other, but only after having worked them separately and differently for a long time.

Of course, it is easy to be in accord with all the serious writers on one fact, namely, that there will be neither a brilliant piaffe nor a brilliant passage without having first gone through the school walk and the school trot.

The piaffe in hand. Nymphéa, 8 years.

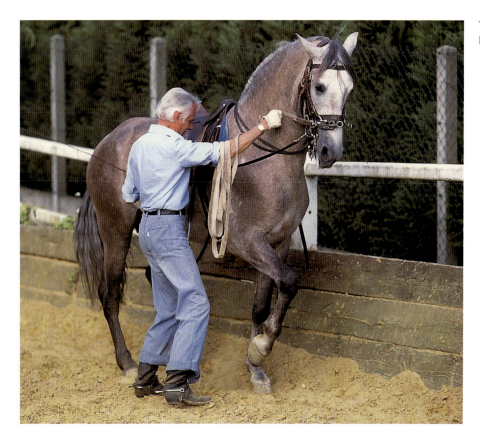

The piaffe in hand,
Fandango, 8 years.

Preparing for the Piaffe

I work the young horse in hand as soon as he has been broken in and is
familiar with the elementary aids.

When working in hand, I can, without difficulty, get the horse to move
to a regular straight halt, to rein back, and move forward straight. When
he executes correctly the shoulder-in and strike-offs at the trot from a halt,
I begin to ask of him a light diagonalization in place and I reward him as
soon as he has given it.

At the second year of mounted work, I begin to seek an active and sustained walk through light half-halts, more shortened for a few strides
before putting him back into a good regular walk.

I mix halts and light rein-backs, executed with the straight and set position of the head/neck ensemble that this work demands. I do a few raised
and shortened steps. One must then avoid letting the horse halt and ensure
that he does not mobilize prematurely in place in order that he can elude
the effort which the reinforcement of the flexion of his strides requires.

I put him forward again at a more ample walk, while retaining his *mise
en main* with contact, but without traction.

As the transitions from the regular walk to the *rassemblé* walk become easier, I slow down the *rassemblé* walk by advancing slightly into diagonalization, and, after a beat in place, I go forward again at a regular walk while maintaining the *mise en main*.

To this work at the walk, and in addition to all the suppling exercises, I add halts from trot and strike-offs at the trot from a halt, reducing the intermediary strides.

In order to engage further the horse's hindquarters when taking off at the trot, I sometimes ask him to take off from a rein-back.

This gymnastic work, brought about with a rigorous adherence to "hand without legs, legs without hand", allows me to obtain quite easily at the end of the second or third year strike-offs at the trot, preceded voluntarily with some diagonalized steps, which are not yet a piaffe because they are neither suspended nor very elevated, but which tie in well with the first strides of the trot.

Here, as with all the other school exercises and airs, it is not only useless but actually detrimental to try to cut short the time necessary to obtain a movement in the air.

The piaffe under saddle. Spartacus, 6 years. 12 to 18 months of suppling brings about a relaxation of the poll as well as a pronounced and improved *mise en main*.

To obtain these majestic slow and elevated steps, even with a most gifted horse, one must have gone beyond *the time to understand* and *to learn* and have reached the time *to do*, in order to have at one's disposal a force that is calm because the horse is confident. This time corresponds to the serene maturity of the horse who has all his ideas in place: he knows that he can.

Orphée, 8 years.

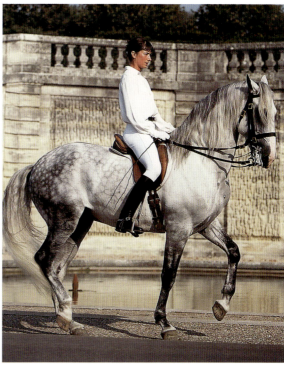

Orphée, 10 years.

Execution of the Piaffe

For the person who has never made a horse piaffe, it is necessary to give an idea of the precise dosage of the aids. One must know that the *piaffe* is *possible only when the horse ceases to lean against the hand*, beyond the simple contact; at the first indication of leaning, a slight half-halt with the outside rein, together with engagement of the pelvis and the indicative rhythm of the legs, and the horse lowers his haunches and elevates his forehand.

One must also be able to predict the usual reaction of the horse who is insufficiently schooled and who, when the *rassembler* is requested, throws his haunches to the inside, especially on the right rein, provoking a noticeable irregularity with the diagonals when touching the ground. It is when a flexion begins to invert into a shoulder-in, that, by maintaining the bend with the inside rein and supporting with the outside rein, one can re-establish the regularity of the diagonals.

Once a straight *rassembler* is obtained, the piaffe is unleashed by the alternate action of the legs, corresponding to the diagonal solicited. Press with the right leg at the moment the right foreleg is put down; likewise for the left. The torso must be raised upwards and slightly backwards, the hand a little raised and light, making only such action as is occasionally necessary to maintain the horse's flexion, but allowing no support from the hand. A pliable seat, a supple waist, will enable one to obtain a pendulous movement then enhance it until a slow, regular cadence is reached, so that one no longer knows if this action emanates from the seat of the rider or the haunches of the horse; when the horse's hind leg flexes on one side and the rider's hip descends on the same side, facilitating the application of the relaxed leg on the horse's flank.

The assistance of a helper with a whip should occur seldom. At the beginning of the horse's schooling, it can bring a little stimulation, supporting the propulsive aids when the horse is languid or hesitant; at the end, it can serve as a brilliant touch. I make use of this only on rare occasions, haunted by the possibility that the horse no longer listens to me when I am alone with him!

If the flexion of the joints and the lowering of the haunches are indispensable to the piaffe, the vertical position of the nose must not be con-

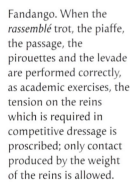

Fandango. When the *rassemblé* trot, the piaffe, the passage, the pirouettes and the levade are performed correctly, as academic exercises, the tension on the reins which is required in competitive dressage is proscribed; only contact produced by the weight of the reins is allowed.

sidered as obligatory with all horses. Some defective necks do not rule out the piaffe, on the condition that one does not force them into an impossible position.

After a promising beginning, the piaffe sometimes gets "stuck", and becomes difficult and lusterless. One must then go back to the base of the horse's preparation: variations at the trot and gentle transitions with reduction of strides up to the halt, taken up again at the *rassemblé* trot.

You should know that the piaffe, which is the carriage of a triumphant stallion, develops with the maturity of the horse; it is foolish to expect it from a creature who is not yet 7 years old.

7. The Passage

Definition of the Passage

The passage comes from the Italian *spasseggio*: the promenade. This elegant promenade is a diagonalized trot with a majestic and cadenced beat, all the more beautiful when the unleashing of each diagonal is energetic and produces the elevation and suspension of the mass.

Fandango in passage.

If I broach the passage after having executed the piaffe, as we have observed when we studied this air, it is because the diagonalization in place, which is the first phase, can be achieved quite early both in hand and mounted. The real passage, which emerges only from a perfect *rassemblé* trot, can only be realized after many years of study and after one has obtained a reasonably good school trot.

The ideal image of a beautiful passage is when a horse, light to both hand and leg, whose total musculature works without rigidity, and whose total joints play with suppleness, allows the rider to meter out the propulsive force as he wishes, from the shortening of gaits up to the piaffe, or a letting out into the most extended trot.

Conception of the Passage

The form of the passage is judged by the regularity of its strides, by the verticality of the foreleg when it touches the ground, and the total flexion of its associated hind leg. The toe of the foreleg in suspension

Nymphéa in passage.

Orphée in passage.

must be raised to the middle of the cannon bone of the other foreleg; that of the hind leg, above the fetlock. The forearm must be held horizontally and form a right angle with the cannon bone. The passage must be straight without any oscillation of the trunk.

Now that we have seen the nature of this air, let us see quickly how the air should not be done… and how it most often is: diagonalized steps with an unequal amplitude of the diagonals. One must then activate further the leg on the side where the strides are shorter, and verify the straightness of the horse.

The "*passagé*" trot is the most tarnished form of the passage because it is the result of a vicious system, or, rather, it is corrupted by premature extensions of the trot and works against the hand. The horse, having adopted the habit of throwing himself "on his nose" whenever he feels an aggressive take-over by the bit and spurs, displaces himself with diagonalized steps but opened forelegs, dragging hind legs, a hollow back and a constant heavy contact against the hand.

To arrive quickly at extension without going through the preliminary phase of lowering the haunches, these horses have been pushed on to their shoulders and blocked by the hand, until they have obtained the infamous "shooting the cuffs" [the forelegs are thrust out stiffly as though the horse were trying to adjust the shirt cuffs within a jacket.]

The true school trot is the non-disputable movement of transition, through the *rassembler*, to achieve the extended trot and the passage. When a horse, who has been rushed into extension without the transitional work at the school trot, finds himself embraced by the enveloping aids for passage, he reacts by producing the false suspensions which Steinbrecht mentions in order to stigmatize this deviant form of passage.

Unfortunately, this is the form one observes most frequently during competitions, even international ones, with about two or three exceptions.

Let us mention at this point another stigma, which occurs when the horse is poorly prepared to piaffe: little disorderly hops; acute spasms provoked by the harsh and awkward interventions of the spur.

Preparation for the Passage

The preparation has been envisaged by many authors, using methods notably varied and different. Each method claims to be the best. Some, such as J. Fillis, make use of a complicated and harsh combination of hand, legs, and spurs. "I incite him to go into the trot by pushing him with strong legs, I hold him back with the hand to prevent him from stretching. The horse unable to stretch his legs, raises them… At the same time, with the aid of the spur, he manages to make little hops from one diagonal to the other." (J.Fillis, *Principes de Dressage* – 1891.) [The English translation is entitled *Breaking and Riding*.] This is rather terrifying and yet Fillis was a well-known world figure. His photos are unequivocal!

The Baucherists take off from the piaffe, which they develop slowly, to the passage, without insisting sufficiently on the close link between the *rassemblé* trot and the passage.

Others recommended arriving at the passage with successive counter-changes on two tracks to the trot – excellent exercises, but far from being able to achieve the passage.

Beudant supports what he calls the "natural passage", the secret of which consists of not letting go the right leg while the left leg acts with greater strength. A secret from which I tried to profit in vain!

In short, I am more and more convinced that the best passage emerged from the school trot and suppling which La Guérinière gave as his first recommendation for the passage: "After having given the horse his first suppling by means of the trot on one track, on a straight line, and on the circle, I rounded him and taught him to place his legs on the ground in the circular position of the shoulder-in" (*School of Horsemanship*, Chapter 14).

Steinbrecht, German counterpart of La Guérinière, wrote the following one hundred years later: "The precise moment to begin work at the

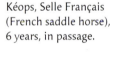

Kéops, Selle Français
(French saddle horse),
6 years, in passage.

passage occurs when the horse…at the school trot has succeeded in moving at a regular gait on one track, as on two tracks." (Steinbrecht, *The Gymnasium of the Horse* – 1885).

The Vienna School also prepares diagonalization in hand and works the transitions of the trot to get to the passage. Maître Oliveira introduces his study of the passage by saying: "The passage is the more artistic form of the *rassemblé* trot" (Nuno Oliveira, *Principes Classiques de l'art de Dresser les Chevaux* – 1983).

Execution of the Passage

The first thing that must be verified before approaching the passage is the preservation of straightness, as essential to the school trot as to the working trot. The *rassembler*, based on compression more than on gymnastics, may provoke a reflex causing the haunches to escape by traversing, which will alter the passage and debase its quality.

When the straightness of the *rassemblé* trot is assured, one verifies the sensitivity of the horse with transitions of the trot. The variations in amplitude produced by the sensitive actions of the aids, in extensions as in shortenings of the trot, serve as a test to indicate the preparedness of the horse to execute the passage.

If any of these points still do not convince, the perfection of the *rassemblé* trot must be sought in an impulsive trot on circles. The flexion of the horse favors the development of the outside diagonal on the circle: circle to the left, inflexion to the left, thus improvement of the right diagonal (right foreleg, left hind leg more engaged).

If straightness and transitions are correct, we will then ask the horse to move energetically from the *rassemblé* trot to the working trot. At the very moment he begins to extend his stride, by means of a steady and gentle half-halt we ask for the return of the *rassemblée* cadence then, with a *descente de main*, our legs are alternately brought at contact, following the rhythm when each diagonal touches the ground: right diagonal, right leg, left diagonal, left leg. These opposing aids (broken up into sequences), bring about one or two moments of suspension, which must immediately be followed by a return to a free trot and a treat.

The diagonalized cadence which now begins has been named the *doux* passage. It has nothing to do with the "passagé" trot wherein the horse is more or less against the rider's hand and drags his hind legs. However, with the *doux* passage, diagonalization is light, the back raised, the haunches function well. Only the elevation is still *slight* and the moment of suspension brief, thereby distinguishing the *doux* passage from the passage itself.

Progressive development and a year or two more work – but without jostling or harshness – will be needed to obtain the superior form of the passage.

If the work is conducted this way, without jabs with spurs or hand, I guarantee that you will not experience any of those horrible little hops or other stompings.

If I can judge on the basis of the contortions of all novices, the passage aids are conceived as very complicated. What is absolutely essential is to have a master direct you and a well schooled horse under you, and to have covered several stretches of territory at this gait in order to capture the simple rhythmic action.

The rider begins to *rassembler* himself above the horse's center of gravity: torso vertical, seat on the perineum and ischia, thighs lowered knees in contact, legs relaxed and free, inside hand low and still, outside rein in support. The rider launches the trot with energetic strides; amplitude is then reduced with the support of loins and gentle half-halts, which encourage the knee and hock joints to take on a heightened flexion, animated but free from stiffness and tension.

Pliable seat and legs, by means of their alternate actions, receive and impart actions of the horse's back and abdominal muscles when each hind leg touches the ground.

It is not the force of the aids which creates or raises the passage, but their precise harmony at the right moment. A caress with the leg at the moment when the hind leg is raised, acts as an animating trigger. A half-halt (take up-yield) on a rein, puts weight on the hind leg and lightens the foreleg. At the passage, as at the piaffe, when the movement is launched, one no longer knows whether it is the movement that unleashes the aids, or the aids, the movement). Indeed, at this point, the aids merely enrich the movement, regulating themselves to it.

Perfecting the Passage

To develop the maximum degree of unleashed elevation, as soon as the horse has gone more than one or two lengths at the *doux* passage, put him into this air on circles of about 15 meters in diameter.

If the horse moves easily at a *rassemblé* trot on circles and voltes, he will, without much difficulty, leave the support of the wall and be able to flex on the curve without his hindquarters escaping and without losing the moment of suspension. The power and elevation of his strides will increase.

As soon as the passage has been correctly established, one attempts the half-pass at this air, which will increase his ease and improve the flexion of his limbs. However, because of the nature of the half-pass, where the difficulty is greater than on circles, a deformation of the quadrilateral figure which the four limbs trace can occur. The diagonal mechanism can, from time to time, be put out of order if the hindquarters manage to escape. One must then take up the passage on a single track once more and begin again. When one feels a loss of amplitude or *tride* [a term used by the former *écuyers* to describe movements that are animated, cadenced, elevated, elegant], one should go into energetic transitions from the passage to an ample and accentuated trot, then return to the passage. One will find once more the animation and brilliance that had become dull with routine.

Transitions of the Piaffe, Passage, and Trot

If one has followed our progression from the beginning of the second year, transitions from the piaffe to the trot, begun with a light diagonalization in place to link on to the trot, should cause no problems. Neither should transitions from the school trot to the piaffe or to the passage cause any. This being so, we must now practice transitions from the piaffe to the passage and back.

The difference in equilibrium between the two airs is a very important factor, and the risk of losing impulsion when doing the transition is a permanent one.

At the piaffe, the haunches are lower, the raising of the forehand is more pronounced and the placing of legs on the ground is executed in place. At the passage, each diagonal throws the mass forwards and modifies the equilibrium by positioning it slightly more horizontally.

At first, during the transition from the piaffe to passage, one must tolerate an intermediary stride that is slightly less raised because it is advancing a little. The transition from the passage to the piaffe is even more delicate, in that it needs the return of the more pronounced flexion of the haunches. It is necessary to re-enforce the propulsive aids, contained by half-halts, the purpose of which is to reduce the amplitude of the strides, and the fingers must be concerned with maintaining the permanent yielding of the jaw and poll.

8. Pirouettes at the Canter and at the Piaffe

The pirouettes at the walk and the demi-pirouettes at the canter are now well executed. They will serve as a basis for the pirouette at the canter and the piaffe.

The Pirouette at the Canter

The conception of the pirouette at the canter is as follows. When executing the pirouette at the canter (360 degrees), the forehand turns around the hindquarters, with the inside hind leg marking the cadence of the canter in place with 6 to 8 equal and cadenced strides.

During and after the pirouette, the horse must maintain the cadence of the *rassemblé* canter unfailingly. Also, if the pirouette has been started from a straight line, the horse should move straight forward on that line upon completion; similarly, if the movement begun from a half-pass, the horse should smoothly take up the lateral flexion of that figure once more.

The pivoting hind leg can describe a small circle while advancing, but this must not exceed 30 centimeters in diameter. With the pirouette, the indispensable lowering of the haunches promotes the raising of the forehand.

Let us now look at the preparation of the pirouette at the canter.

During our study of the quarter and demi-pirouette, we saw that the half-pass at the canter, together with the canter in place, serve as its foundation, and that when one brings the pivoting hind leg beneath the center of gravity, the forehand can turn around the hindquarters.

One prepares this very slow canter with demi-voltes on the haunches and small voltes that are very *rassemblées*, reinforced by the inside leg. The inflexion of the ensemble is made with the shoulder-in at the canter, first on fractions of diagonals, then along the tracks, combined with demi-voltes on two tracks to continue with croup to the wall.

Each time one notices that the quality of the canter is being affected because of difficulties confronting the horse, halt him in a flexed position, lighten him, and take off once again in the same position.

It would also be excellent to reduce the forward movement and obliquity of the horse with the half-pass at the canter on diagonals, ending up with the half-pass without advancing, [which comes close to being a full pass] almost parallel to the long sides. If one notices that the haunches present considerable inertia in the lateral movement when executing this exercise, one returns to reversed pirouettes at the walk and to circles at the counter-canter with a strong bend to hold the haunches to the outside of the circle. A certain amount of linked work, of which examples follow, prepares for the execution of the pirouettes. One first chooses those exercises which best accommodate the horse, and one then insists on those which present the greatest difficulties.

The circle is reduced progressively at the canter, haunches-in, together with halts, strike-offs, and fractions of the pirouettes at the walk.

One rides at the counter-canter on a circle, followed by moving onto a diagonal without a lead change, at the end of which one makes a tight demi-volte on two tracks, ending up with a pirouette.

One strikes off at the counter-canter, then passes through the two corners of the short side, turns and goes to the center line across the *manège*, does the half-pass head to wall (travers position) until the first corner of the other short side, where one asks for a few steps of the pirouette, which one terminates at a walk.

"The passade and croup to wall" described by the Vienna School, with pirouettes at the corners. At the end of the track, one does a tight half-turn around the hindquarters, describing a semi-circle. One keeps the hindquarters on a parallel line at 3 meters from the long side up to the first and second corners of the short side, which one passes doing a pirouette at the canter towards the outside; one continues at a counter-canter passing the third corner, croup to wall, and one straightens.

On the circle at a canter, with a volte within the circle. When the volte is executed easily, with the outside lateral aid one makes first a tight half-turn on the haunches, then, later, a demi-pirouette. One finds oneself at a counter-canter on the circle: this time one does the volte towards the outside, then a half-turn and, later, a demi-pirouette, One gets to the full

BELOW, LEFT AND RIGHT
Fandango. Pirouettes at the canter.

pirouettes in the same manner. *In the meantime, between these exercises, one maintains impulsion by means of riding energetically forward at the canter.*

To introduce the execution of the pirouette at the canter, one starts out with a combination of a pirouette at the walk and strike-off at the canter from a halt. That is to say, once the horse can pirouette in good form on both reins at the walk, and can depart from halt to canter, one puts the horse into pirouette at the walk – to the right, for example – then, after a couple of steps, one asks him to strike off into right canter and to perform one or two steps of the pirouette in canter before halting. Should the horse show the slightest sign of misunderstanding or error, one returns to the pirouette at the walk. When all goes well, one progressively increases the number of steps ridden at the canter.

Finally, to correct the tendency horses to have to step backwards when executing pirouettes, one makes them react to the impulsion engendered

BELOW LEFT Orphée.
Pirouette at the canter.

BELOW RIGHT Spartacus.
Pirouette at the canter.

by the inside leg. An excellent exercise for achieving this consists of riding each of the four quarters of the pirouette at each corner of an imaginary square of about 15 meters. On covering each quarter of the pirouette, one rides the horse forward 15 meters, and begins the next quarter pirouette at the next corner.

Execution of the Pirouette

This is a delicate exercise and one that most rarely succeeds. At the same time, it demands all the qualities that have been mentioned here.

One must sit perfectly on the horse's axis, one's torso slightly turned inwards and a little backwards, one also puts weight on the inside buttock. The outside leg envelopes without force; the inside leg is active at the girth to maintain the cadence of the horse's inside hind leg. The inside rein indicates the movement and the light bend; the outside rein is held at the base of the neck towards the inside, *without pulling*.

The lateral flexion must be moderate, otherwise one risks contractions and a veering of the haunches. *The descentes de main are essential, as one cannot force a pirouette, one can only indicate it.*

The horse is put to the test with this exercise; one must not repeat it too often, for opposition of hand to legs can have grave consequences.

The Pirouette at the Piaffe

If one owns a horse with a good equilibrium and sensitivity, one can achieve this movement. It is a superb air, which expresses well the skill of the horse and the talent of his trainer. It contributes to the equilibrium in general, especially to pirouettes at the canter.

When the horse executes the piaffe easily, one places oneself on the track along the wall. One starts the pirouette in piaffe by gently bringing the horse's forehand to the inside by means of very light rein aids and giving him support with gentle actions from the inside leg. As soon as he has displaced himself with two steps *one lets him piaffe in place to restore his equilibrium*, one the takes up the movement again, and so on, until one has executed first a quarter, then a demi-pirouette. When the exercise has been understood on each rein, one goes back to the center line.

If one has a skilled assistant, one asks him to contribute his attentive presence and a discreet and subtle application of the whip, to the horse's hind leg or, where necessary to prevent any veering or backward movement.

Should the horse become unbalanced, it is important to return to a light piaffe in place.

9. The Levade

The levade is an air wherein the horse "raises the forehand quite high, in one place. He must bend his haunches and hocks underneath his body... He must bend his upper forelegs in such a way that his feet turn up almost to the elbow" (La Guérinière, *School of Horsemanship*).

It is the first of the airs above the ground and, in a way, the basis, for the others.

Until the 18th century, only the pesade was mentioned, wherein the horse raised his forehand up to 45 degrees above the ground. In the 19th century, the term levade described the same air, executed with an elevation of about 30 degrees. One must not confuse the levade or the classical pesade – which are achieved with the most complete suppling up to the piaffe – with the *cabrer* (rearing) which is, at most, a requested defense, wherein the horse raises himself almost vertically and rigidly up on his hocks.

Initially, these airs above the ground, or school jumps, were intended to help a rider surrounded by infantrymen to free himself in one bound, by means of a lançade, a cabriole, or a courbette. How artistic and wonderful war must have been in those days!

Characteristics School Jumpers Must Have

In principle, horses with rather short backs, powerful haunches and joints are best.

Paraphrasing La Guérinière, I would say that these horses must, of their own accord, show a natural inclination for this air. That is, they must execute work in hand without undue effort, *rassemblé*, and be able, quite naturally, to pick up their forelegs from the ground when one pushes them into a very engaged piaffe, with light oppositions from the hand.

La Guérinière emphasizes, however, that it is more important for the horse to have an even disposition and be attentive, rather than to be strong, and vigorous, yet worried and nervous. "The horse endowed with mediocre strength, but with a great deal of courage and lightness, is unquestionably better because he gives what is needed willingly." (La Guérinière, *School of Horsemanship*.)

Of all the horses I had at my disposal, only one seemed to have the necessary mental aptitudes for the levade, despite his large size of 1m 70 and his somewhat long-limbed conformation, which could make one doubt. His levades were quite correct.

It is obvious that if one works at the levade as a prelude to the caprioles and courbettes, mounted, a tremendous athletic force is called for.

The Levade at the School of Versailles

At the School of Versailles, work between the pillars was the usual train-ing method for preparing a horse for the *rassembler*, being used to dis-cover and develop "his resources, vigor, generosity, his lightness and his disposition" (La Guérinière, *School of Horsemanship*). In a word, to put him on his haunches and get him ready for the piaffe. They maintained the same technical logic in preparing the horse for the levade.

Having attached the horse between the pillars, shortened the rein attached to the pommel of the saddle "as much as was necessary to keep the horse's head in the correct position" (the *placer*); the *écuyer* placed himself behind, facing the croup, clicking with his tongue and swishing his whip.

When, tied between the ropes, the horse began to raise his forehand, an assistant, standing next to his shoulders, touched him with the whip on his chest or on his forelegs. The horse raised himself, bent his forearms, and lowered and placed his haunches under himself, incited by the whip of the *écuyer*. At this point, La Guérinière says: "No matter how little he raises himself, one must stop and caress him."

Orphée at the pillars. Mobilization in place.

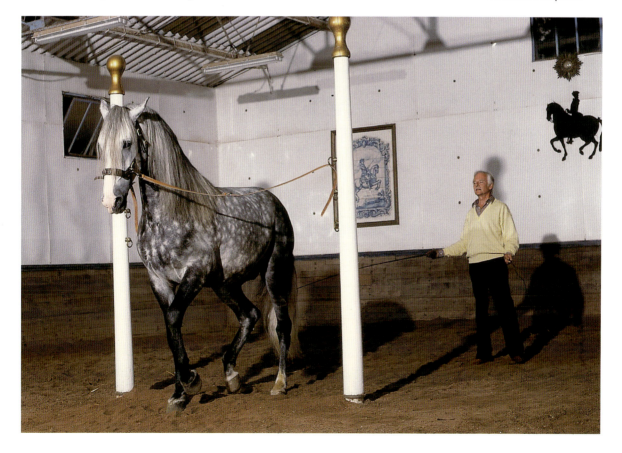

Fandango at the pillars, in piaffe.

As soon as he was in the position of the pesade, one refrained from using the whip so as not to unleash any bounds. One untied him, mounted him and, riding on straight lines, touched his shoulders, holding him back gently with equal reins; one brought one's calves closer to him and asked him to execute a pesade, followed by a piaffe.

If, after coming down from the pesade, he went into a half-pass, La Guérinière recommended that one "rein back, and go into another pesade and caress him". If he resisted and over-bent, one made him go forward.

The great master concluded "that they ought not to be pushed to the limit of their capacities executing this air, because they might become hardened".

Preparation for the Levade without Pillars

The horse must have already obtained a good piaffe, mounted. One can then move on to the pillars to perfect him and raise him further.

For the first two or three lessons, I attach long reins to the snaffle without side reins; a skilled assistant takes hold of these, while I take the short, guiding lungeing line of the cavesson in one hand, the whip in the other.

The assistant holds the horse straight and with a forward inclination along the wall, with equal contact on both reins. When I ask for the forehand to be raised, he increases his supporting contact. I intensify the piaffe in place using the whip behind the hocks and request the raising of the forehand with the guiding lungeing line.

It is normal that, during these early lessons, the horse becomes annoyed and tries to throw himself to the right and to the left; one must often interrupt this work and reassure the horse.

The horse may sometimes detach himself from the ground by raising the forehand too high and extending his hocks. One tries again until only the forehand is raised.

If he throws his forelegs rigidly forwards, one touches them, giving little quick taps with the whip, until he bends them backwards towards himself. At this point, reward him generously.

One first gives this lesson a few days in a row, then every two or three days.

Once the horse performs calmly, and now having only to find his equilibrium and stability when raised, one abandons the long reins, retaining only the guiding lungeing line and the whip. If the horse goes above the bit, one can install side reins. When he raises himself, he must neither bend to the side nor incline towards one. Six to eight months are necessary to obtain an equilibrium more or less appropriate to this air.

The Levade, Mounted

One intensifies the mounted piaffe, preserving an honest contact, while maintaining lightness. One raises the wrists slightly and one accentuates contact with the legs, bending the torso slightly backwards although this must remain perpendicular to the ground once the horse is up. [Once the horse is in levade, in order for the rider's upper body to be perpendicular *to the ground*, it must be angled forwards in respect of its relationship *to the horse*.]

The horse raises his forehand slowly, steadying himself on his flexed hind legs. When he has reached the point of his equilibrium, lightness has become total; if he loses balance on the forehand, one brings it back only with one's fingers, if he loses balance towards the back, it is restored with the legs.

It is by yielding with the fingers and contact with legs that one re-establishes the lowering of the forehand.

If the rider is awkward or rough, or if the horse is insufficiently prepared, he will defend himself, rear, and over-bend.

While not yet very experienced at this air, but prudent and working

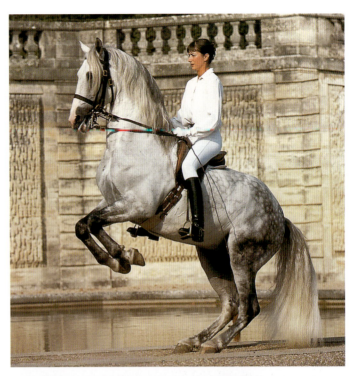

Two pictures of
Orphée in levade.

progressively, I never experienced the slightest defense – at the most, some excitation.

Each time he tries to avoid going into the levade or out of it, the horse should be brought energetically forward at the piaffe.

A well-executed levade is evidence of a natural progression towards the *rassembler* of a gifted horse, in harmony with his trainer.

10. Recapitulation Model of "The Time to Perfect"

Our three horses are now 7 and 8 years old. Here is a recapitulation model, bringing together the exercises and airs with which they have begun to be familiar. The abundant material at this level of schooling makes it almost impossible to work at everything every day. Two or three times a month, after some relaxation, one can link together all the airs of the program, which, in about fifty minutes, represents a considerable amount of concentration and energy. To do this daily would lead to fatigue and disgust, which would tarnish the *brio* of which the horse is capable.

After warming up and suppling the horse, a rational training program should lead to working alternately those points which are the weakest. One should be satisfied to work the principal airs in outline, or even omit those which work well, but perfect those which need it.

Apart from the airs, one must not forget the essential goal of one's school work, which is the constant perfecting of the three natural gaits on one track. To that, one must also devote a great amount of time, not only in the *manège*, but also outdoors, on good and varied terrain.

This recapitulation model is thus a summary, from which one must choose daily what is most essential and most urgent, while not leaving out a repetition of all the elements, if only to verify their accuracy and to keep them in mind.

Time to Relax

The walk must be stretched, ample, straight, and regular, the reins fairly long, yet having sufficient contact for the neck to be in a horizontal position; when this occurs, one must begin without delay the dialogue between a confident mouth and a supple poll.

At the trot, the same conditions apply, and, regardless of the *quality* of the cadence, one must verify that the cadence the horse gives us is our own, the one we decided upon, and not the one the horse decided to do, even if it is correct.

At the Walk

After eight or ten minutes of relaxation at the walk or trot, to which we added a few circles at the canter, we return to the *rassemblé* walk. On the right rein, we execute a volte at the second corner of the short side to prepare a right shoulder-in, covering two-thirds of the long side, which we then leave at a quarter circle, doing the same shoulder-in.

When we reach the center of the *manège*, we slow down the movement to transform it into a rotation of the haunches around the shoulders, still with the same bend, the horse pivoting around his inside foreleg.

We continue doing a quarter circle at the shoulder-in, which brings us to the track opposite the one we have just left.

Maintaining the bend to the right, we leave the track doing the half-pass with the horse parallel to it, from left to right, up to the center line where we execute a complete pirouette, which we leave by going forward on the center line. We regain the outside track in the middle of the short side, execute a transition, extending the walk and lengthening the neck.

The recapitulation work of *the time to perfect* must be founded upon work on the three gaits, and transitions within and between the gaits.

One executes the same program on the other rein. From one day to the next, one can vary the precise movements, with counter-changes of hand from the center line going here and there, the half-pass in each direction on the center line and circles with haunches-in. Verify also the halt, and do a straight rein-back on the center line.

At the Trot

Take off at a working trot, seeking regularity. It must be free, if not, go back and try again. Control the steadiness of the haunches, but also their sensitivity on circles, with no veering or contractions. Ride transitions at the *rassemblé* trot; pay attention to the cadence on one track; do a volte of 6 meters to control the sensitivity of the horse within the aids. The volte at the *rassemblé* trot is more difficult than the shoulder-in at the same rhythm.

Go from a straight *rassemblé* trot to a *rassemblé* halt, then, without any period of immobility, link on to a straight rein-back, then go forward at a *rassemblé* trot, still without a period of immobility.

You can obtain a strong propulsion from the haunches at strike-offs by means of legs and seat but without fingers, alternating with half-halts with fingers.

Ride transitions from the *rassemblé* trot to four beats of the piaffe; go forward from the piaffe to the *rassemblé* trot two or three times in succession.

Relax, with reins long. Then take up the *rassemblé* trot again, do a counter-change of hand on two tracks; circle on two tracks, haunches-in; go large, do transitions from the *rassemblé* trot to a working trot with an absolute maximum of impulsion, returning to a most energetic *rassemblé* trot. From the start of a long side or a diagonal, extend the trot. At the farthest end, return to the *rassemblé* trot, with an accentuated flexion of the haunches.

Go to inside track at 1.5–2 m from the wall, remaining parallel to it, verifying whether the horse keeps straight or whether he is attracted to the wall. This is an interesting test, indicating whether the horse is well channeled between the aids. Finally, still at the trot, turn and go down to the center line at the shoulder-in and at the half-pass.

The Canter

At a working canter on one track go large around the *manège*, then on to circles and voltes. Execute the half-pass on the diagonal and, at the end of the *manège*, do a circle at the counter-canter, leave the circle on the diagonal and, at the center of the *manège*, take advantage of the horse's equilibrium being now ready to execute a demi-pirouette.

Go large at canter, then turn down the center line, halt, rein back, and strike off again, straight into the canter.

Change lead and canter on inside tracks, a little away from walls, and straight.

Ride a transition from the *rassemblé* canter to one or two steps in place, quite straight, then go forward.

Move on to the half-pass, head and croup to wall (travers and renvers positions), with a quarter pirouette in the corners.

Execute the half-pass on median lines and diagonals, then at X execute a pirouette.

The Piaffe

From the walk, ask for a piaffe on the track, then, on inside tracks, verify the regularity of the diagonal movements which are rarely evident in the horse's natural state, and thus require constant attention under saddle.

From the trot, execute a transition to the piaffe then, from the piaffe return to the trot. Execute a demi-pirouette and pirouette at the piaffe, retaining the outside haunch well, and paying attention to all this in the mirror.

The Passage

From the walk, then from the *rassemblé* trot, execute transitions to the passage.

Do the passage on circles. Do the half-pass at the passage. Do transitions from the passage to the piaffe and from the piaffe to the passage. Should the horse drag his hind legs, return to an energetic *rassemblé* trot, requiring considerable energy from the hind legs. To succeed with these transitions, rather than alternating the movement with one's legs as is recommended with diagonal gaits, close both legs simultaneously.

Recommendations

Link together, and vary, the possible combinations of exercises on two tracks, utilizing the bends of the shoulder-in, then passing on to the half-pass and vice versa.

With all this gymnastic work, and regardless of the gait, be greatly concerned with a certain requirements, noted below.

The steadfastness of the cadence at all transitions is essential, including – and above all – when you go from a straight line to a two-track movement.

Note the symmetry of your horse's flexion. Horses almost always tend to bend the neck more easily to the left than to the right: *do not let yourself be fooled, pay attention to the flexion to the right, regulate the one on the left*. Equality of contact on each side of the mouth is the best indication. It is an especially delicate matter to maintain it with counter-changes of hand, but it is essential at the piaffe and the passage.

The symmetry of movements: note the equality of strides, equality of the distance traveled between each counter-change of hand, the constancy of the angle formed between the horse and the long side relating to two-track exercises.

The straightness at this level of schooling must be perfect at all gaits, whether on inside tracks or along the wall, with rein-backs as with forward strike-offs.

The different elevation and length of step in the gait variations must not be forced or precipitated, neither should there be false strides.

The *mise en main* is the result of putting the horse in the correct equilibrium through co-ordination of the aids, alternating with seat and fingers. If it is not achievable within the gait, halt, lighten, and move off again on the other rein.

CHAPTER FIVE

Forgotten Exercises and Rejected Airs

U NTIL THE END OF THE 18th century, equitation was still considered to be fundamentally a martial discipline; however, it was already beginning to be considered as a moving art form. This view initiated a certain number of exercises which gave the horses a greater facility to develop certain combat positions with greater precision and speed. La Guérinière stated it in the following manner: that the martial arts and the art of horsemanship owe a great deal to each other.

When one considers all the training and exercises that have been designed to develop a horse's speed and agility, one realizes that some of them have been forgotten today because they are too rigorous and difficult for many horses. They would, nonetheless, give a greater brilliance to the very best of them.

I will present here some of these exercises, from which one could profit without any serious contra-indications.

1. The Two Ends-in

This is more an equine posture than an exercise; rather, it is a position to be prepared, which one can utilize later with certain exercises. One flexes the horse for a while, giving a considerable lateral bend to the ensemble, wherein one holds the haunches in almost as much as one does the shoulders, neck, and head. The *écuyers* of the past utilized this position "to shorten the base [frame] and make those horses, whose chest and neck were too long, appear to be on their haunches" (La Guérinière).

La Guérinière recommended this at the passage "so that the horse could become rounded in his whole body, forming a semi-circle". It is a posture which shortens the base of horses and puts them on their haunches when they have difficulties with the *rassembler*, which puts them virtually on two tracks.

I find it quite a help in disposing of the haunches more efficiently at the stride that precedes the start of the half-pass, when the horse is still on one track along the wall. With the first step on two tracks, this flexion of the ensemble gives a cohesion that is not always attainable when one brings first the shoulders forward, then the haunches.

Of course, one must avoid giving the horse an exaggerated incurvation and not place the haunches farther in than one places the neck. The aids are more pronounced use of the two points which hold the bend around the inside leg: the inside hand sets, but without pulling, the required flexion of the front end; the outside leg sets the bend of the haunches. The outside rein controls and keeps the shoulders to the track, then regulates their lateral displacement.

Executing the two ends-in is above all a preparatory gymnastic exercise, which loses its usefulness once the horse and the rider have understood the organization of the elements of the ensemble.

One can consider it as a precursor to Baucher's flexions.

2. La Guérinière's Square

Today, the expression "volte" is commonly assumed to designate a circle of 6 meters diameter. In the 16th century, however, this term also applied to a movement on two tracks, haunches-out or haunches-in, which a horse described on a square, each side measuring three horse's lengths. This exercise can already be found in the work of Salomon de la Broue in 1593; it continued to be honored two centuries later by the School Versailles, and is perfectly described by La Guérinière. His sketches and his text describe squares of about a dozen meters on each side. One covered them at a walk, trot, canter, and at the passage.

This exercise supples the shoulders and haunches of horses, while also giving them a sensitivity to the aids for lateral movements. Indeed, if the horse maintains an equal angle and movement with respect to the forelegs and hind legs on all sides of the square, this is not the same at the corners, where one must set either the haunches or the shoulders in place, depending upon whether one covers the square haunch or head towards the outside. It is when one arrives at the bisection of the angle that one sets the "pivoting" part.

This exercise is broached only on gifted horses, who are already quite suppled on both one and two tracks and at the three gaits. It sets the final seal on their brilliance.

3. The Passade

If, in the 18th century, the "passade" signified a short liaison in the domain of love, in the *manège* it was also a rapid going-and-coming on the same line.

"To execute a passade", says La Guérinière, "is to put the horse into a canter on the length of a terrain, and, at each end, change from right to left, then left to right, passing and passing once more on the same line".

The purpose of the passade was to move towards an adversary, attack him and, if necessary, promptly go back at him. In the *manège*, the passades were composed of a succession of demi-pirouettes at the canter at the far ends, with a fast lead change between each one.

The passades were practiced at a "petit galop", with the horse *rassemblé*, at a shortened "galop" or a furious "galop". [In the era referred to "galop" generally referred to the gait of canter – although it also signified the four-time gallop, when this was ridden. Here, "petit galop", shortened "galop" and furious "galop" would pretty much equate to a slow, collected canter, a shortened working canter and either an extended canter or gallop, respectively.]

Although the passades are not part of dressage tests, this is an excellent exercise to test and "finish" a horse and, when he has reached this point, it is also a very nice movement.

4. The Long Reins

These come in the same category as the lunge; a means of relaxing the horse and channeling him better. They can be used in the preparation of *manège* figures, from the volte, the demi-volte, the reversed demi-volte, to the figure of eight. They allow one to initiate the horse into obstacle jumping by guiding him better with the long reins than is possible with the simple lungeing line. One can also use them when working in hand, parallel at the shoulder with the snaffle, as we already attempted at the outset of our study, for lateral work, the shoulder-in, the half-pass, and the *rassemblé* airs: pirouettes at the canter, the passage, the piaffe, not to forget lead changes. Long reins are also a way of presenting a horse who is perfectly schooled and gives a beautiful performance.

One sometimes uses them with a surcingle to which rings are attached, through which one passes each rein, allowing one to work from a distance, putting one out of harm's way from possible kicks made out of fear. This arrangement also prevents the reins from dragging on the ground or

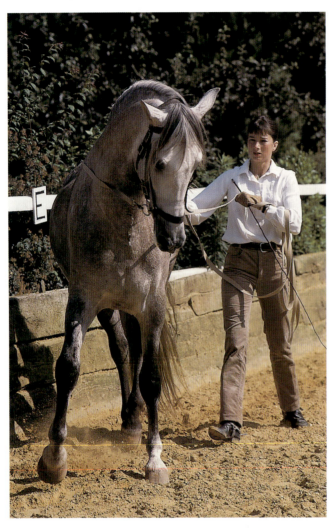

Fandango at left shoulder-in, in long reins.

getting caught in the horse's legs. The only inconvenience is that the rings transform all the rein effects into direct effects.

At the School of Vienna, horses are worked on long reins without a surcingle with rings, and without a lungeing whip – with only the dressage whip. The trainer places himself twenty centimeters from the horse's hocks, his outside shoulder against the inside buttock of the horse. On the left rein, he holds a rein in each hand, with the whip in his left hand.

He places his right hand at the base of the tail, where he can also steady his hand with his little finger. He holds the outside rein, the right rein, somewhat aside, the inside rein with a semi-tension, his hand at the same level with the point of the horse's left buttock.

The School of Vienna chooses horses who are sensitive and impulsive, since the means of moving them forward are reduced. They are also creatures who respond with absolute confidence, for their trainers' position is such that there is no possible evasion from the trajectory of the hind legs! For this work, one must also have horses who are relatively small if one does not want to work with one's hands level with one's head.

The reins for this work are 5 to 6 meters long. The horse is put in an egg-butt snaffle, and one can utilize the rings of the surcingle or not. We have already broached the technique of using long reins without rings in a preceding work.[1]

In any case, if one does not want to destroy the sensitivity of the horse, a great deal of experience and skill is required, as is being in excellent physical condition. To begin with, working behind the horse whom one must animate, then take up again, guide on a circle, on the straight, laterally, at the three gaits, hands level with one's chest, is very tiring. Further, the risks of damaging the horse's mouth are serious, for the following reason. When

1 M. Henriquet, *Le Travail à pied*. Opiprest. Connaissance du cheval, 1987.
P. Karl *Emploi des longues reines*. Maloine, 1990.

Fandango at the piaffe in long reins.

Fandango at the passage in long reins.

one is mounted and one moves the horse forward, the whole of one's body rests on the horse and is obliged to follow all the horse's displacements. Only awkward hands can cause a loss of impulsion. However, when, in hand, one drives the horse with long reins and asks of him an excess of impulsion with an imperfect co-ordination, it is the total inertia of one's body, feet on the ground, which will weigh on mouth and tongue.

Long reins, used as a means of expressing classical schooling in a performance which entails academic airs up to lead changes at every stride, requires horses who have been perfectly schooled, including all the mounted work. This does not mean that it is therefore easy with a horse already academically trained; rather it assumes a very serious apprenticeship for both trainer and horse.

5. The Rejected Airs

Re-reading the excellent work of General Decarpentry, which presents peremptorily the "academic" *écuyers* and the "circus *écuyers*", reminds me of the evolution of human ideas in general and riders' ideas in particular.

The former, "whose sole aim is the perfection of their art" are compared by Decarpentry to the latter, "whose only aim is to fill the cashbox and obtain, no matter what, the applause of the crowds who have little or no appreciation of the artistic merit".

Other times, other fashions; fifty years of demagogy has changed objectives! It is true that the circus and its *écuyers* have disappeared and that the "academic" *écuyer* "working at the perfection of the art" is rare...

Let us try to understand what is meant by fantasy airs, artificial gaits as opposed to the classical airs of high school equitation.

One somewhat arbitrary classification has excluded from the "respectable" field all the airs which are no longer part of the defined program of the F.E.I. Consequently, if, in a freestyle test, you do a transition from a slowed-down canter to a canter in place, or a piaffe going backwards linked to a forward-flowing piaffe, you will be considered a second-rate performer and treated as such.

So, even principles evolve: in the 19th century, great lords and performing artists were mingled together in mutual esteem and throughout several centuries names such as Pluvinel, La Guérinière, Baucher, d'Aure, Franconi, and Fillis were honored without reservation.

During the 1900s, military *écuyers* of renown, such as General Faverot de Kerbrech or Captain de Saint-Phalle, did not hesitate to introduce into their works such arcane movements as the Spanish walk and trot, the piaffe backwards, and canters on three legs.

Rather than condemn such and such an air in particular, General L'Hotte criticized eccentric equitation whose methods were "in poor taste", resulting in unnatural movements.

My own response is to give the opinion of one of the best judges, namely, that what is intolerable is not the Spanish walk, which brings about a splendid activity of the haunches, but any form of equitation which compromises a horse's balance and mutilates his natural steps and gaits.

One can frequently see young horses at liberty playing, throwing their forelegs forward, which are nothing but natural jambettes, from which the Spanish walk is simply a sophisticated development.

The Spanish Walk

This can be useful gymnastic exercise if it is cadenced and regular, at an equal four beats, with an energetic propulsion of the hind legs.

It is taught in hand: the horse is halted straight along the wall. One supports the snaffle on the inside; one touches gently the foreleg on the same side with the whip, where the horse is most sensitive. At the same time, one maintains contact with the outside rein and brings the horse forward as soon as he extends the required leg. When he responds easily in each direction, still along the wall, one must ask for these jambettes mounted, several times on the same side, going forward at each extension. When he executes a few such steps in succession correctly on each side, one requests them alternately. This is the Spanish walk. One must confine oneself to sustained signals from the fingers and avoid arm movements and heel actions, which can make the horse traverse and contract.

The Spanish Trot

This is a trot wherein the horse projects his forelegs and holds them up high at each step.

Since the horse was energetic at the Spanish walk, one asks him to move himself quickly forward, with the leg opposite the extending foreleg in support. When he freely takes a step forward, one asks him for the same gesture on the other diagonal.

It is by *starting with a very impulsive passage*, together with repeated jambettes on the side of the wall, with diagonal effects, that one begins the Spanish trot. When the horse does several jambettes on the same side

The Spanish trot. Andaluz, pure-bred Lusitano, 6 years. The position of the rider in 1966 to be worked at.

easily, with passage steps on the other diagonal, one works the inside of the horse in the same manner. To avoid any confusion with the passage, one must hold one's wrists up and keep one's legs more forward.

The Trot Backwards

To trot backwards is actually to go from the piaffe in place to a piaffe going backwards.

This air is acceptable only on two conditions: that, from the halt, the rein-back is easy, immediate, and flowing, using only the weight of the reins, and that the piaffe is executed with absolute lightness and a regularity. Under these conditions, when the horse does the piaffe, one inclines the torso slightly forward to lighten the back of the seat and, with fingers only and without pulling, one alternates the delicate signals on the reins.

As soon as the horse executes one step backwards, one straightens the torso and goes back to the piaffe, advancing by a few centimeters before doing the piaffe in place again.

This air is only admissible and presentable insofar as the horse goes forwards as easily and as regularly as he did when going backwards. In the contrary situation, the consequences could be an over-bent horse. Throughout my life, I have only seen a trot backwards well executed only once or twice. For this feat – and the canter backwards is another one – the horse-*écuyer* relationship must be exceptional.

Postface

HERE I AM, ALREADY submitting a conclusion to this treatise on equitation when I have barely completed my last sentence. This conclusion was written as a definitive and satisfying reflection on a work thankfully completed, yet without any presumption on my part.

On the other hand, I wish to bid farewell in an urbane manner those who persevered in following the development of this work to its very end. It is for them that I want to close by saying a few words; yet I cannot do so without ignoring our mutual dissatisfaction.

Over forty years ago, in the middle of the desert which described the equestrian landscape, I discovered literary fragments and illustrations dealing with high school equitation, which gave me a doctrine founded on reason and reflection, with different objectives which inevitably preoccupy the horseman.

This equestrian art of the Age of Enlightenment [the 18th century] had not yet become falsified by the scientism [faux science] of the 19th century and the simplistic military theories which, after the Revolution of 1789, monopolized the thoughts of successive masters and thus gave us, two centuries later, nothing but indistinguishable leftovers.

The only documents attesting to the level attained by the School of Versailles came to my notice resembling far too much the outline sketch of a lost treasure. Thus the question which concerned me was to find out which aspects of these texts – which were presented too summarily, but which included superb engravings – were idealism, and which were realism.

Luck had it that, while I was studying passionately the works and documents which seemed to conceal the equitation of French tradition, I met the man who was aware of this equestrian wealth, and with whom I never ceased to work.

Nuno Oliveira, whom I consider the first and foremost equestrian talent of our times, was able to reunite the qualities and the methods which, alonc, could reproduce faithfully the image that one made of the *Maîtres Ecuyers* of the Royal Manège.

A devouring passion, an immense culture, a tact emanating from his whole self, a burning sensitivity that finds its equal only in its own dissatisfaction, were only part of the qualities of Oliveira. He was lucky to have been born in one of the last countries where the horse was still in use and to have had as his godfather Joaquim Miranda, a man who was a master of tradition and who, in his early childhood, had at his disposal those Andalusian horses and their marvelous natural balance.

After more than a half century of study and reflection, my ambition (and, perhaps, my illusion), was to try to make more feasible and as clear as possible a body of ideas and a means of applying them the value of which lies more in the finesse with which they are applied, than in the technique itself. Very few things are of my invention. I have tried above all to present a text and reflection that are my own, free from imprecision, fuzziness, and contradictions, which I so often had to endure during many years of practice and research.

I hope that everyone can discover, as I did – even in the absence of the perfect equestrian equilibrium, which I still seek – this entrance into another universe where largesse opposes utility, play opposes routine, and imagination opposes reality.

Index